Conversations
in Psychotherapy

Conversations in Psychotherapy

Ways of Working with Individuals, Couples, and Families

R. V. Fitzgerald, M.D.

JASON ARONSON INC.
Northvale, New Jersey
London

Production Editors: Adelle Krauser and Leslie Block

This book was set in Garamond by Lind Graphics, Upper Saddle River, New Jersey, and printed and bound by Haddon Craftsmen, Scranton, Pennsylvania.

Library of Congress Cataloging-in-Publication Data

Fitzgerald, R. V., 1922–
    Conversations in psychotherapy : ways of working
    with individuals, couples, and families / R.V. Fitzgerald.
      p. cm.
    Includes bibliographical references and index.
    ISBN 0-87668-561-0
    1. Psychotherapy. I. Title.
    [DNLM: 1. Psychotherapy—methods. WM 420 F554c]
  RC480.F5566 1992
  616.89'14—dc20
  DNLM/DLC
  for Library of Congress   91-33335

Manufactured in the United States of America. Jason Aronson Inc. offers books and cassettes. For information and catalog write to Jason Aronson Inc., 230 Livingston Street, Northvale, New Jersey 07647.

To Margaret

Contents

Part II: Individual Psychotherapies

Part III: Couple and Family Psychotherapies

Acknowledgment

It would be impossible to thank personally all of those who have contributed to the writing of this book; they are a multitude. They include all my teachers over the years and all those whom I have talked with about my and their therapeutic experiences. Although I cannot name each of you here, please accept my sincere thanks. My wife Margaret has been her usual supportive self and I am deeply grateful for her patience and forbearance as I agonized and displayed irritation when the writing was not going well. She also made many helpful suggestions as I read the manuscript to her, piece by piece. I also appreciate the encouragement given by many of my colleagues at the Department of Psychiatry of the Medical College of Ohio. Dr. Marijo Tamburrino was especially helpful, as was our chairman, Dr. Joel Zrull. Mrs. Gerry Kujawa used her word processing expertise to get the manuscript in final form.

I must also give credit to Lorelei, my trusted computer, who helped immensely with word processing, searching databases, organizing references, and preparing bibliographies. Margaret named her Lorelei, because my computer so often lured me and held me in her grasp. Siobhân, my English cocker spaniel co-therapist, spent long hours curled up asleep as I wrote. Occasionally, she became impatient and hassled me till I stopped and gave her some attention.

Ms. Anne Patota of the Jason Aronson staff offered many fine editorial criticisms and compliments and I thank her for both.

I feel indebted to all my patients who taught me most of what I know about being a therapist. All of you and none of you will find yourselves in these pages. I have not used any case material directly. Rather I have combined and/or massively disguised patients' histories, characteristics, dynamics, and experiences in therapy. Although I based it on real people, I made up all the case material.

I hope that younger generations of therapists and their patients will profit in some way, however small, from what these therapists learn from my book. And I thank them all, for they served as one of the most powerful motivations for my writing it.

Part I

THE CONTEXT OF DOING PSYCHOTHERAPY

Because this book presents readers with the opportunity to learn several ways of doing psychotherapy for individuals, couples, and families, some preparation is necessary at the outset. This section offers that preparation, beginning with a statement of my objectives and a description of my image of the audience of readers. The first chapter also summarizes current trends in psychiatry and psychotherapy, and views about the agents that bring about change in all forms of psychotherapy. It provides, as well, a very concise summation of my psychoanalytic foundations in conducting all psychiatric treatment.

The next two chapters discuss the initial diagnostic interviews and cover both the nosologic and psychodynamic aspects of the assessment of patients. The most urgent initial concerns relating to decisions about treatment, and how to plan for and begin it, are also considered. I then review ways to educate patients about treatment and I stress the critical importance of the therapeutic alliance, the therapeutic contract, and the setting of goals in all psychotherapies. It is my hope that this material will prepare readers to better understand and integrate what follows.

1

Current Trends

Objectives
Current Trends in Psychiatry
Current Trends in Psychotherapy
Change Agents in Psychotherapy
Psychoanalytic Core

Objectives

I would like to invite each of you into my office, preferably one at a time, to observe and to learn what you choose to take from the kind of psychotherapy I do. I am reasonably sure that it has much in common with what many other therapists do, but it bears my personal stamp as well. I make no claim that this is the best or only way therapists should practice. It has worked well for me and for most of my patients. Salvador Minuchin was once asked why he called the type of family therapy he originated Structural Family Therapy. He is said to have replied that he did so for the same reason designers put their names on the backs of blue jeans. What do I call the psychotherapy I practice? I have no special name for it but like to think of it as exhibiting an informed and selective eclecticism, surrounding a solid core of psychoanalytic information. The basics of the latter I will summarize later.

Today's psychotherapist serves many kinds of patients and operates in an environment that is not particularly friendly. Some Managed Care providers (Health Maintenance Organizations, Preferred Provider Organizations) continue to pay hundreds of thousands of dollars for various transplant procedures but limit payment for outpatient psychotherapy to six visits or so. With great difficulty and much red tape, it may be possible to get a few more. There will therefore be many more patients than in the past who will receive inadequate treatment compelled by cost containment that bears *no* relationship to clinical reality. Psychotherapy should be as brief as possible without sacrificing quality. To fool ourselves about the efficacy of very brief "drive-through" psychotherapy would represent denial of the worst kind. Many of my colleagues, who are diligently attempting to provide quality inpatient care for their psychiatric patients, are in great distress about this issue. Nevertheless, briefer methods of therapy deserve to be used when they are *clinically* indicated. For this reason, I will consider them here.

I hope to inspire you to learn about the field of psychotherapy in a generic sense. In time, what methods we plan for a particular patient will have increasingly precise indications. If, for example, cognitive–behavioral therapy fits Mrs. Jones's personality and her psychopathology, we should offer that method to her. If, on the other hand, analytically informed marital therapy is indicated, clinicians should know that it is indicated, even if they don't practice it; thus they can make an appropriate referral to a colleague who does. When the clinician evaluates Mr. Jones, he may prove to be suffering from Obsessive Compulsive Disorder; for him, currently, a serotonin re-uptake inhibitor is indicated. Clinicians who are psychiatrists will usually prescribe the medication and integrate the pharmacotherapy into the individual, marital, or combined psychotherapy planned for the patient. Non-medical therapists will work closely with a psychiatrist who prescribes and monitors the proper medication for Mr. Jones while they conduct his psychosocial treatment. How to proceed with these kinds of treatment plans will be described in the chapters devoted to specific forms of psychotherapy.

In summary, my objectives are that the reader will be able to do the following:

1. Conduct a thorough assessment of an individual patient, couple, or family.
2. Think through and write out treatment plans that consider all levels of the biopsychosocial model, including the use of pharmacotherapy.
3. Formulate a dynamic diagnosis using psychoanalytic, general systems theories and concepts gleaned from the main schools of marital and family therapy.
4. Plan the overall treatment strategies based on all aspects of the assessment, including probable or predictable complications and tentative ways of pre-empting or dealing with them.
5. Carry through to completion the treatment planned.
6. Revise formulations and plans as comprehension of patients' problems is amended and enlarged throughout the therapy process.

I hope that what I have written here demonstrates many of the treatment alternatives currently available. Most of what I write about, I have had first hand experience with. But, although I mean to be diverse in the procedures I discuss and explicate, I do not know enough to be encyclopedic. In the modes of psychotherapy I do consider in depth, I cannot give you examples of what I do and say under all possible circumstances. I do, however, provide enough by way of specific examples to help you extrapolate to other clinical circumstances.

Audience

The audience I have in mind as I write is youthful, in attitude if not in chronological age. I picture you as open-minded and curious. So that I can avoid writer's phobia, I imagine you as benign and I anticipate that your criticisms will be civil, mild, and thoughtful. Most of all, regardless of the amount of experience you have had, you continue to learn. And I must confess to a special place in my heart for trainees and the less experienced among you. This bias will affect *how* I write more than anything else.

What should you, the audience, bring with you to get the most out of what you will read? Certainly, you should have completed the basic courses in your respective mental health disciplines and in the forms of treatment you will conduct. Physicians should, at the least, be in the second year of their psychiatric residency programs. For preliminary reading, I would recommend some introductory text on psychoanalytic theory and some material on Engle's biopsychosocial model and general systems theory as it applies to our disciplines (Brenner 1974, Engel 1989, Frosch 1990, Kris 1989). Also I have provided summaries of the theoretical constructs of the foremost schools of family psychotherapy. Although I have taken care to use ordinary language wherever possible, some sections may prove confusing to readers who do not yet understand these notions and terminology. For those of you with the luxury of time to read extensively, I am appending a list of my favorite books and articles on the subject at hand. (Appendix A).

Current Trends in Psychiatry

The nature–nurture controversy among those who tend
to reductionism in their thinking continues ad nauseam.
Many theorists and clinicians remain prisoners of Carte-
sian dualism and of our very language, which requires us
to think in certain ways and provides no way to think in
others. Beware also of those who reify concepts and then
get into disputes about their structure and function. To
discuss the etiology and treatment of psychiatric conditions, it is necessary for us to identify and intervene at
several different levels. Many clinicians apply the biopsychosocial model in diagnosis and treatment. They rely
upon observations that significant change in one level
leads to a change in all other levels, in a circular rather
than linear fashion. Positron Emission Tomography has
demonstrated that brain metabolism is selectively altered
in different areas of the brain, according to the emotion,

thought, or fantasy experienced by the subject (Gott-schalk 1990). Psychological factors (under the influence of social ones—the conditions of the experiment) affect brain chemistry. Changing brain chemistry with psychoactive agents affects emotions, thought, and behavior—anxiety, depression, obsessions, compulsions. And a change in a person's behavior will influence her or his family and other groups of which the person is a member.

Other developments in the neurosciences, especially an understanding of the physiological processes of perception, learning, and memory, have demonstrated that psychotherapy changes brain function in transitory and more enduring ways. If enduring changes in function can be thought of as a change in structure, then psychotherapy can indeed modify brain structure. What a thought! Psychotherapy is an *organic* or biological treatment (Mohl 1987)—and creative innovations in the neurosciences have proved it so.

Over the past three decades biologic psychiatry has produced several families of psychoactive medications and a beginning comprehension of their mechanisms of action. A discussion of these is beyond the scope of this book, but no psychotherapist can function properly today without sufficient knowledge about what conditions may respond to one medication or another. It approaches malpractice for any of us to treat, for example, bipolar patients or certain unipolar, depressed patients without apprising them and their families of the availability, efficacy, and indications for the use of medications for these conditions (Klerman 1990, Stone 1990). The chief usefulness of the nomenclature and classificatory system of the Diagnostic and Statistical Manuals is in the identification of those conditions that are likely to respond to pharmacologic agents. Recent developments seem, however, to suggest a classification based on families of disorders that respond to certain families of medications, which cut across conditions as classified in DSM-III-R and its previous editions.

Computer programs are already available that assist clinicians in making DSM diagnoses and in patient management. In one of the former, *Decisionbase,*[1] clinicians answer the structured interview questions "asked" by the program, based on the decision tree branches selected by the clinician. The program then sorts through the criteria for the various diagnoses on the clinician's differential and "concludes" which ones do and do not meet them. Further, the software compiles a report including the data about the patient and the diagnosis or diagnoses established. Problem Knowledge Couplers combine a current database compiled from the most recent literature with data about the patient requested by the program (Weed 1989). It puts the two data sets together and formulates treatment options in terms of "Pros for the use of . . ." and "Cons for the use of . . . ," together with reasons for these conclusions.

Soon researchers will have totally mapped the human genome. Already, evidence suggests genetic linkage of some mental diseases, such as some cases of schizophrenia and manic-depression, to certain chromosomes. We can therefore fantasize about treatment through genetic engineering. Enhanced awareness of the association between abnormal perinatal factors and mental illness has also influenced our thinking about the vulnerabilities with which certain people begin life.

Congress has declared the 1990s to be "The Decade of the Brain." Since the brain and mind are one, psychotherapists have as much to celebrate as do those of a more biologic outlook.

---

[1]Copyright 1990 by P. W. Long, M.D.

Current Trends in Psychotherapy

I enjoy doing and teaching psychotherapy. I have been doing it for more years than I like to admit to and teaching it for almost as long. At first, I taught as a consultant to various community mental health and family service agencies. Their staffs consisted mainly of social workers; there were also a few clinical psychologists and counselors. For over twenty years I have taught and supervised psychiatric residents as they struggled to learn the craft of psychotherapy. Perhaps it would reflect less by way of hubris to say *not* that I taught but that I talked with these people about what I thought I was doing in my psychotherapy. Many of them seemed to take some of the things I had to say seriously and used them with their clients and patients. Throughout my professional career, therefore, I have been in continuous and enlightening contact with one younger generation after another. It was and is a fine tradeoff. I received and continue to receive more than I give.

11

At first I worked only with individuals, as did almost everyone else then. Later I treated couples and families. My training was, throughout, psychoanalytically oriented. In those days it was the only game in town. It was and *is* a good game! In its deep understandings about human development, in its equally thorough and scholarly description of individual and group dynamics, and in its careful and thoughtful attention to the therapist–patient relationship and other critical dimensions of the treatment process, psychoanalysis has served us well. Most of what clinicians do in their practice of dynamic, expressive, or uncovering modes of psychotherapy, they have borrowed from psychoanalysts. In the borrowing, most of us have changed the technical rules to fit our own styles, the briefer forms of therapy we practice, and the patients we treat. Those who employ supportive modes of psychotherapy also borrow from psychoanalysis in terms of what to support and how to do it. Early on I fell under the influence of Alexander and French and their Chicago school of psychoanalytic therapy. To this day I use many of the methods they taught in their 1946 book.

During my professional career I have seen many schools of psychotherapy burst onto the scene with great acclaim. When I was a resident at Menninger's, a group of older and bolder trainees (following Wilhelm Reich's specifications) built and experimented with an Orgone Box; it didn't make any of us feel any better. None of us was willing to talk about whether it affected our orgasms. Had it made any favorable difference in anything, we would not have abandoned it as quickly as we did.

Other systems of psychotherapy have enjoyed some popularity through the years. Even Primal Scream therapy has, unfortunately, endured. Encounter groups have attracted many people, as has Erhard Seminars Training (EST), now called The Forum. At the final session of the weekend EST ordeal (according to a patient of mine), the attenders' sponsors gathered at the back of the room and, in fulfillment of the leader's promise to tell the group all they needed to know about sex, shouted in unison: "When it's hot it's hot, when it's not it's not!" That's about the only thing in this form of therapy that made any sense to me. Most of these new forms of psychotherapy (if, indeed, any of them deserve to be graced by the term) have waxed and waned, some more quickly than others.

In a different class and quite respectable were E. Berne's Transactional Analysis and Fritz Perls's Gestalt Therapy (Berne 1972, Perls 1969). The former seemed to me to be a form of psychoanalytic treatment, using different language, guided fantasy, and a more directive approach. Behavior therapy gained a strong foothold in the field of psychotherapy and continues to grow in use and usefulness. Beck was one of the most influential proponents of cognitive–behavioral psychotherapy (Beck 1976). Psychoanalysis developed three perspectives in addition to drive-defense concepts: ego psychology, interpersonal or objects relations, and self-psychology (Pine 1987). Under the charismatic leadership of Milton Erickson, hypnosis and allied techniques enjoyed a renaissance (Haley 1973). And Erickson influenced the Neurolinguistic Programming of Bandler and Grinder (Grinder and Bandler 1981). He also influenced the theorists and practitioners, Bateson, Jackson, Haley, and others, who originated so-called paradoxical strategies and a system of family treatment based on theories about human communication (Bateson 1972, Watzlawick et al. 1967). Nathan Ackerman, Murray Bowen, and others developed analytically oriented family therapies (Ackerman 1958, Bowen 1978). Carl Whitaker dazzled us all with his very personal form of experiential family psychotherapy (Napier and Whitaker 1978).

On the level of theory, many clinicians emphasized the differences among various schools or systems of psychotherapy. Therapists, on the firing line, seemed to borrow freely from each other and became more alike. For example, dynamically oriented therapists used the behavioral method of prescribing tasks for patients to do between sessions, and behaviorists attended to relationship and transference issues. Currently, theorists are at work attempting to integrate further the disparate theories of psychotherapy. One promising approach is the effort to find common ground at a level of abstraction that involves therapeutic strategies (Arkowitz 1989, Beutler 1989).

From whom have I borrowed? In the foregoing review I have included many who influenced me in a positive or negative sense. Probably I have neglected some and I cannot now recall where I have read about certain procedures. I can only ask forgiveness of those of you from whom I have unknowingly plagiarized—and request that you contact me, if you recognize something for which you deserve credit, and I'll insert it in the next printing of this book. To specify precisely where I learned each item I will discuss is impossible. Much of what I write about is generally accepted practice. Some is my own, although I make no claim that I originated it. My reference list will therefore be parsimonious.

Those who do research in the field of psychotherapy have been at work demonstrating its efficacy (Glass et al. 1989, Luborsky et al. 1986, Manos and Vasilopoulou 1984, Pilkonis et al. 1984, Robinson et al. 1990, Smith and Glass 1977). Some are making strenuous efforts to define more precisely the specific indications for the various modes of psychotherapy (Karasu 1990a,b). Little progress has been made in sorting out which psychotherapies are more effective for what disorders since they occur in different kinds of people living in distinctive environments, including their families, cultures, and societies. We clinicians are left to our own devices in evaluating each patient, couple, or family and choosing the psychotherapy that will most likely succeed. Since the mutative power of most psychotherapies that have earned credibility and respect are approximately equal, our task is easier than it sounds (Altshuler 1989). This conclusion about similarity of outcome was determined by researchers using statistical methods and is useful at that level of analysis. What therapy will prove effective for my patient, Mr. John Doe, *I* will have to decide, using all of my clinical acumen. And all of you will have to do the same for now.

Change Agents in Psychotherapy

It may seem that attempts to integrate various systems of psychotherapy have occurred only recently. In fact, however, finding common denominators among psychotherapies began long ago. Thomas French read a paper at a 1932 meeting of The American Psychiatric Association contending that operant conditioning was a part of the psychoanalytic process (London and Palmer 1988). What a furor *that* caused among both analysts and behaviorists! Many clinicians/authors have found aspects common to most successful psychotherapies (Marmor 1979a, Strupp 1986). I have emphasized these points throughout this book and summarize them here.

A Good Enough Therapist–Patient(s) Relationship

A good enough relationship between therapist and patient depends upon what both bring with them to the relationship. It is the most critical and powerful of all the factors that foster change, the *sine qua non* of a continuing therapeutic process. Without its nascent presence by the end of the first interview, there will be no second one. This is why I have accentuated, perhaps redundantly, this aspect of psychotherapy. It includes the average, expectable therapist behaviors and attitudes as well as carefully planned corrective emotional experiences. All of these I will describe and exemplify later.

I often articulate this to patients, as follows (depending on how many of us are present):

> Whatever happens here can be stated in an equation. It consists of A—what I put into it, plus B—what you put into it, Joe, plus C—what you contribute, Ann—and that will equal X, which is some kind of an outcome, desirable or undesirable. Each of us must take responsibility for our share. Because I'm the professional in this situation, my A is somewhat bigger that either your B or your C.

This statement stresses the importance of the relationship between or among the participants in a shared endeavor. Also I hope to set a tone that discourages the all-too-common human tendency to blame and that promotes an atmosphere of cooperation and shared responsibility.

Therapists bring their personalities, warts and all, their training, knowledge, and skill to their work with patients. For some, doing so comes naturally and easily; other therapists are more reserved. Cold therapist is an oxymoron. Most patients respond positively to an appropriate degree of warmth in their therapist's manner. We also learn, however, that a few patients are frightened by warmth and we find that it is necessary to set a cooler tone. Perhaps it would be more accurate to say that therapists should be able to warm up to patients as they get to know them. Warmth at first sight is probably as uncommon as is love at first sight.

If a therapist brings as much as is necessary to form a good professional relationship with another person, what is the patient's part? A few patients have been so damaged by some concatenation of genetic, biologic, perinatal, and early parental neglect or abuse that they are unable to build a meaningful bond with another human being. At the other extreme, there are patients who come assuming they will be treated decently by a professional whom they believe, unless proven otherwise, is reasonably competent. And then there are all the shadings of difficulty between the impossible and the relatively easy. Some patients will not allow us to treat them. Some are afflicted with mental diseases that do not permit them to forge realistically based relationships with anyone, for example, a severe psychotic state with little or no intact reality testing. At first, treatment may have to be imposed by force of law against the patient's will. If the psychotic state is effectively treated, then it may become possible with effort and skill to build an enduring relationship with such a patient.

Demoralization and Hope

For a patient, to call one of us for help is a very difficult decision! Calling the plumber or the electrician is easy: the only concern is how much it will cost and how much of a mess they'll leave to be cleaned up afterward. People, of course, vary in how hard it is for them to call upon a mental health professional. Many people must reach a state of demoralization before making that call. Often some event of the "straw that broke the camel's back" type has occurred. True, there are less desirable moti-vating factors, even destructive ones. Those who present repeatedly with factitious illnesses have complicated mo-tivations involving extreme need for care and intense hostility toward caretakers; their conditions are in fact quite serious diseases over which they have little or no control. Some come to pacify others (e.g., a spouse has issued a "get help or else divorce" ultimatum), and some come to avoid the consequences of criminal behavior. Others come under various kinds of duress. It is therefore very important to explore the reasons patients are coming for help; ancillary sources of information are sometimes of critical importance. Occasionally, when patients come with less than desirable motivation, we may influence them to try therapy, and the therapy may stimulate their latent desire to do better or to be better human beings.

Fortunately, most patients who seek our help are suf-fering and experiencing some degree of demoralization. Once patients have made the decision to come for help, their suffering sometimes eases promptly. Some hope has already been mobilized. Again, fortunately, we can help most patients in some way and to some degree. It is usually possible for us to project an optimistic outlook without being dishonest or promising guarantees. Occa-sionally I say something like the following:

> I believe that if you wish to give therapy a fair trial, the chances that you will benefit are very good. Of course, I can't guarantee results; there is some risk in whatever we undertake in life.

I assume many clinicians do likewise—yet I think it is honest enough to say the first sentence and omit the second. Chances that are very good are, after all, not certain. For some cases I make a more cautious prognosis that nevertheless still offers hope:

In your situation, you have not told me that you were doing reasonably well until recently. On the contrary, you have said that you have been having these difficulties for a very long time. I'm not saying there's no hope; there definitely is now that you've decided to do something about it. But it will be more difficult because it is a chronic condition and will probably take longer than if it were of more recent origin.

It's important to be as honest as possible while still holding out some realistic hope. For hope itself is a powerful generator of change.

An article I read a long time ago—too long to be able to retrieve the citation—documented that over a short run at least, student social workers treating schizophrenic patients in a state mental hospital had better results than experienced therapists did. The former didn't know enough to appreciate how grim the prognosis was for some of these chronic patients!

Faith

Hope and faith are intimately connected. Faith constitutes the content of hope stated as, for example, "If Dr. Jones gives me an antibiotic, soon my infection will be cured" or "If I exercise to the advised aerobic level, I will be less likely to have a heart attack." Modern-day therapists need not be ashamed of our kinship with native healers and medicine men. Patients' belief in us is an important factor that contributes to their changing for the better. If we happen to have a good reputation or if we are associated with a facility that has, patients' faith in us is bolstered. Thus names like Mayo and Sloan-Kettering inspire faith in all who work there. Be not dismayed if patients express doubt about you because you are in training or young. The stance that will have the best chance of building confidence in the patient is a nondefensive one, stated casually:

> Yes, I am young and I am learning. I will be discussing your treatment with Dr. Marijo Smith and she will be guiding me. If any of this gives you a problem, I'll help you find a more experienced person to work with.

More often than not, your realistic acceptance of your position and your calm confidence will mobilize patients' potential faith in you. After all, we are all learning continuously and your sincere desire to learn with and from your patients and teachers will induce confidence in you.

Heightened Emotion and Its Expression

We do everything we can to make it easy for patients to express their feelings freely. We tell them this. We watch and listen for emotions to show themselves in patients' nonverbal behaviors, as in the pace, tone, and volume of their voices. At the proper moment, we may offer encouragement or say:

> You seemed about to show me how mad you are and then stopped yourself. What led you to shut your feelings down?

There are other tactics we can use to heighten emotional tension in therapy as well as tactics to dampen feelings when too much is contraindicated. We will discuss these in the sections devoted to techniques in supportive and expressive modes of psychotherapy. Except where danger is associated with patients' experiencing too much emotion, abreaction and catharsis are both significant agents of change in psychotherapy.

New Learning

Cognitive learning about ourselves and the dynamics of our difficulties and symptoms is another major factor contributing to change. As long as this new learning makes sense, is based on a body of knowledge constructed honestly from observed data, and is internally consistent, patients profit from it. Insight has been valued too much by some clinicians. Its specific content cannot be as compelling as some believe. Patients who learn to formulate their problems with concepts derived from Jung, Freud, the neo-Freudians, ego psychology, object relations dynamics, or self-psychology seem to do equally well in dynamic psychotherapy. Thus the *specific* theoretical orientation of clinicians is not of crucial importance, but it is critical for clinicians to have *some* respectable and credible theoretical orientation. Scientists now deviate from Newtonian concepts but they *know* what they are.

Operant Conditioning

What happened to the model of analytic neutrality? It never existed in an absolute sense. Certainly, when therapists are visible and active, patients learn much about us. None of us is so obscure that we do not display some of our values, feelings, attitudes, and beliefs, as well as what patient behaviors we approve and disapprove of. In very supportive treatment we do so overtly, deliberately, and for good reasons which will be discussed. In more expressive therapies we reveal ourselves in much more subtle ways, including nonverbal cues. For example, our selecting a piece of a patient's behavior (action, thought, way of thinking, feeling, attitude, conviction, etc.) to explore strongly suggests our opinion that the patient should change it. An old adage maintains that silence gives consent. But here we must remember that patients experience therapist silence as meaning many different things, according to what they project onto it.

We guide patients to understand their dreams in certain ways. Patients of Jungian therapists, therefore, dream Jungian dreams and those of Freudian therapists, Freudian ones. I am not denigrating the process; I am setting forth what I think happens in therapy. If we keep patients' needs in mind and frequently check out whether we are serving only our own, then the way we influence patients through operant conditioning will be for *their* benefit.

Using suggestion, persuasion, and direction are so intimately connected with operant conditioning that they do not need separate consideration here. Again, these procedures should be used with regard for their effect on the therapist–patient relationship and the individual needs of each patient.

Identification with Therapists

In all of our behaviors, how we think, our ethical principles and values, our attitudes, our feelings, we serve as role models for patients. This is another way we influence people to change. We are human and do make mistakes, and it is important for us to take responsibility for them. Our duty to patients is an awesome one akin to that of being a parent. It would be unwise to underestimate the power of patients' identification with us. When the identification has been helpful, we can justifiably take the credit provided we also take responsibility for any harm we have unwittingly done in this way. When we catch ourselves setting a bad example for patients (using sarcasm in expressing disapproval is one of mine), or if patients comment on such, we may say:

> That's not a particularly desirable trait of mine and one I hope you will not emulate. I'm working on getting it under better control and think I'm gaining on it.

It is a very good feeling to have a patient say or do something more adaptive, based on an identification with us. It is pleasant to recognize ourselves reflected in our patients' words and deeds.

Practicing New Learning

Once patients have learned new, more adaptive ways of dealing with themselves, with others, and with life, they make them their own through trying them out. It is necessary for patients to put these new strategies into effect in their daily lives, not only vis-à-vis the therapist. It's expected that patients will use the therapy situation as a safe haven to take risks and use these new tools, but if they do so *only* in therapy, they have gained little. Therefore, we must see to it that patients transfer what they have learned into their daily lives. It is a good idea to prepare patients for failures at first, especially interpersonal ones. I say something like this:

> Remember that you have a certain image or reputation with your boss. If you use what you have learned here

about being appropriately assertive with him, it probably won't work. At first, he won't notice or believe the change in you. Secondly, it's likely that a change in you, once he's acknowledged it, will make him uncomfortable and his first move will be to try to get you to change back to the way you were. If you stick with it, you may make him even more uncomfortable, so he'll up the ante to get you to back down. If you can stick with it through all of that, then we'll know that you have really made it. So be careful! And if it doesn't work out, we'll have to revise our plans.

Note that I've given the patient an out and made it a joint enterprise in saying "we'll" and "our." Note also how supportive that statement is. If patients are to succeed in integrating new behaviors into their repertoires, they require consistent support as they test their updated version of reality. Other methods for facilitating patients' use of coping skills learned in therapy into their day-to-day experiences will be explained later.

Jerome Frank's Summary of Change Agents

Frank (1976) stated all of what he believes to be present in all effective therapies as follows:

1. Strengthening the therapeutic relationship
2. Inspiring the patient's hope for help
3. Providing opportunities for both cognitive and experiential learning
4. Stimulating emotional arousal as a motive power for change in attitudes and behavior
5. Enhancing the patient's sense of mastery by providing or stimulating success experiences

6. Encouraging "working through" and applying what patients have learned in therapy to daily living

"Working through" originally meant overcoming patients' resistance to the therapy process. It has gradually also come to mean, what is more important, methods (encouragement, prescription, persuasion) by which therapists help patients overcome their fear and avoidance of change itself.

Jules Masserman's Summary of Change Agents

Masserman (1976) has stated these notions in the form of his "Seven R's of Psychotherapy."

1. Reputation of the therapist
2. Rapport
3. Review of history—assets as well as liabilities
4. Reorganization of adaptive patterns
5. Reeducation and rehabilitation
6. Resocialization
7. Relief of symptoms

Psychoanalytic Core

Having summarized the sources of my eclecticism and the change agents operative in most, if not all, forms of respectable psychotherapy, I will now explain what I mean by my solid core of psychoanalytic information. Although much of Freud's metapsychology has been questioned, what we use of his clinical understanding and interpretations in our day-to-day practice continues to be most useful (Holt 1989). The following is only a sampling of those features of psychoanalytic thought that I rate as most worthy on a practical level. Later they will be elucidated in more detail and clinical examples will be provided.

The Therapist's Human Needs

I'm not sure how much of what I will now say has been derived from psychoanalysis and how much is just good common sense (more accurately called *un*common sense). Therapists, like most humans, need their share of security, success, warmth, closeness, affection, sensuousness, tenderness, and lust. Most of these we satisfy in our roles as persons with other persons. Therefore, therapists must have gratifying and full personal lives, as well as consciences that demand exemplary ethical behavior, to serve as insulation between us and our patients. Professional success, therapeutic and financial, does arise from our work with patients. To preclude excessive financial dependence on a few patients, we need a large enough number of patients, or income and opportunities for success from another source, to protect our patients from any overweening cravings.

Understanding

The predominant purpose of psychoanalytically informed therapists is to understand the people they treat. Were we proceeding in a strictly classical manner, we would impart our understandings to patients and regard interpretation and the insight they gain as the most powerful mutative factor in psychotherapy. I have already called this postulate into question, thereby joining many others who have demoted insight from its position as the major change agent in psychotherapy. Many psychoanalytically oriented clinicians disagree with me. Eventually you will make your own judgments about this matter.

However, I believe strongly that we should understand our patients and what we ourselves do in psychotherapy. Of all the explanations of the development of the individual, psychopathology, and the process of therapy, I favor psychoanalytic theory that is closely connected with clinical realities. And if we neglect a deeper understanding of ourselves, which we can attain only through personal therapy, we do so at some risk. Our own blind spots may limit our understanding of certain things that are crucial to know to help our patients. And our ability to monitor ourselves with analytic tools further ensures against our acting out our own needs with patients. We need the inner voice of our current or former therapist saying: "Hold it! Before you do (or say) that, let's try to understand what it means and whose needs it will serve."

What we comprehend in analytic terms goes beyond common sense. The mechanisms we seek to understand take place automatically and outside of our awareness. You will know this if you have already studied sufficient psychoanalytic material. In asking for our help, patients present us with their *solutions* to their problems. We start with these solutions, look at them as they are manifested in patients' current behaviors toward us and others, and find out how these solutions developed in patients' personal histories. In this manner we gain a recognition of the function and meaning of patients' problematic attitudes, thinking, feeling, behavior, and relationships. And we fully accept, at the outset, that none of us surrenders these solutions easily. True, the suffering that issues from these precious solutions gets patients into treatment. Overcoming their avoidance of feared and unpredictable changes leads to improvement, an end to therapy, and loss of the therapist. Analytic comprehension teaches us and patients that change is difficult and that to win, we must risk losing and bear the pain of it.

As I shall demonstrate in the body of this work, therapists can use analytic understanding regardless of the form or mode of therapy they conduct. I regard psychoanalytic comprehension as *a* way of understanding the dynamics of all human relationships, especially psychotherapeutic ones, but including those based on behavioral and learning theories as well.

Responding to Patients' Need for Treatment

Clinicians respond to patients who seek their help. Although some clinicians do conduct epidemiological studies to determine the prevalence of mental disorders, they do not use them to proselytize for patients or clients. Except for those who require treatment because of their danger to themselves or others, or their inability to care for themselves, mental health professionals do not force their services on others. Even in these special cases, we do not do it on our own; society and the law require us to treat such people against their will, if necessary.

In all other instances we do not gratuitously tell prospective patients that they *need* our help. Patients determine their need for help. We help them decide the kind of help they require for their particular ailment. In doing otherwise we run the risk of stimulating regression and dependency, and the latter may incite intense fear and rage. Our eagerness to treat those we believe to be in need should be tempered by our realization of these perils. We should assure ourselves that patients voluntarily solicit our help or, at least, wish to explore the possibility that we have something of value to offer them.

The Meaning of Silence and Talking

For many, to be listened to is an honor and a sign of respect, acceptance, and potential understanding. Others experience silence, especially lengthy silence, as rejecting and threatening. On a deeper level, some patients savor words as if they were food given by therapists lovingly.

Continuing the metaphor, other patients seem to chew up our words and spit them out. When some patients are spinning out a theme they want their therapist to hear, they feel an interruption as jarring and invasive. We may need to listen longer to discern the meaning behind the meaning. With each patient, then, we have to learn what silence and words mean. We will also discover that they mean different things on different days: the patient's frame of mind may have changed in the interim. What makes our work difficult also makes it interesting and challenging. For sure, we can't take anything for granted!

Significance of Objectives

Long ago I heard a story, perhaps apocryphal, about the well-known pianist Oscar Levant. A friend said to him that although Oscar had been in treatment with an analyst for several years, he didn't seem to have changed a bit. The friend then asked him why he continued something that seemed worthless. Mr. Levant replied, "It gives me somewhere to go." Without objectives, there can be no meaningful therapeutic alliance. Therapists and patients do not get together for their mutual amusement or gratification. By definition an alliance must have a purpose. What about those patients who are sincerely interested in pursuing psychotherapy but at the outset are unable to delineate goals clearly? In this event the first objective will be for the patient to define one or more goals, with the therapist's help.

Primacy of Process

Most of the time, when we attend to process properly, the material that is grist for our therapeutic mill will emerge naturally. This is another way of saying that we vote with our feet or what we do is usually closer to "truth" than what we say. Then, having been caught dancing, we sing. The other day I was interviewing a patient for the first time. In exploring a suicide attempt, I asked how close she had come to succeeding. She replied, seriously, "Very close." However, one corner of her mouth turned upward in what looked like partially suppressed amusement. When I commented on what I thought I had observed, the patient said that I was wrong, it wasn't amusement: "Every psychiatrist makes such an issue of that and it's not my problem *now*!" I was then able to understand that my questioning had distressed and angered the patient. Consequently, I acknowledged and empathized with her feelings and invited her to tell about what was on her mind *now*. Had I missed the process, I would have also missed an important piece of content and thereby might have put the interview in danger of failing to achieve its intent.

A blatant example of what can happen when an interviewer ignores process occurred recently when I observed and supervised a resident psychiatrist's diagnostic interview of a patient. (This particular resident usually did very well in conducting such interviews, and I later found out that he had been preoccupied with a serious personal crisis.) The patient seemed to be trying to tell him something. Each time, the resident interrupted the patient with an item from his own agenda, and each time he did this, the patient looked over at me appealingly. I had to intervene and found out that what the patient was trying to say was that her husband was bisexual and had infected her with AIDS. As it turned out, the woman was delusional. The trainee seemed to be on his way to missing a very significant diagnosis.

Because we update and amend our psychodynamic

formulations throughout psychotherapy, it is of great significance for us to take note of and talk with patients about what they do. What they do during therapy sends us powerful messages. More often than not, patients' actions are reactions to something we have said or failed to say. These actions are designed, unconsciously, to lead us toward or away from consequential material. Patients not only long to be truly understood, they also fear revealing unpleasant facts about themselves. First, they are loath to know them. But knowing them, they are very reluctant to reveal these "shameful" secrets to us. It is hard enough for all of us to say *to ourselves,* "What a horse's ass I made of myself." It is much more difficult to admit it to another person. There may be times, of course, when we purposefully ignore an aspect of process because, for example, we believe that a patient is not quite ready to go in the direction they are evading or that to go there would be too dangerous for the patient. The latter is an example of how we use psychoanalytic judgment to provide support by eschewing an uncovering tactic.

The Importance of an Aseptic Therapeutic Field

Psychoanalysts believe that the most aseptic therapeutic field is the kind they create by behaving with virtual neutrality toward patients and the data they reveal. What these classical analytic clinicians present to patients is the so-called blank screen. Patients usually lie on a couch and the analyst positions herself or himself at its head, out of sight. Presumably, whatever the patient reads into this situation is the patient's material only. Analysts have reduced their actuality to a minimum. However, some patients have strong reactions to this experience. These clinicians intend to provoke a certain degree of frustration, regression, transference feelings and attitudes, and, ultimately, a strong transference neurosis.

To apply this concept to the broad range of psychotherapy discussed in this book, we must maintain a relatively sterile therapeutic field differently. Although our presence, as persons, is more evident and sometimes purposefully used as a therapeutic tool, we endeavor to make a clear cleavage between our roles as therapists and our other roles. The principle of tailoring our interventions to satisfy patients' needs maintains this separation of roles and keeps the therapeutic field free from contamination.

The Power of Transference

Psychoanalysis has taught therapists who have taken transference seriously to treat it with great respect. Transference is one of the most important facets of the patient–therapist relationship. When patients experience a therapist in an excessively negative way—for example, if the therapist represents someone hateful from the past—the therapy can be destroyed. To sustain patients, especially during difficult times in therapy, sufficient positive feelings toward the therapist are crucial. You will find ample discussion in pertinent chapters about how to be sensitive to and manage transference from the beginning and throughout psychotherapy. Psychoanalysis also teaches us that it is important to differentiate transference from manifestations of patients' characters. The latter reflects how patients behave toward others "normally." Our interventions, as I shall discuss later, vary accordingly.

An Equitable Division of Responsibility

If therapists seem to be working harder at therapy than their patients are, something is seriously wrong. Looked at differently, we can confidently expect that some patients will try to induce guilt in us for their failure to improve. They thereby may make the outcome of their psychotherapy more important to the therapist than it is to them. We must be on guard to avert this situation, which is equally toxic to us, to patients, and to *their* therapy. Those of us who have a tendency to be too conscientious should keep this possibility in mind and make adjustments in our attitudes as necessary. I make this next pronouncement so often that I must need to hear myself say it. We are responsible *only* for conducting the therapy in as competent and professional a manner as possible. The rest is up to patients or what's written on the wind!

Our Actions Must Validate Our Words

Dissonance between our words and actions shadows our images as therapists and as persons. If serious enough, such dissonance may ruin our credibility. In making contracts and establishing alliances with patients, we set forth certain expectations, such as that patients be on time; therefore, we must be on time or offer a compelling reason for our lateness. In our expectation that patients will speak freely and fully to us, we imply that we will listen to and hear what they say. Consequently, for instance, we tell patients far enough in advance about our inability to meet with them at a scheduled appointment time. By doing so, we give patients ample opportunity to express their thoughts and feelings about the change in scheduling. We do *not* wait till the end of a session to say: "By the way, next Friday I'll be away and won't be able to meet with you. So, I'll see you in two weeks." If we do this ostensibly by "accident," then we need to look at how we are feeling toward this particular patient. If we do this repeatedly, we will have to conclude that something is seriously amiss with the way we are doing psychotherapy. Perhaps we have deluded ourselves into believing that we are receptive to receiving patients' displeasure and anger. In this example, we may be demonstrating that we are not!

2

Diagnostic Consultations

Meeting Strangers
Diagnostic Considerations
Treatment Considerations

Meeting Strangers

It is possible to have a therapeutic conversation with anyone, anywhere, anytime. It should be easiest to have such a conversation with spouses, children, other family members, best friends, and colleagues. I don't mean treating them. I mean listening and responding in a caring, helpful way. The trouble is that we need things from all the people we are closest to. It is difficult to set aside *our* needs and be truly compassionate toward them. We *can* do it, and often do, but probably not on Friday night. What facilitates our empathy for these people is familiarity. We're starting within a continuing relationship. Mustering a bit of empathy for those we know, care about, and most resemble comes naturally. Doing likewise for strangers in distress is another matter. Let's think together about how to do this task as effectively and painlessly as possible. Doing this is of great importance! How skillfully clinicians conduct the first session sometimes determines whether patients return for a second.

The first step in the process is the diagnostic consultation (see interview outline in Appendix B). At its conclusion, one of four outcomes occurs:

1. The consultant advises against treatment.
2. The consultant recommends treatment, but the patient rejects the recommendation.
3. The consultant advises treatment and refers the patient to another therapist or agency (perhaps admission to an inpatient psychiatric unit).
4. The consultant recommends outpatient treatment and offers to accept the patient for it.

Diagnostic Considerations

Beginning any relationship is difficult for the therapist and much more so for the patient. (The therapist in training, caught between patient and supervisor, may experience great difficulty.) How can therapists ease those first few moments? We can help by welcoming our patients warmly and graciously. I generally say, "How do you do, Mrs. Smith? I'm Dr. Fitzgerald. Please come in, have a seat, and make yourself comfortable." Then I like to continue with social chitchat for a few minutes. That helps me and many patients get more comfortable. For all but a very few patients, my canine co-therapist, currently an English cocker spaniel named Siôbhan (Shiv-*on*), helps immensely to make those first few minutes relatively relaxed and often revealing. I begin observing patients and my interactions with them as soon as we greet each other in the waiting area.

Now it's time to shift into a professional role. As I enter the necessary data into the computer billing program, I get my second peek at patients (my first was during the brief initial screening interview on the phone): where they live, with whom, where they work, and so on. As clinicians begin to get to know their patients, it is good to keep in mind the journalists' list of questions: Who? What? Where? When? Why? So I pick up pen and clipboard and start with these questions. To orient myself to the patients, couples, or families, I start by drawing a genogram of their nuclear family, recording the answers to these journalistic questions in a diagrammatic and easily accessible form. With this kind of record, it never becomes necessary to plow painfully through a record to find out how many times a patient has been married, for how long to each spouse, how many children were born of each union, and where everybody is now. Questions flow naturally as I sketch out the genogram: "So this was the first marriage for both of you. Do you have children? Did all three pregnancies and deliveries go well? Any pregnancies end in any other way?"

The strangers become, little by little, more familiar and often begin to respond positively to this first display of interest in their lives.

Nosologic Diagnosis

Experienced clinicians glide smoothly between the rational-active mode of interviewing and the sensuous-receptive mode. The rational-active mode employs questioning, attentive listening, reasoning, and a classificatory system. Its aim is to determine what psychiatric condition troubles the patient. It is akin to the mental procedure an internist uses to make a diagnosis of, say, a myocardial infarction. In the sensuous-receptive mode, therapists defocus and listen to the patient and to themselves. The patient's meaningful themes hide, just under the surface. Therapists use feelings, images, fantasies, and wishes that they notice in themselves as tools to understand the patient's material.

Clinicians use the rational-active mode to obtain the most important information, logically and sequentially as the interview unfolds, and to delay seeking the less important. First I like to find out the sequence of events that led to the consultation. Is the patient here at her or his own initiative? If not, whose idea was it? Does the patient wholeheartedly agree with the reasons for the referral? If not, what led the patient to come? What is the patient expecting or hoping to gain from the consultation?

Next I ask the "chief complaint" question, usually in a very general way: "Please tell me about the situation that brought you to see me."

Inquiring in this way gives patients much latitude in responding. It usually elicits the patient's central concerns. If the patient's thinking is reasonably clear and well organized, I thoroughly explore all the clinically relevant aspects of these concerns. If the patient's thinking is poorly organized, tangential, or circumstantial, I provide structure and focus lest interview, patient, and I become increasingly more confused. As the information obtained from the patient requires and as tact permits, I actively seek the data required to make any treatment plan that must be put into effect promptly. Is the patient suicidal or homicidal? If so, how imminent is the danger? In like manner I follow the patient's leads and/or raise questions designed to establish a DSM-III-R diagnosis (American Psychiatric Association 1987). This can also be done within the framework of a structured interview or with a computer program written for this purpose. Or clinicians may follow an internalized outline flexibly as time and the patient's status permits.

It is important for several reasons to know what disorder the person is suffering from, so as, for example, to prescribe proper medication. It is equally important to know what kind of person is afflicted with the disorder. We get some sense of this as we watch and listen to the patient responding to us, although we are aware that much of what we perceive, at first, is a defensive veneer. To develop a deeper understanding of patients, we will make a "dynamic" diagnosis, which will be discussed later in detail. Psychiatrists performing diagnostic procedures may conduct a review of systems and perform physical and neurological examinations. All mental health professionals should perform a complete mental status examination. These procedures will not be discussed here in any detail; many excellent books and articles discuss them thoroughly. All mental health professionals should use the biopsychosocial model and grant equal weight to all three dimensions. And each of the mental health disciplines has its special expertise in one or more of these dimensions.

It is better not to hurry the diagnostic process. Two hours are better than one. These may be sequential or several days to a week apart. In particularly difficult cases I may ask the patient to spend more time with me before I offer an opinion and recommend a treatment plan. Occasionally I refer patients for a psychological test battery. If a physical or neurological examination is indicated, I refer patients to their physicians or to specialists. Every step of the way, I keep the patient fully informed about what I am doing and why, using language that is at the patient's level of comprehension. For example, to an electrician, I might say, "Your circuits could benefit from a few resistors" or "Your symptoms are like fuses blowing." I make it clear to most patients that we are partners in this diagnostic endeavor and that I want them to participate in any decisions that must be made. Patients whose conditions preclude their giving informed consent are exceptions to this rule.

The Clinician's Behavior

While going about the task of arriving at a formal diagnosis and treatment plan, the clinician makes every effort to attend to the patient's discomfort. In addition to the tactics mentioned above, therapists listen intently and display respectful interest and restrained curiosity. It might be remiss *not* to ask, "Has your mood influenced your sex life in any way?" However, asking for explicit details too early might be inappropriate.

Experience enables therapists to feel calm and confident. Regardless of how upset, hostile, or uncooperative a patient is, the proficient therapist retains control of the interview. Talking with patients about the behaviors they manifest leads to an understanding of the feelings, attitudes, and experiences behind these troublesome behaviors. This understanding then permits therapists to say or do whatever is necessary to calm the patient down. For example, suppose the patient reveals a bad experience with a previous professional caretaker. Talking with the patient about this experience and empathizing with his or her feelings about it often gives the patient enough courage to give another therapist a chance. Saying something like the following may also help: "Well, you'll have to watch me closely then; telling you I don't intend to do anything like that won't help much."

It is contrary to good practice to *agree* with the patient by attacking the person cited, for we do not yet know how much the patient has distorted what happened or has projected his own disowned characteristics onto this other person. Nor do we know what more fundamental transference experience the patient's attitudes, feelings, and behaviors may be grounded in. Significant, forgotten childhood experience with family members is probably involved. Unless we're very careful, the patient is likely to experience us in a similar manner, and we must prepare ourselves to deal with these negative reactions aseptically. We must deal effectively with any impediments that stand in the way of our attaining the goals of the consultation. In rare and extreme cases the therapist must terminate the diagnostic process:

> Well, it's clear, Mrs. Jones, that you have a strong belief that you're in the wrong place. You are convinced that you don't need to talk with a psychiatrist at all. If you change your mind about that, I'll be here if you need me. If you wish, I'll report back to your doctor and she can take it from there.

This outcome is unfortunate but occasionally we have to bring it about.

We can express empathy toward patients in several ways (Havens 1978, 1979). We cannot manufacture it. For empathy to be perceived as sincere, therapists must feel it. When I feel empathic—imagining myself being the patient, feeling what the patient felt or feels—I hear myself making barely audible guttural sounds that signify the feelings. What I say audibly may be very parsimonious or consist of much longer responses; I might say any or all of the following things: "Of course." "Naturally." "Ow!" "That hurt." "That must have been difficult for you." "That sounds sad." "No wonder you did that!" "Who wouldn't be upset and mad under those circumstances?"

If I do not feel empathic, the patient may be hitting something in me that I will need to understand and overcome if I am to work with this patient. It may mean, however, that the patient is massively distancing himself from me for some compelling reason.

Concluding Abbreviated Consultations

We sometimes limit the initial consultation to making a nosologic diagnosis (e.g., Panic Disorder with Agoraphobia), creating an abbreviated dynamic formulation, and offering recommendations to the patient and to the referring professional. In concluding this type of consultation, I usually summarize the essential elements of what I have heard and give the patient an opportunity to make any corrections or amendments. Then I make an explanatory statement, such as the following:

> Your suffering seems to fit the picture of the kind of depression that is caused, in part, by problems with the regulation of moods by certain chemicals in your brain. The treatment that is usually effective involves taking medicine and entering into psychotherapy. The medicine will work on the chemical aspect of your difficulty. Psychotherapy will help you understand yourself better so that you can make any necessary changes in your attitudes, thinking, or life-style.

Using language the patient can grasp, I often expand on this explanation, especially if patients ask.

I next address the question of who will undertake the treatment. Currently, a social worker or a psychologist sometimes conducts the psychotherapy while a psychiatrist does the medication management. If I agree to do the treatment and the patient concurs, I go on to explain the terms of the treatment contract, about which more later. If one of the objectives of the consultation is to evaluate and prepare the patient (and therapist) for psychotherapy, a thorough dynamic and genetic assessment is made.

Psychodynamic Diagnosis

Within some sections of this diagnostic interview, the therapist will encourage patients to free-associate; the therapist will shift into the sensuous-receptive mode of listening.

> Now I need to hear you think out loud for a few minutes so that I can observe how your thoughts go from one to another, then to another, and so on. Even if you ask a question, I may not reply so that I can listen for *your* next thought.

We need to be careful in the use of this method. It should be used only with patients functioning on a "neurotic" level with relatively strong egos, who employ more mature defenses. If the patient shows any signs of decompensation, such as loose associations, free association should be replaced with structure. In this case I say:

> That's enough of that kind of talking for now. Let's return to a more detailed exploration of what happened at work just before you became anxious.

By focusing on details of the patient's history, I provide the required structure.

Early in the second session I bring out the necessary data from patients to draw a family-of-origin genogram.

The information elicited about family members is pregnant with meaning. For example, I find out the ages of parents at the time of death, month and year of death, cause of death, and the status of the parental marriage at the time. If one or both parents are living, I find out their occupation, where they are living, and the like. Next I ask about each child of the parents' union and about any other parental marriages. You get the idea. Try it and see how useful data will practically jump off the page at you. And think of how easy it will be for a subsequent clinician to review the case.

Next I explore the nature of patients' past relationships with significant family members and I probe for the feelings within these relationships:

> As you were growing up, from as far back as you can remember and until the present time, what was and is it like between you and your mother? How did you *feel* about each other at the various stages of your development? . . . Good, that's a complete description, but I didn't hear anything about feelings.

I continue the questioning until all sections of the outline are complete or time runs out. If necessary, I schedule additional sessions.

Some therapists-in-training are reticent about taking the history of patients' sexual development in these early interviews. If we are matter-of-fact in our questioning, most patients will have no difficulty in responding.

> How and by whom were you prepared for menstruation? When did you have your first period? What was it like for you? Did the preparation you had help you avoid being upset or embarrassed? When and how did you learn about masturbation? How did you feel about doing it?

Naturally, if the patient displays too much dysphoric affect, the therapist should inquire into the reasons and might elect to defer further exploration of the sexual area. If the patient has been sexually abused or raped, the clinician's approach should be especially gentle and non-intrusive.

Many therapists do not inquire about dreams until therapy is well underway. Early dreams, before patients become defensive, are often very revealing. I ask about recent dreams, especially any on the night before the interview or between the first and second session. These very recent dreams can dramatically reveal patients' anticipations about and reactions to the therapist. For example, a patient may dream of going on a trip by air. If the patient creates a scenario in which the plane crashes, we can strongly suspect that the patient is extremely frightened about our piloting the therapeutic flight.

Near the end of the session I ask what these interviews have been like for the patient. I also inquire directly about how the patient has reacted to me: "What feelings have you noticed about my approach in these interviews? And what feelings in regard to my personality?"

Most patients will state their reactions to the actual behaviors of the clinician, relatively uncontaminated by transference distortions. If the latter are present, especially of a negative sort, the therapist should talk with the patient about them.

> What did I do or say that led you to believe that you didn't answer questions in ways that I expected? Have others been critical of you in the past? Who do you remember as being most critical?

Later on I will discuss the rationale for addressing negative transferences promptly especially in supportive and brief psychotherapies.

Therapists should now be ready to make recommendations to patients and their families. The first question is whether to advise treatment at all. We will consider this question next.

Treatment Considerations

To Treat or Not to Treat

When therapists take patients into treatment, they make a major commitment of time, energy, and dedication. Patients make an equally heavy investment, and they or third-party payers invest substantial amounts of money as well. Decisions in favor of therapy require careful evaluation of the gravity of the condition to be treated, the prognosis, and the ratio of benefit to expenditure. I would reassure a patient who presents, for instance, with a simple phobia of tigers, and I would then tell the patient that avoiding tigers is a simple and inexpensive alternative to psychotherapy.

Any circumstances that contribute to a very poor prognosis may dictate a recommendation against treatment. Chronicity, absent or poor motivation, minimal or no apparent suffering on the patient's part, inadequate or absent family or other social support, each suggests a relatively poor prognosis. With two or more of these present, the prognosis may be grim. We know, however, that there are many chronic patients who never get much better; they will be patients for life. If maintenance treatment keeps a patient out of a hospital, it is worth the expenditure. Some conditions we can control but never cure, such as Bipolar Disorder. Here too treatment will continue for as long as the patient lives. Certainly it is worth the continuous, bilateral effort to keep bipolar patients stabilized, with normal mood and good functioning most of the time. All contraindications to therapy are relative. It is difficult to know where to draw the line. When in doubt, clinicians can recommend a trial of psychotherapy for some reasonable time.

In certain situations we also have to consider the balance of risk and benefit of psychotherapy. For example, with patients who present with a serious marital conflict as a central concern, successful individual psychotherapy often increases the chance of divorce. Family psychotherapy is indicated in such a case. If one or both spouses reject this recommendation, we should inform them both of the risks involved. Nor can we omit telling patients that treatment could make matters worse for them in other ways. If we believe that psychotherapy is powerful enough to help, it follows that it can do harm. For example, a therapist may help a patient see some unpleasant aspect of herself or himself that is very painful and cannot be changed. In retrospect, we conclude that certain patients would have been better off with their self-deception left in place.

To warrant a positive recommendation for psychotherapy, patients must have a strong belief in its value for their condition. At the very least, their minds must be open enough to embark on a trial of psychotherapy. This is no time for proselytizing. In the presence of inadequate or questionable motivation, the therapist should counsel the patient to think the matter over carefully before deciding about treatment. Therefore, I state:

> You seem unclear about what will prove to be best for you to do. It would be better for you *not* to make a decision now. Give yourself enough time to think about it; talk it over with someone you trust. If you decide to give psychotherapy a reasonable chance to work, give me a call.

Clearly, patients who are convinced that their conditions are organic are not suitable candidates for psychotherapy.

> Mr. Jones, your doctor apparently believes that your condition is related to stress and to your emotions. On the basis of the short time I have spent with you, I tend to agree. What is most important is that you believe that our opinions are correct. Before undertaking psychotherapy, you must find a way to settle that issue for yourself. If and when you do, you may be ready to begin this kind of therapy.

Patients of this sort frequently do better with frequent, reassuring visits to their primary-care physicians than they do with us anyway.

In the role of consultant to a physician who is treating a patient with a "psychosomatic" condition, therapists can serve to enhance communication or relieve tensions between patient and caregivers. The consultant can also be supportive to the patient without saying anything about psychosocial factors related to the patient's suffering. Some patients will acquire motivation to enter treatment through this "back door" left open for them by wise and skillful therapists. If I have helped such a patient in a very specific and concrete way, I now make myself available to the patient by saying, "We can talk again, if you like, to see if there are any other ways I can be of help to you."

To assist patients to overcome the primary gain of their symptoms is a formidable task. Had patients been able to face their issues and the intense fear, guilt, or shame associated with them, symptoms would not have ensued. The symptoms, however painful, must have seemed preferable than that alternative. These processes are outside of awareness. In the presence of secondary gain, our task may be impossible. Can the patient afford to get better, give up a disability pension, and get a job that pays *less?* That's very unlikely! Most of the time it would be rendering a disservice to the patient to advise treatment in the face of massive secondary gain.

Less blatant secondary gain is pervasive. Patients do not get sick to get some unexpected payoff. Rather, they discover various advantages in being ill. Consider the case of the young man with Obsessive-Compulsive Disorder whose wife, intimidated by his anguish, agrees to wash the dishes three times after every meal, satisfying his need for control. Unless we attend to the wife's unwitting reinforcement of her husband's symptoms, he may not develop adequate motivation for change.

Patients who do not themselves suffer but who cause suffering or worry to others are often not treatable. Some of these, if their deviant behavior can be controlled, begin to suffer enough to make treatment possible. Treatment, therefore, may have to begin with the patient confined in a closed psychiatric unit long enough to convert acting up into dysphoric feelings. Only very affluent patients or their families can afford an adequate stay in an inpatient unit for this purpose. Family therapy, concurrent with individual psychotherapy, sometimes helps these very difficult patients and their families.

But what of the therapists' preferences, limitations, and need to set limits for their own welfare? Some therapists do not like to treat the kind of patient who will require emergency care in the middle of the night. These therapists will rule out patients who are likely to act up or act out in serious ways. They will also refer alcoholic patients elsewhere, except for members of Alcoholics Anonymous. When therapists are already treating several patients with very serious disorders, it may be wise for them to accept no more. Also, we are human and may dislike a certain patient for no reason we are able to identify; rather than struggling to overcome this mysterious countertransference, it might be better for us and for the patient to refer this patient to a trusted colleague. When a patient must be rejected for therapy or referred, we should do it gently.

> Presently all my therapy hours are filled. As I told you at the outset, I was able to see you for consultation only. Fortunately, your condition has a good outlook, but you should not delay getting help. I checked with Dr. Randolph and she would be able to accept you for treatment. Naturally I did not use your name, so tell her when you call that you are the patient I talked with her about today.

It is because of such eventualities that we should commit ourselves to only a few visits at first, so we can determine our suitability to treat a particular patient.

I have not yet touched on the question of the indications for family as opposed to individual treatment. First, the therapist must be interested in and capable of conducting one or more of the family psychotherapies. Otherwise, a referral should be made. I will briefly consider the indications for family, as opposed to individual, therapy. In the chapters devoted to couples and family treatment, these will be discussed in some detail.

Whom to Treat

At the time of the initial phone contact, therapists should be mindful of any compelling indication for family psychotherapy. Or, in some cases, we may find an indication to involve the family at some level in the diagnostic or treatment process. There are only two relatively unequivocal indications for individual therapy. The first is if the patient is an emancipated adult living on her or his own. The second is if the patient has a strong wish to deal mainly with her or his individual issues. There may be cases where individual treatment is the treatment of choice but where it is important to involve a family member (or close friend) from time to time to act as a support for the patient and report to the therapist as needed. For example, a patient with Bipolar Disorder may need a tap on the ego when a manic episode portends. Sometimes the patient's friend or relative may have to call the clinician. I will supply additional explanations about this important topic when I discuss the outpatient management of very disturbed patients.

During my telephone intake interviews, which I conduct myself, I ask probing questions to determine what form of psychotherapy is indicated. For example, I ask:

> Are you saying, Mrs. Jones, that difficulty between you and your husband is one of your main reasons for seeking treatment? How receptive is your husband to attending with you? No, it would be better to meet with the two of

you first. Then, depending on the result of that consultation, we can decide together what would be best to do next.

Although I am tactful in these cases, I am quite firm.

The caller may be a parent seeking treatment for a child or adolescent. Although the young patient may require evaluation and individual treatment by a child psychiatrist, family therapy may be the treatment of choice. Therefore, I declare:

> For starters, Mr. Smith, I like to meet with all family members to get as much information from everyone as possible. What form the treatment will take after one or two family consultations, we'll talk about then.

Any problems this parent or other family members have with this advice, I handle immediately on the telephone. Further discussion may be required before it is possible to schedule an appointment with the family. Or they may not like this approach and go elsewhere.

Of course, if the person calling for the appointment is asking for family therapy, the only thing that needs to be determined is which family members should attend. A brief exploration with the one calling will usually make this issue clear. Families seeking family therapy are easier to deal with on the phone and in early sessions.

Therapists should tailor treatment plans to fit the individual needs of each person and family. At the outset or later, one or more family members may require individual psychotherapy, so the treatment plan often includes some mix-match of individual and family psychotherapy, concurrently or sequentially. I will explain these procedures in more detail in the chapters that follow.

Having recommended some form of psychotherapy and accepted the patient(s) for treatment, we are now ready to consider how to *continue* the treatment, what the therapeutic alliance is and how to promote it, and how to make and guard a therapeutic contract. I say "continue" advisedly, because treatment, whether we or someone else undertakes it, began when we uttered our first words to the prospective patient. All along we have displayed interest, concern, respect, compassion, understanding, and our wish to understand more and be helpful if we can. We are now ready to begin treatment formally.

3

Beginning Treatment

Planning for Degrees of Support and
   Expression
Strategic Planning
Educating Patients about Psychotherapy
Protecting the Therapeutic Alliance
Initiating and Guarding the Therapeutic
   Contract
Determining Goals

This chapter will discuss briefly and in general terms some of the most important elements of the beginning phase of psychotherapy. Subsequent chapters will expand on these topics.

Planning for Degrees of Support and Expression

Individual Treatment

To begin planning, we place the therapy on a continuum which reflects the blend of supportive and expressive strategies we intend to use at first (Luborsky 1984). I assume that all sensible psychotherapists are supportive, especially when patients need support. Some patients experience support aversively. For example, a patient who has experienced excessive parental "encouragement" (to do what the parents believed to be best) will likely react negatively to our well-intentioned encouragement. Unfortunately, we may not know patients' idiosyncratic sensitivities until we hit them. Nosologic diagnoses can serve as rough guides to how supportive or expressive our treatments can safely be. Usually, the more serious the

61

condition the more supportive the therapy needs to be. Unfortunately, there is no predictable relationship between ego strength and many of the disorders classified by DSM-III-R criteria. Therefore, we must use other clinical grounds to estimate patients' ego strength and their ability to profit from more expressive interventions.

Therapists need to know the signs of stronger and weaker ego functioning (Adler 1982, Buckley 1986, Colby 1951, Gustafson 1986). To do so we ask a series of questions about patients:

1. Relative to the stress the patient has been under, to what degree have the patient's social and occupational functions been impaired?
2. What has been the patient's most serious pathological behavior?
3. Are the defenses the patient uses most often those that we classify as more mature or more primitive? (See Table 3-1)

We must also separate those patients who are introspective and capable of understanding dynamic concepts from those who are not. Patients may possess relatively good ego strength but lack intellectual curiosity about or the introspective capacity to explore their mental lives. Some who seem naive or ignorant are capable of learning psychological formulations. Others who are bright and sophisticated prove unable to profit from more expressive, insight-aiming treatment.

I make an educated guess about the sum of these factors and tentatively rate the therapy on a scale of 1 to 10, with 1 being most supportive and 10 being most expressive. I find that I never use either extreme. Rather 1 gives meaning to 2 and 10 to 9. Most of my therapies I rate as 3 to 7. Whatever plans I make in this regard are very tentative. As soon as I find that a patient cannot tolerate the degree of expressiveness I have used, I become more supportive. And as soon as I find that a patient requires and can tolerate more uncovering, I restructure the treatment accordingly.

Family Treatment

Planning family psychotherapy is similar in principle to preparing for individual treatment. Now we operate zoom lenses on our clinical cameras so that we can change our focus back and forth from individuals to the family group. The first step is the same, to decide the degree of supportiveness indicated for a particular family. What must we consider here? First we evaluate the status of the primary patient (if there is one) as if this person were entering individual therapy. Then we evaluate the status of the family in terms of its assets and liabilities. Families who present with chaos, disorganization, emotional volatility, and anger need more structure. Another significant variable is the number of family members who will attend meetings. Larger groups typically need more structure than do smaller ones. As with individual therapy, I consider all these factors and decide how much support seems to be indicated to begin with.

Have you ever attended a disorderly committee meeting? Members discuss one issue after another. They solve no problems, make no plans, vote on no motions, and take no actions. Therapists who conduct family treatment cannot allow such disasters to occur. A few families require maximal organization to be provided. For these sessions, I write out rules and agendas; the chapter on family psychotherapy contains a detailed example. A few families require minimal structure; most families are rated somewhere in between.

TABLE 3–1*
A Theoretical Hierarchy of Defense Mechanisms

I. **Psychotic Defenses:** Common in healthy individuals before age 5; normal in adult dreams and in projective testing.
   1. Delusional projection: Frank delusions about external reality, usually of a persecutory type.
   2. Psychotic denial: Denial of an easily perceived external reality.
   3. Distortion: Gross reshaping of external reality to suit inner needs, e.g., hallucinations or wish-fulfilling delusions.

II. **Immature defenses:** Common in healthy individuals aged 3 to 21, in character disorders, and in adults in psychotherapy. (Slight alterations in the definition of these mechanisms allow their translation, with the exception of "splitting," into the mechanisms that, according to Kernberg, underlie borderline pesonality organization.)
   4. Projection: Attributing one's own unacknowledged feelings to others.
   5. Schizoid fantasy: The autistic use of fantasy to create comforting or controllable people in one's own mind or to resolve conflicts with others in secret.
   6. Hypochondriasis: The transformation of reproach toward others, first into self-reproach and then into exaggerated complaints of pain, somatic illness, and neurasthenia.
   7. Turning against the self (passive aggression or sadomasochism): Aggression toward others expressed indirectly and ineffectively through passivity or retroflected toward the self.
   8. Acting out: Direct nonspecific expression of an unconscious wish or impulse in order to avoid being conscious of the affect, or the ideation accompanying the impulse, or the object toward whom it is directed.

III. **Neurotic Defenses:** These mechanisms are common in everyone, especially those with neurotic disorders and in individuals mastering acute stress.
   9. Dissociation (neurotic denial); Temporary but drastic modification of one's character or sense of personal identity in order to avoid emotional distress.
       N.B. Although placed with neurotic mechanisms, dissociation, unlike the other mechanisms in this section, is associated with maladaptive outcome.

TABLE 3–1 *(Continued)*

10. Isolation (intellectualization, undoing): The thought is conscious, but the associated affect is unconscious. Present in most obsessive thought and compulsive behavior.

11. Repression: In contrast to isolation, the affect is often conscious, but the associated ideation is unconscious. Present in seemingly inexplicable naiveté, amnesia, and conversion hysteria.

12. Displacement: A redirection of conscious feelings and ideation toward a less-cared-for (less cathected) object than the person or situation arousing the stress. Present in many obsessions and conversion reactions.

13. Reaction formation: Ideation and affect are conscious, but opposed to an unacceptable, unconscious impulse.

IV. **Mature Defenses:** These mechanisms are common in healthy individuals from age 12 to 90. Whereas mechanisms in the other three categories ignored at least one of the four components of conflict (conscience, impulse, object, or reality), each of the mature defenses ingeniously synthesizes the four components.

14. Altruism: Vicarious, but constructive and instinctually gratifying service to others.

15. Humor: Overt expression of affect and ideation without individual discomfort or immobilization and without unpleasant effect on others. In humor, the forbidden wish is expressed, but not acted upon.

16. Suppression: The conscious or semiconscious decision to postpone paying attention to the idea and affect of a conscious impulse or conflict. Unlike repression, suppression temporarily puts the conflict out of mind and then remembers to deal with it.

17. Anticipation: Realistic experiencing of both the idea and affect associated with future conflict or loss.

18. Sublimation: Indirect or attenuated expression of instincts without adverse social consequences, frustration, or guilt.

*With the permission of and my thanks to George Valliant, M.D. (1971). Theoretical hierarchy of adaptive ego mechanisms. *Archives of General Psychiatry*. 24:107–117.

Strategic Planning

Individual Therapy

Having listened for at least two hours to autobiographical material and the psychiatric history elicited from patients, therapists should be ready to plan general therapeutic strategies and tactics. To do so we make tentative psychodynamic formulations. At this point we should have the equivalent of an aerial photograph of the dynamic terrain we and the patient will traverse together (Alexander and French 1946). Now is the time to think through what we know about the patient's dynamics, how they developed, and what sustains them. If we force ourselves to put these inferences in writing, we will have to organize them. Usually a clear picture will emerge, although it may be incomplete and tentative. As we get to know the patient better, we will revise and amend this first psychodynamic formulation (Perry et al. 1987). Clarity and brevity often go together. The following is an example:

This young lady, who will be called Jane, suffered from a specific form of parental deprivation. Her mother was often seriously depressed and her father, who rarely spent time at home, was too preoccupied with business matters to give of himself to his wife or children. They often failed to satisfy Jane's needs or they met them only partially. When she was physically ill, her mother took good care of her. Naturally, Jane came to use physical complaints of various kinds to command her mother's tender care. At times, even her father would join in and spell his wife in looking after their daughter. At the same time, Jane developed the conscious attitude that she was quite an independent person and strongly avoided becoming too dependent upon others. It was only when she was ill that she felt justified in allowing others to care for her. That Jane married Henry, who was obsessive-compulsive and alexithymic, was not surprising. Although unable to articulate his feelings, Henry had a tender spot for and took good care of anyone who was suffering. Jane and Henry were at their closest when she was ill with her frequent headaches, indigestion, and other somatic symptoms. When Henry accepted a promotion to a more demanding job he became less available to Jane, and this replication of earlier painful experiences was the precipitating event that led Jane to seek psychotherapy.

It can be expected that Jane, as my patient, will probably avoid dependency on me or, at least, keep any dependent longings out of awareness. She will attempt to command my attention as a physician through "physical" symptoms. I will need to display more interest in Jane when she is "well" and less when she is "sick." I will be alert to Jane's need to test and reject me so that she can protect herself from her expectation that I will abandon her. When Jane becomes more aware of her dependent wishes, I may increase the frequency of her sessions temporarily. Because of her fear of dependency, I will honor Jane's choice of weekly or biweekly sessions at first. If Henry cannot accommodate to changes in Jane, such as more direct requests for nurture, I will consider, with Jane, including him in the treatment. I will meet with Jane and Henry early on to make an alliance with him and secure his cooperation.

Family Therapy

After one or two family sessions, the therapist's impressions about what is transpiring on the family level should be firm enough to write out. What dynamically oriented clinicians refer to as a psychodynamic formulation, family therapists usually call constructing hypotheses (Selvini-Palazzoli et al. 1980). I combine and integrate the two operations. Here is an example of a formulation I wrote after two consultations with the J. family:

> This family has been at work launching the children into the wider world. Jeff has been away at college for two years, Mary is leaving home next year, and John will follow in two more years. This transition had been going smoothly until Mr. J. had a serious myocardial infarction six months ago. The family has always had a kind of stoical, "stiff upper lip" tradition which, until recently, helped them adapt to various losses. Recently this tradition has prevented their ventilation of their fear of losing the father. It has also impeded the father's grieving the loss of his good health and confronting his mortality. Mary has

reacted with more depression than she is able to share openly, and her school grades have dropped to a serious degree. For the first time in her school career, she is in danger of failing. The family is now focused on Mary's problems. Mother and father take turns helping her with her homework. John offers his suggestions, as does Jeff by long-distance telephone. My task at first will be to join with the family in their efforts to help Mary. Gradually I will lead the family to get in touch with Mary's feelings, which seem most accessible. Later I will address the family's fear and grief. The danger of their bolting from therapy would be high if I were to confront their stoical coping style directly or too early.

Note that in this fairly straightforward example, I considered two of the main aspects of family life: (1) At that time, in what stage of the family life cycle was this family? and (2) What crisis led to an imbalance in the family's equilibrium (Fitzgerald 1982, Fleck 1983, Rapoport 1962)?

Educating Patients about Psychotherapy

Individual Therapy

All the behaviors exhibited by clinicians during the consultation sessions give patients their first instruction in what therapy is all about. Patients who have had previous treatment present different and often more difficult problems. If they had good experiences, our task will be easier; if they had a bad experience, we will seek to understand why and try to give the patient a better one. Some patients, however, regardless of how benign and skillful the therapist, will not have a favorable experience. It's almost as if these unfortunate people are foredoomed to experience repeatedly what they already believe. Let's assume that this is the person's first experience with therapy.

If we were leaders of an "Outward Bound" group, we

would conduct many training sessions before we allowed the inexperienced to set foot in the wilderness. That's a life and death matter. Similarly, patients require training in the ways of psychotherapy. They need maps of our wilderness. Sometimes they need to be set straight because they have read or heard such absurd things about therapy that it's a wonder they came at all. Often I say the following:

> This kind of treatment is like going to school to learn about yourself. Everything you think or feel is important to talk about. No matter if it seems trivial; it may prove to be a small missing piece of a big puzzle. If you feel uncomfortable, ashamed, or embarrassed when you think of something, please be sure to say it. Your feelings are telling you how important it is. We're not here to talk about easy things, and people usually find in the long run that it has been worth it to discuss difficult matters.

With this introduction I am structuring a moderately expressive therapy.

For a more expressive therapy, I will encourage introspective communication that is very close to the free association of psychoanalysis:

> I need to listen to paragraphs, even chapters, of your thoughts and feelings before I will have anything very helpful to say to you. I need to hear how your thoughts go from thought one, to two, to three, and so on, perhaps for a long time. Silence or censoring your thoughts will work against your therapy. So please say everything, no matter how painful it may be to reveal. I may not even respond to direct questions you ask, because I'll be waiting for your next thought. This way of talking is so different from ordinary social conversation that it will probably lead to your having troubling feelings. It is even more important

to talk about those, because an ounce of feeling is sometimes worth a pound of thought.

If the therapy has been planned to be more supportive, the conversations between therapists and patients will resemble social ones in their form. The therapist may talk almost as much as the patient and will answer most questions. To start more supportive therapy, I say:

> Now I'm ready to turn the floor over to you. Where would you like to begin? You have already identified several concerns. You may wish to begin by going into one of those more deeply.

A good rule of thumb is that the more chaos the patient begins with, the more structure the therapist provides. I will consider both kinds of strategies in more detail later.

Family Therapy

Most of the time I begin working with couples (Fitzgerald 1990) by using the following explanation:

> These sessions are different from the ones in which I met with each of you alone. Now I need to settle back and watch, listen, and think for a while before I'll have anything helpful to say to you. It is not possible for us to stand back and monitor our involvement with others, especially when feelings are running high. That will be my role. I'll seek to understand aspects of your relationship that you can't because you're too close to it to see clearly. Toward that end, speak mainly to each other rather than to or through me. Pick any issue you wish to address. At first, until you get used to this uncomfortable way of talking, consider one of your less difficult problems.

If I find that the couple can't handle this much freedom because, for example, they become too verbally abusive toward each other, I will intervene by working with each in turn. When they calm down enough to deal with each other more constructively, I will again ask them to talk with each other.

With family groups who are ready to look at their relationships, a similar beginning can be employed. Otherwise, it is necessary to begin by tacitly accepting the family's agenda and exploring the problem they bring. As we do so, family members will begin to interact with each other spontaneously. Taking advantage of these opportunities, therapists can intervene in ways that are indicated. With the J. family, I might say:

> Well, you certainly have tried very hard in many different ways to help Mary. I've noticed that she sometimes looks troubled. But you know Mary better than I do. Do you think she might be struggling to keep some difficult feelings inside?

Note that I do not explain explicitly what family therapy is all about with families that are not ready to hear it. Rather, I demonstrate it bit by bit, tentatively.

As has been mentioned, with some families that need maximal supportive structure, I write out rules and agendas. These will be detailed in the chapter on family psychotherapy.

Protecting the Therapeutic Alliance

Individuals

Most of the therapist behaviors already discussed support the therapeutic alliance (Colby 1951, Saul 1972, Wolberg 1954). Therapists who are empathic, interested, concerned, respectful, and optimistic and who display an intellectually curious attitude strengthen their bonds with the healthy, reasonable, adult facets of patients. We should be sure enough of ourselves that we come through to patients as informed and capable. We are fallible experts; we do not patronize others and we acknowledge that patients know more about many things then we do.

Those of you who are trainees or young therapists will usually feel less than expert. Appreciate what you do know and the experiences that you have already had. Also understand that listening carefully to patients will enable you to hear things that you can put together in ways they cannot. And it will help to acknowledge, without apology, that you are learning and will be consulting with a more senior person. We, who consult with you, hope to remember what it was once like for us. The only way to learn is to clock the hours doing therapy, expect to make your share of mistakes, and learn from them. You will survive and so will your patients. It may surprise you to find out that, no matter how confident more experienced therapists may appear, we feel puzzled and confused more often than we like to acknowledge.

With some patients whose dynamics require a type of quasi-parental guidance or that we maintain distance by being a personage, such as the doctor, we will continue as the expert. It is better to display this role by means of a somewhat formal, didactic manner than to state it. For example, some patients have intense feelings that are easily activated in the treatment situation. Therapists may need to regulate the distance between themselves and these patients. Patients afflicted with serious character pathology often call for this kind of "cool" atmosphere.

Unless there is a definite contraindication, I prefer, through my words and demeanor, to invite patients to be full and equal partners in the treatment process. I might say, "First *we* have to decide what the objectives of your therapy will be and how often we need to meet." Later I continue this approach by framing interpretations in words like these: "Most of *us* . . ." or "It's a natural part of human nature that *we*. . . ." Most of these measures apply equally to working with families, but there are some special differences.

Families

With families who have sought help for one of their members, clinicians diagnose relationship or transgenera-

tional issues (Bloch and LaPerriere 1973) and will therefore recommend meeting with all family members. Sometimes no one attending the consultation wants to be there.
Building an alliance with such a family is always difficult
and often impossible. How firm we choose to be about
our recommendations for family therapy depends upon
how critical we believe it to be for a successful outcome.
I prefer to send the family on their way, graciously
accepting their rejection of my advice, rather than getting
into a prolonged struggle with them. Alternately, it is
sometimes possible to sneak in a modicum of family
therapy by doing individual treatment with the identified
patient and having family "interviews to exchange information" at regular intervals. Families with a very disturbed family member are often receptive to a psychoeducational approach; this will be discussed in Chapter 4.

One of the pillars on which the therapeutic alliance
rests is the therapeutic contract. For this reason, it must be
clear and carefully maintained.

Initiating and Guarding the Therapeutic Contract

The most tangible and dramatic loss of a patient occurs when the patient quits treatment. A more subtle and more malignant loss of a patient occurs when the patient stays in therapy but fails to honor the contract. The contract includes the following:

1. The form of the therapy (individual, couple, family, or some mixture of these).
2. The time, length, and frequency of sessions.
3. The amount and time of payment of fees.
4. An understanding that patients rent scheduled appointments.
5. Agreement about when and under what circumstances cancellations are acceptable.

In establishing this contract, I say:

So, we have agreed to meet regularly at this time every week. We have already discussed the amount of my fee; I bill people monthly and will furnish you with a completed form for you to send to the insurance company. Unless you have some financial difficulty, which we will have to discuss, I expect patients to keep current with payment of fees. You pay me and your insurance company will reimburse you. Our appointments are like reserved seats at a football game or concert; I require that they be canceled three days in advance to avoid payment of the fee. If you have any problem with any of these terms, please tell me now so that we can talk about it.

When dealing with families rather than individuals I will add something like the following:

The whole family will attend every other week. On alternate weeks, Mom and Dad will come without the kids to focus on marital issues. Any of you who wish to see me alone in addition to the family meetings may ask to do so.

If you belong to a managed insurance plan, you will have to alter the part of the contract concerned with fees as required by the specific plan.

This contract may, of course, be changed and renegotiated if all the parties agree. But all must respect it. Therapists who permit contract violations are thereby saying: "My word means little or nothing. You may ignore it if you wish."

It is supportive for patients to know that we mean what we say; we must strictly meet our responsibilities and must require patients to do the same. Therefore, when patients bend the contract, we must respond! Lateness can be used as an example here. Suppose that at the first visit after the contract has been explicated a patient arrives five minutes late. Should therapists let this pass as trivial?

Never! I often ask, "Did you have some problem with the traffic or something?" I want to let the patients know that I've noticed the lateness, but I refrain from making an issue of it then. Next time I will up the ante by asking, "You seem to be having a problem getting here on time. What is that all about?" In therapies that are planned to be both strict and less expressive, I may say, "I don't like lateness." And to the apologies and justifications that usually follow, I reply, "Apologies and reasons don't help me like lateness any better."

I charge for most missed appointments and freely acknowledge that part of my reason for doing so is to protect my income. Exceptions to this rule are at my initiative. I *never* say, "If you are very ill, I will excuse the fee if you have to cancel at the last minute." I don't want to argue over the definition of "very ill," because doing so would complicate the contract and the aseptic handling of failed appointments. Patterns of failed appointments, especially if patients do not respond to these tactics may call for terminating the treatment.

There are, of course, exceptions to this tough approach. With patients for whom I have chosen a more permissive strategy, I may state, "It seems difficult for you to make it here on time," or "It's too bad that you are cheating yourself out of some of your therapy time." At the extreme end of the permissiveness continuum, I say, "Well, better late than never!" Again, it is of critical importance to react to every contract violation in some way.

In family therapy we should deal with the absent member issue in some forceful way. When one spouse of a couple doesn't show for an appointment, it is usually best to abort the session. If the absent spouse is in the hospital in traction or something equally serious has prevented attendance, canceling the session would be a serious mistake. If, however, the absent spouse stated that he or she is delayed at the office—and has had previous extramarital involvement—it would be a serious mistake to allow the couple to repeat their pattern with the therapist. In setting up the contract with couples and families, I say at the outset:

> From now on, this will be a family therapy. All (or both) of you will attend unless we have agreed ahead of time to change the plan.

It should therefore come as no surprise when I cancel and charge for the meeting because the couple or family has violated the contract. Note that those who arrive have participated in the breach of contract and that I hold all the adults equally responsible. So far as the children are concerned, it is clearly a parental responsibility to ensure their attendance. With some couples and families it is possible to get to a level of trust and cooperation and be able to say:

> You people have progressed to the point in your therapy that I can count on you to determine what issues have priority. I now feel comfortable leaving to your judgment which family members should attend.

For many therapists, dealing with fees is difficult. Nevertheless, doing so is part of our therapeutic job. Our work is not structured such that one aspect of it serves patients and the other only ourselves. Our society grades products and services in dollars and cents, and most people believe that nothing worthwhile is free. Therefore, neglecting the collection of fees is a threat to the integrity of the therapy. Transference and countertransference feelings may underlie patients' failure to pay within a reasonable time and therapists' failure to address this matter with them. I resent it when patients do not meet their only responsibility to me, and I know that my resentment is not good for me, the patients, or their therapy. With some difficulty, therefore, I force myself to handle this trying subject. You should do likewise.

Determining Goals

If we were starting out on a trip, "I don't know" would not be an acceptable answer to the question, "Where are we going?" (Madanes and Haley 1977). Except in those instances when utmost structure is indicated, I say:

> I'm like a travel agent. You tell me where you want to go and I'll try to get you there safely. I might tell you that a certain goal is beyond what can be expected from this kind of treatment. It is important that you state your goals clearly and that they be attainable. Once we have agreed upon general goals, we can think together about how to break them up into smaller segments. Then we can chart our progress as we go along. Remember that those who plan to climb Mount Everest have a grand design, but they plan day by day.

It is especially important to capitalize on goals in the more supportive therapies in order to keep the therapy focused and grounded in patients' actual experience in life. Therapists also use goals to facilitate and acknowledge progress. The next section of this book considers the strategies and tactics of conducting individual psychotherapy.

Part II

INDIVIDUAL PSYCHO-THERAPIES

Introduction

There are some who would eliminate the terms denoting that psychotherapy is supportive or expressive; others believe that these forms of therapy merit separate consideration (Buckley 1986, Conte and Plutchik 1986, Heim 1980, Ornstein 1986, Werman 1984). The former argue that all therapy is supportive and that all therapy promotes expression on the part of patients. I agree that all therapists give (or should give) support and encourage patients to talk. Classical psychoanalysts could rightly claim that analytic therapy is supportive. Again, I agree. What could be more supportive than having the undivided attention of a compassionate human being for three to five hours every week! But herein lies the definitional problem. Analytically informed therapists who undertake to treat patients with the aim of understanding their dynamics and imparting this understanding to them would deliberately avoid many of the treatment strategies and tactics described in Chapter 4, about the more supportive psychotherapies. For example, a more analytic therapy requires that intellectual defenses be *weakened* not strengthened, so that patients may become aware of the feelings, wishes, and impulses against which their intellectualizations had defended. What happens in the more expressive therapies is so different from what happens in the more supportive ones that it is of critical importance to think about the particular rationales, indications, and techniques of each separately. Those at an early stage of their training must attain as much clarity as possible about how to proceed with a wide variety of patients. Before we can appreciate that a therapy plan includes using 60 percent supportive measures and 40 percent expressive ones, we must understand the application of the full measure of each approach.

In day-to-day practice, of course, we neither dichotomize nor implement therapy in the ways in which we need to think and talk about it for purposes of learning. Nor should we fall into the error of holding up one method as the ideal to be striven for and regard all departures from it as the mark of a second- or third-class treatment. I have seen what a disaster can result when beginning therapists attempt to emulate their images of the analytic model. Psychoanalysis has its specific indications and methods, as do the more expressive, analytically informed psychotherapies. And the latter, the subject matter of Chapter 5, are distinct from the former. Clinicians who see patients once or twice per week cannot expect to carry out the technical rules the psychoanalyst does in treating patients more intensively. Because I discuss supportive therapy and expressive therapy as two discrete entities, I need to remind you again that supportive–expressive psychotherapy exists on a continuum!

What we actually do day in and day out is a blend of the two. To blend the two well we must learn to do each well.

Although individual therapy and couples and family therapy have much in common, especially the change agents that are present to varying degrees in all therapies, there are notable differences. Therefore, the couple and family therapies will constitute the subject matter of Part III.

4

More Supportive
Psychotherapy

To demonstrate how crass it would be to withhold supportive responsiveness under some circumstances, I offer the following example:

> This patient had been in insight-aiming, intensive psychotherapy for several months. At the time of this episode, she was working on issues of self-esteem and guilt that had led her to remain in an abusive marital relationship too long. When she arrived for her Monday morning session looking terrible, I greeted her in my usual fashion. She said, "Oh, you don't know, do you?" She then explained that her son had been killed in an accident the day before. At that point she started weeping and moaning as she walked toward me. I found my arms opening to embrace her, and she wept and wept with her head resting on my shoulder until her grief abated for the time being.

My suspension of professional "neutrality" by holding the patient in this way did *not* contaminate the transference (Nicholi 1988). We had behaved like two human beings who felt close to each other. We acted within the actual relationship between therapist and patient. Had I not responded as I did, I might have damaged the therapeutic alliance. The transference would have turned negative because of my cold and unnecessary frustration of the patient's exceptional and intense need.

In conducting supportive therapy, therapists do for their patients many of the things that good parents do for their children. It follows, therefore, that supportive interventions must coincide with the emotional status of the patient at the time. A parent who forcefully pulls a child of 5 to safety from in front of a moving truck is acting appropriately. The same parent will encourage this child to read a simple sentence and offer no more help than is needed. Following is a clinical example of fitting the response to the patient on the basis of her "psychological age" and emotional status at the moment. This intervention was also based on the patient's developmental history and on observations I had made during a family diagnostic interview:

> Sally, a college student, began her session by telling me that over the preceding weekend she had slept with seven different young men. Her manner was defiant. I saw red, and pounding the arm of my chair I yelled, "You will never do that again!" Early in this patient's therapy I had met with her whole family. Sally had told me that her father didn't seem to care about her and offered her no guidance. I directly observed his exceptional passivity during the family interview. When I reacted strongly to the patient's acting-out behavior, I did not (consciously) have Sally's relationship with her father in mind. My intervention was the proper thing to have done. She did not repeat this behavior and several months later brought her boyfriend along for a session. She wanted me to meet him and be reassured that he cared about her and treated her decently.

The psychoanalytically informed reader will realize that what I did in this instance could be viewed as a "corrective emotional experience" (Alexander and French 1946). We must individualize supportive tactics. With another patient this same reaction could be inappropriate and antitherapeutic. Imagine what might have happened if the patient's parent had consistently reacted with excessive emotion to this patient's misbehavior! Supportive psychotherapy is, indeed, based on psychoanalytic understanding of the patient and of the therapeutic relationship. It is also based on the premise that most patients tend to grow and become stronger and healthier under the proper conditions. I am, of course, mindful of "resistances" and will consider this topic below.

To construct these proper conditions, therapists attend to all the relevant systems conceptualized within the biopsychosocial model (Beitman et al. 1989, Rhoads 1988). We intervene within those systems and subsystems in which we identify problems. These interventions seek to ameliorate conflict, identify and stimulate strengths, and facilitate natural healing processes.

Supportive psychotherapy has specific indications for which it is a first-class therapy (Buckley 1986, Heim 1980, Winston et al. 1986). Poor workmen do not hesitate to use their wrench as a hammer when they have left the hammer in their truck. Therapists who use more expressive therapies when more supportive therapies are indicated are like this workman using the wrench instead of a hammer. Unfortunately, some clinicians continue to think of supportive therapy as a stepdaughter of the more dynamic therapies. It is not! Also recent studies have emphasized the efficacy of forms of supportive treatment for many patients (Burstein et al. 1972, Lempa et al. 1985).

Indications for Supportive Psychotherapy

Practiced in the way described here, supportive psychotherapy is a universal treatment in the same sense that
Type O, Rh negative blood is universal for transfusion. It
is probably the safest form of psychotherapy and as
efficacious as any other form, regardless of the patient or
condition. Its versatility lies in the fact that the degree to
which therapists employ supportive strategies and tactics
lies on a continuum. Therefore, we can apply it flexibly to
a wide range of patients and psychiatric disorders (Adler
1982, Berger 1983, Bloch 1977, Foerster 1984, Freyberger 1977, Pinney 1981).

Fragile Personality Organization

Visualizing the patients for whom supportive treatment
is the treatment of choice will help you see that this form

of treatment makes sense. It makes sense especially for this group of patients, who may not be able to make use of any other form of psychotherapy, however skillfully used. If we focus on the DSM diagnosis alone, we may not identify these patients. Consider a patient who tells of viciously punitive delusions and auditory hallucinations he has experienced for the past five years. Pursued by enemies out to destroy him and beset by voices that command him to kill himself because he is so evil, the patient is still alive! I'm not saying this patient is a candidate for less supportive psychotherapy. I'm making a point about relative ego strength and the factors that go into assessing it. It is safe to say that we are likely to find ego deficits and fragile personality organization in patients who have been or could become psychotic and in patients with severe character pathology.

We ask ourselves, "What is the worst this patient is capable of?" (Gustafson 1986, pp. 281–282). If our answer is psychotic breaks with reality, serious suicide attempts or intent, homicidal actions or preoccupation, severe drug or alcohol addiction or abuse, deep depression with psychotic features, or deep depression alternating with equally extreme highs, supportive psychotherapy will probably be the treatment of choice. It will also be the treatment of choice for patients with any diagnoses who have been unable to sustain a gratifying long-term relationship and whose ability to form a reliable therapeutic alliance is therefore limited (Buckley 1986). These patients are vulnerable to regression, are unable to tolerate even a modest degree of frustration, and are exquisitely sensitive to any suggestion of abandonment, rejection, or criticism. The self-observing aspect of their ego functions inconsistently. They depend excessively on the primitive defenses of denial, splitting, and projection. No one patient has all of these characteristics; three or four of them are all that would be necessary to make a therapist cautious about applying uncovering methods.

Presence of Extreme Stress

If someone is starving, we don't usually seek to find out why they have been so improvident; we give them some food. For patients under extreme stress, we must be there with comfort, compassion, empathy, and all the strength we can give to help them stave off emotional collapse, despair, and demoralization. People experience extreme stress at certain times: during terminal illness, and during and after natural disasters such as earthquakes and floods as well as man-made ones such as fires, mass murders, rapes, and genocide. In these days of high technology, I also include here patients in intensive care, those undergoing dialysis and transplant surgery, and their waiting, watchful, frightened families.

Serious Systemic Deficits or Problems

We must offer maximum support to people who are living under conditions of such extreme poverty that survival issues predominate, if they seek us out at all. The same is true of strangers in a strange land—recent immigrants, for example, who have lost connections with their families and native lands and have not yet formed strong human bonds in their new homes. A homosexual patient, depressed and fearful about his HIV status, totally rejected by his family and not yet integrated into a homosexual community, would be in a similar position, as would members of a persecuted minority. These and any patients living in a hostile social atmosphere, whatever the reasons for it, would qualify for very supportive psychotherapy.

Because of the high probability of misunderstandings, communication problems, and consequent difficulties in management, patients hospitalized with a medical illness adversely affected by psychological factors, and with somatization or somatoform disorders, often require psychiatric consultation and/or continuing psychotherapy. This is one of the main functions of the consultation-liaison psychiatrist, who employs mainly supportive strategies and tactics. Indeed, the definition of the term *liaison* indicates that the interventions are of a systemic nature and involve communication between groups—in this case patient, family, and staff.

Procedures that Make Supportive Therapy Distinctive

In the Therapeutic Alliance

For therapists who learned first how to do more expressive treatments, shifting to supportive modes is difficult. We must restrain our intellectual curiosity at times and *not* ask certain questions. We must also restrain our need to point out certain obvious aspects of patients that they themselves do not apprehend. Thus, in supportive therapy, fostering and strengthening the therapeutic alliance often requires that we treat patients' defenses gingerly, especially at first. Let me emphasize this point by offering an example of a mistake I made:

A single woman in her forties told of some childhood experiences with an older male relative that implied sexual abuse. I was aware of this patient's exquisite sensitivity to any questions or comments that she experienced as my finding something "wrong" with her. Nevertheless, I asked, in a gentle manner, "Is it possible that [this person] did something of a sexual nature to you?" The patient decompensated promptly and several sessions were required to help her reconstitute.

In doing supportive family psychotherapy, we must be especially careful to avoid any procedure that parents might misinterpret as blame. For this reason, questions that begin with "Why" are dangerous (*why* is a semantically contaminated word, in that it is usually experienced as critical, so it is usually better to find another way to ask). For example, in a first consultation a father severely criticized his teenage son. Rather than asking the father why he was so critical, I said:

> Mr. Jones, what John did must have been very painful for you and it's certainly your job to try to set him straight. And, John, Dad's words must have been very painful for you to hear. So right now you are both hurting.

Distributing the empathy equally to father and son will comfort each and serve to build a supportive alliance with both. Subsequently, I will plan to be alert to the first signs that a similar sequence is about to repeat, and move to prevent it.

In the Therapeutic Contract

In Chapter 3 I discussed initiating and enforcing the therapeutic contract. It is important to appreciate how supportive it is for patients to have firm boundaries within which to feel and operate. The contract serves as part of the framework of the safe haven or "holding environment" that some patients urgently need (Adler 1982). It is in the best interest of patients to know what we expect of them and to find out that we react promptly and firmly when they test our resolve.

The therapeutic alliance and the therapeutic contract belong to the "real" or "actual" relationship between clinicians and patients. Therapy cannot proceed without their being intact. They constitute the adult-to-adult aspect of the therapist–patient relationship. Both can, of course, be invaded and compromised by the "transference" aspects of the relationship. I will consider transference later in this chapter.

In the Use of Goals

As therapists we should have goals for ourselves, not for our patients. For patients, it is essential for us to estimate how much they can accomplish, on the basis of our understanding of their resources, liabilities, and motivation. I elicit the patient's (or family's) objectives as follows:

> What would you like to get out of your therapy? Please be as specific as possible. Tell me now what your top priority is or name two or three. These do not have to be written in stone. As we go along, you might change your mind, amend, or add to the list. From time to time we will review your progress so that we'll have a reading of what we've accomplished and what remains to be done.

In this introduction I am laying the groundwork for goals to be used for support, to spur the patient on or to note and congratulate patients for having attained one or more of their aspirations. If, by monitoring goals, we determine that a treatment is at an impasse, this knowledge should impel us to take a close look at what we are doing, not doing, or could do differently. Goals therefore act as the rudder of the therapy, keeping us and patients headed toward patients' ports of call.

Clarity and Structure

I have indicated that the more structure and clarity about the treatment process therapists provide, the more supportive the therapy is. Therapist silence promotes obscurity and patients usually feel frustrated by it, a feeling that stimulates regression. Frustration and regression often trigger unwanted negative transference. And the "sicker" the patient, the more important it is to avoid unnecessary complications provoked by the form of the treatment itself. Wise therapists therefore titrate silence and limit it strictly with those patients who cannot safely tolerate it. Later on, as the relationship becomes stronger and the patient gains in ego strength, he or she will require less support; then we can use more expressive strategies.

Transference Maintenance and Repair

Positive versus Negative

In supportive psychotherapy, the reasonably positive facets of patients' transference feelings, attitudes, and behaviors toward the therapist govern the therapy. I say *reasonably* positive advisedly, because excessively positive transference is better viewed and treated as negative. If patients perceive therapists as awesome figures and endow them with superhuman attributes, the patients are in a very regressed state. They are like very young children experiencing us as omnipotent, omniscient, ideal parents. The therapy takes on a fairy tale quality. For these reasons, this kind of transference is undesirable.

I also regard patients' seductiveness and transferences that are too sexualized as negative. It is a mistake to think of these feelings and behaviors as arising from sexual wishes alone; hostility is the stronger force. The patient who unseats the therapist from her or his position as therapist has scored a victory in an interpersonal war. How empty a victory it would be, the patient may never appreciate.

When patients are in genuinely positive transference, they feel trusting, confident, friendly, appropriately dependent, and respectful toward the therapist. They display these feelings and attitudes by meeting their responsibilities to the therapist and to the therapy. They make sincere and diligent efforts to cooperate, because they realize that doing so is in their best interest and because they seek to please and earn the respect and admiration of their therapist. The child in all of us wants a literal or figurative loving hug. Why then do patients *seem* to fight our efforts to show them more accurate pictures of themselves, the change they solicit, the therapy itself, and us? These so-called resistances often elicit strong feelings or countertransference in therapists and I will discuss them more fully below. Here I will consider only the transference aspect of the problem.

In supportive psychotherapy it is vital to address negative transference at the first hint of it. To allow patients, for example, to fight us because they put us in the place of a demanding parent they want to defy or a sister toward whom they feel vengeful, will wreck the therapy. In a first (diagnostic) interview a patient seemed guarded and angry, admitted that he was reluctant to reveal much about himself, and mentioned his "rebellious streak," so I interrupted the diagnostic process and said:

> I'm very concerned about the difficulty you're having in talking about yourself. It will prevent my getting the information I need to be helpful to you if you want me to work with you. You said you have a rebellious streak.

> Help me avoid stirring up your rebelliousness by telling me
> right away if I do something that makes you mad. I don't
> know where your corns are and I want to know if I step on
> one!

The patient then aired his feelings and grievances against
previous "pushy" and "bossy" caretakers, to which I
responded:

> Well, I'm sorry you've had so much difficulty getting the
> help you want and need. I don't want to be pushy or bossy
> with you or anyone. If I sound that way to you, let me
> know. I can have a bad day like anyone else.

For most of us therapists, it feels good to be lionized by
our patients. However, because putting us on a pedestal
will interfere with patients' sharing with us unpleasant or
shameful aspects of themselves, we must speak to these
feelings. One effective way to do this is to say, "As you get
to know me better you'll discover that I'm quite human."
Another, perhaps more effective way to cut ourselves
down to size is to reveal some personality foible to the
patient, saying something like, "On *my* bad days I think
that I'm in the wrong field and picture myself as a forest
ranger."

Helping patients with their seductiveness or their erotic
feelings toward us in ways that won't hurt, humiliate, or
sound rejecting is difficult. If patients are unaware of their
sexualized feelings or behaviors, our first step must be to
lead them gently to become conscious of them. Then, or if
the patient is bolder and more aggressive and says something like, "Just this once, Doctor, give me a little hug; it
would help me get through these terrible feelings about
my boyfriend's dumping me," I reply:

> I can certainly understand your need for comfort and
> reassurance right now in the form of a hug. Your wishing

for that and talking about your wish is fine! However, this is a place where it is of the utmost importance for the good of your treatment that neither of us put our feelings into action.

Male patients can be seductive with male therapists as well as with female therapists. The former situation is not necessarily a homosexual overture, but can be a more subtle form of seductiveness, such as "What did you think about the Tigers' loss of the pennant in the ninth inning last night, Doc?" Our replies to questions of this sort must conform to the therapeutic plan. If we have planned a very supportive therapy in which we will answer most of the patient's questions, we will briefly discuss the baseball game. If answering would be detrimental to the therapy, then in supportive therapy we would answer in some way without getting drawn into a conversation about the topic.

To deal effectively with patients' negative transferences, therapists must first resolve their own countertransferences.

Negative Countertransference

What is difficult for us to keep in mind is that therapists are responsible *only* for meeting their professional obligations to patients. This means keeping our part of the therapeutic contract and conducting therapeutic sessions skillfully. We will, of course, make our share of mistakes. It is generally the *patient's* responsibility to acquire enhanced self-awareness, to make the necessary changes in attitudes and behaviors, and to profit from the treatment generally. All patients encounter intense fear of change that leads them, in spite of their sincere desire to cooperate, to oppose change. We then feel thwarted by patients' opposition or resistance to change, the therapy, and us. As a consequence, we often feel hurt pride, diminished self-esteem, and anger toward patients. Understanding these dynamics and regaining our perspective about this division of responsibility will help us to resolve these unpleasant feelings and thus free us to be with patients as they struggle with *their* demons. When patients are reacting to mistakes we have made, correcting the mistake will relieve the resistance. For example, we sometimes expect too much too soon and unwittingly put excessive pressure on the patient. Easing this pressure will usually resolve this difficulty.

Other forms of countertransference, in which therapists respond to patients out of their own unresolved feelings, require continuing self-examination and self-analysis. How many people are in our consulting room? In individual treatment, the patients bring in many people from their recent and more distant pasts. In family psychotherapy, there are the actual family members plus all the images of each other and the other people who are or have been important to each. *We* bring in our host of people as well. It is wise for us to be especially familiar with our leftover childhood feelings about the significant people with whom we interacted during our developmental years. Those who can acquire this knowledge without personal therapy are indeed fortunate and unusual individuals. Nor should we neglect people close at hand: I often ask myself how I'm feeling about my wife today. You should ask yourself analogous questions about important people in *your* current life.

What to Support

Survival

We cannot treat people who have put themselves beyond our reach, for example, by committing felonious assault or murder. With patients who have the potential for violence, we must buy time. Whether we decide on inpatient or outpatient treatment, we can elicit a protective, limit-setting, no-harm contract from the patient. The form I prefer is to ask the "healthy side" of patients to make a firm pledge to themselves.[1]

> I am now speaking to your healthy side, Mrs. Smith, the part of you that brought you here to ask for help. I'm going to ask that part of you to make a contract with yourself.

---

[1]The essential features of this contract, I read long ago. I have been unable to find the source in order to give the author credit.

Please repeat after me what I will say. You may insert a time limit and any exceptions. "I will not, accidentally or on purpose, do anything to harm myself or anyone else for–you may put a time in here—unless—you may put anything that might happen to change your mind in here."

While patients repeat this, I listen to and observe them for any verbal or nonverbal signs of indecisiveness, substantial ambivalence, or deceptiveness. Nothing, of course, provides certainty, but this good-faith pledge bolsters patients' strengths. I mark the ending date of this contract in my appointment schedule in red, underlined. In using this format, I hope to avoid taking responsibility for patients' survival and their using any angry feelings that they will form toward me, against me, or against themselves by breaking a promise made to me.

Symptom Reduction

In certain extreme situations it is impossible to conduct psychotherapy because of patients' profound disturbances. Have you ever tried to talk down an excited, extremely angry, manic patient? Patients must be on a stable biological platform before they can respond to our psychological interventions. In less extreme circumstances, we must ameliorate any symptoms that cause serious suffering before patients can make maximal use of psychotherapy. Some clinicians believe that suffering is the only force that drives motivation for treatment and that patients who become too comfortable will terminate prematurely. According to these clinicians, we should therefore use medications sparingly, if at all. I have found this to be incorrect. Patients who have been properly informed about treatment, along the lines I have discussed, usually continue in treatment for a reasonable time. Besides, patients are grateful for the symptom relief they experience with the skillful use of pharmacotherapy, and their appreciation strengthens the alliance. How to combine pharmacotherapy with psychotherapy will be discussed later in this chapter under Using Pharmacotherapy.

Reality Testing and Other Critical Ego Functions

Reality testing may be impaired to minimal or profound degrees, from the misinterpretation of a nonverbal cue to a full-fledged delusion. Even the former may have serious consequences. An insecure and dependent woman may worry for much of her day because her husband left in the morning without kissing her goodbye and had a scowl on his face. If she is jealous besides, she may imagine that he is having an affair with his secretary. These feelings are extremely painful for the person who has distorted the reality of the situation and for the mate as well. Such a situation may ultimately lead to divorce. If one accuses the other of infidelity and the second is provoked into the position of "I might as well have the game as the name," the couple will be on their way into an escalating circle of destructive transactions. Situations like these underline the importance of our confronting these small distortions of reality promptly and effectively.

Patients who project their own judgments, feelings, wishes, and impulses onto others will soon do likewise with therapists. Clearly, very negative material put off onto therapists has the potential for seriously compromising and even destroying the treatment alliance. Preventing projections of this kind or reversing them promptly is therefore of crucial importance.

Delusional thinking in affective disorders, paranoid states, and schizophrenia often seems quite intractable. Delusions and other psychotic productions of patients often intimidate beginning therapists and less experienced ones as well. However, delusions frequently yield to a combination of the appropriate medications and supportive psychotherapy. The delusions do not, of course, vanish into thin air; patients may merely view them differently. Delusions are not usually present (or attended to) continuously; at times, patients become intensely preoccupied with them and at other times they fade into the background. Because delusional thinking is usually so intensely frightening and because it can seriously impair patients' functioning, we must counteract it effectively in supportive treatment.

Also, patients who lose control and abuse others physically should be quickly helped to control their impulses. Therapists must also help patients stop being abused. Before intervening forcefully, we must be sure, of course, that the therapeutic alliance is strong enough for such interventions. Whatever the dynamics of the victims of abuse, we must help them to protect themselves from it.

The capacity to sort items into a hierarchy of importance and deal with each in turn—the organizing function of the ego—is vital for people to be fit to conduct the ordinary affairs of everyday life. In any states in which the person is overwhelmed, this ego function is impaired to varying degrees. When patients' productions are chaotic as a consequence, therapists must act to help patients organize their material; to be successful, therapy must proceed in an orderly fashion.

Most of us go through difficult times. Were we not able to close our mind's door on our troubles temporarily, we would not be able to do our work at all. Suppression or the ability to live our lives in compartments is a useful and, at times, necessary ego activity. I do not say to myself:

> Now I'm on my way to work. I must put my concern about my sister's scheduled breast biopsy out of my mind for now. What I am obliged to think about now is my first patient, Mary Jones, what transpired at her last session, and what to do with her today.

For most of us, fortunately, this process is automatic, occurring on a preconscious level. We may continue to be prone to apprehension and be a little distracted. We may, I'm sure, forgive ourselves for occasionally operating with only six or seven of our eight cylinders. For functionally impaired patients, the ability to live their lives in compartments is often defunct. One of our first therapeutic tasks is to restore patients' occupational and social functioning in attainable stages.

It is also necessary for patients to develop some ability to postpone gratification and tolerate the resulting frustration in order to be able to perform average life tasks. Another aim of supportive therapy is to fortify these important ego functions.

Our language is constantly being revised by usage. One unfortunate recent change is that the word *feel* has become synonymous with think or believe, as in the sentence, "I feel that the stock market will quickly recover from this week's decline." Some people will not notice this shift in usage because they suffer from alexithymia; for them there never was a difference in meaning. When we ask some patients how they feel, they often reply with thoughts. Supportive treatment offers these patients an opportunity to learn the language of feeling and, perhaps, to know what some of their feelings are.

Sometimes parents who consult because of their children's behavior problems are ego-deficient in the sense that they do not know how to discipline. A thorough evaluation of the children and the family reveals that, except for the presenting problems, all are reasonably healthy. Neither conflicts nor a pathological family organization seems to have contributed to the difficulties. What treatment will have to attend to in these cases is the parents' deficits in the disciplinary aspects of child rearing.

Alleviation of Guilt and Shame

Granted, the capacity for experiencing reasonable amounts of *anticipatory* guilt and shame serves to regulate behavior for many. Excessive guilt and/or shame, however, are the hallmarks of many mental conditions and stand in the way of reasonably happy and successful living. In our society, people offer praise sparingly but criticize almost immediately when a person does not measure up. Under expectable circumstances, people vulnerable to guilt and shame have a very difficult time in life. When children do things parents disapprove of, some parents are quick to induce guilt or shame by saying, for example, "Shame on you!" or "What will the neighbors think of you (or us)?" Patients who anticipate that we will react along similar lines will have to test us repeatedly before they reveal many things about themselves for which they feel guilty or ashamed. Therefore, therapists must be prepared to use all the ways at their command to combat these powerful and destructive feelings.

Self-Esteem Enhancement

Patients usually have no recognition that their "failures" in life, which have lowered their self-esteem, may have stemmed in part *from* low self-esteem. It's a circular process that feeds upon itself. Usually, the act of seeking help, especially from a psychiatrist, deals another blow to most patients' self-esteem. They now picture themselves as "crazy" or as likely to be so labeled. As therapists, we must understand the power of damaged self-esteem and, at the very least, know how to avoid contributing to it. We must know that *anything* we say to patients can be screened through a denigrated self-concept and be processed as demeaning. Helping patients fight low self-esteem and its consequences is our formidable but achievable duty.

The More Adaptive Defenses

Usually, the more mature the defenses that patients commonly use, the more adaptive are their behaviors. Mental processes that people use as defenses have acquired a bad name and we sometimes automatically view them as pathological. I assure you that none of us can do without them. What I am doing right now is intellectualizing and, I hope, you are doing the same. In our diagnostic assessment of patients, we determine which of their defenses are "best" for them, that is, most adaptive. Unquestionably, reaction formation is better than projection. It is better for me to believe that I am very kind (it is clear to you that I'm very hostile) than to believe that a group of enemies is out to kill me. So please support my belief in my kindness if I am your patient. Or reinforce my ability to intellectualize so that I can better use it defensively if what I need to protect myself from will devastate me and impair my function.

Alternative Ways of Coping

Another way of looking at ego strengths and weaknesses and at the defenses is from the adaptive point of view. However maladaptive or out-of-date certain behaviors may appear, at one time they probably were adaptive. The notion of learned helplessness illustrates this point of view. For example, if pleading helplessness worked with his or her mother, a child will learn that it is profitable to do so. From a subjective perspective, this person, now an adult, learned a successful coping strategy and, given the right fit with another person, it *still* works. At the same time, this way of coping causes suffering and functional impairment. Therapists are often confronted with the very difficult job of helping patients give up or modify attitudes and behaviors that have satisfied their needs and are deeply entrenched.

How to Support Patients Directly

Treating Concurrent Medical Conditions

It sometimes becomes the responsibility of the psychiatric consultant to pick up on the possibility that the patient has an undiagnosed medical condition. I am not speaking here only of the medical conditions that present with psychiatric symptoms (e.g., AIDS, Addison's Disease) or that cause or contribute to the etiology of psychiatric conditions (e.g., subclinical hypothyroidism in depression). What I mean is a concurrent medical condition that needs attention regardless of its relationship to psychiatric symptomatology. Psychiatrists take the time to listen to patients carefully and for an extended time. It is no wonder that we come to suspect things that were missed by others. A recent study of clients referred to social agencies documented an alarming incidence of undetected physical illness in them (Corney 1985). All mental health professionals must be mindful of the general health of patients. It is very important in any kind of psychotherapy to refer patients for attention to their physical conditions. It is especially supportive to encourage, advise, or persuade patients to seek such medical attention. Out of defensiveness, some patients are reluctant to find out the truth about their physical condition. When ordinary measures do not prevail, therapists must persistently confront and explore the patient's opposition until it is overcome. For example, one 44-year-old patient thought that she had felt a lump in her breast during her periodic self-examination. She jumped to disastrous conclusions and was having great difficulty calling her gynecologist for an appointment. After approaching this problem unsuccessfully in several different ways, I said:

> When I have something very unpleasant to do, I ask myself if I'm going to do it or not. If my answer to that question is positive, I do that unpleasant thing right away. You have already decided that you will get an appointment with your doctor. So, when are you going to call him? Make that decision right now. It won't be any easier two hours, two days, or two weeks from now! Here's the phone. Call right now.

Acting almost as if she were in a trance, she made the call. She kept the appointment and had a good experience. All that the gynecologist had to do was aspirate a cyst and reassure the patient.

Using Pharmacotherapy

Usually we call this *psycho*pharmacology and with good reason. Therapists who prescribe medication must explore the meaning of medication to patients and be acutely aware of the transference implications. Prescribing medicine without a strong enough alliance in place is tantamount to making a painful interpretation or an unwelcome confrontation in the absence of a very strong trusting relationship. With very suspicious patients, some of whom very much need medication, we may have to delay suggesting it. In less difficult circumstances a brief exploratory excursion commonly proves sufficient. When I raised the question of medication with one patient, she looked and sounded doubtful and apprehensive while verbally expressing agreement. So I said:

> You look frightened. Taking medicine is frightening for many people. I wonder if you have had any bad experiences with medicine or know someone who did? Tell me what's bothering you about it. Naturally, your feelings and attitudes about taking medication are very important. And remember that you're a voting partner in this endeavor.

Fortunately, these questions led the patient to tell the story of her brother's near death from aplastic anemia caused by an antibiotic. After ventilating her feelings about this experience, the patient was able to consider more rationally the pros and cons of her taking medication. She decided to take the antidepressant. Memories of experiences from the more distant past may also be in the way of patients' accepting medication. Most pediatricians don't know how far into the future the impressions they leave on children will reach.

After patients agree to start medication, therapists should listen carefully to the material they offer for any veiled allusions to medicine. As is usual, dreams can be very revealing. Nonmedical therapists are in a particularly good position to pick up on patients' negative feelings about medication prescribed by collaborating physicians or psychiatrists; out of fear of retaliation, patients may conceal their negative feelings from the prescribing doctors. Both caretakers must talk with each other and with patients about the latter's fears and other negative feelings. To do a good job, our collaboration must be thorough and continuing so long as the patient is being treated by both of us.

I mentioned earlier the fear of some clinicians that if patients become too comfortable, they will terminate prematurely. A few more words about termination are in order here. I no longer use the term "termination," but rather talk with patients about *interrupting* their therapy. If patients require long-term maintenance medication, I meet with them at widely spaced intervals and conduct very limited supportive psychotherapy. In this way I can review with them their psychosocial functioning and they can resume the interrupted psychotherapy as indicated. Others know that they can resume psychotherapy at any time they deem it advisable to do so. I *never* say, "Remember that it's okay to call me if your symptoms get worse or if an emergency arises. I'll be here if you need me!"

I don't believe in inviting people to have emergencies in order to get back on the therapy train. Rather, I say:

> Remember that I expect you to seek an appointment if you become aware of any new issues you need to address, or old ones that need further work, or if you develop curiosity about any difficulties in living that you may encounter. We can review things at that time and decide together if you need more psychotherapy and how much more might be required.

Providing Structure and Limits

Winnicott's felicitous metaphor, "the holding environment" that therapists provide for patients, evokes images of parents protecting their children from harm (Richard-Jodoin 1989). If we are firm, tough, and resolute about the structure we provide and the limits we set, most patients will honor them. Our expectations are more powerful than we realize. When patients push on the boundaries we have set, we push back as we would for children, and we do so as often as is necessary to get our message across. Much of this limit-setting relates to the keeping of the therapeutic contract and to the therapeutic alliance discussed earlier. Much of it relates to our not allowing patients to intimidate us or to call the shots. If we choose to act as an auxiliary ego for patients in crisis, it must be clear that doing so is our choice. Suppose a relatively new patient calls in crisis at 3:00 A.M. I deal with the crisis briefly and direct the discussion of any issues that can wait to the next therapy session. At this next session I say:

> Today we'll have to understand as much as possible about what led up to the difficulties you called me about the other night. It will be better for you to take care of as many difficult situations as possible between sessions. Your own muscles could get flabby if you rely on me and don't give yourself a chance to learn that you were strong enough to have done it yourself. So call me if, and only if, you are convinced that you have made every effort to deal with the trouble yourself. And, by the way, in saying this to you I am also protecting myself; I like my free time to be as free of work as possible.

I would definitely *not* say, "Call me at any time you get worried that you might do something to harm yourself."

First, that's too vague. But more important, the patient will likely read that statement as, "To get attention around here, you have to be really sick!" or "That's the way to get at him; he just told me where to put the knife." I'm not being cynical; this is the way human nature works (ours too, not just theirs). We should invite, encourage, and support *healthy* behavior, not its opposite.

Both participants in repetitious physical abuse will be asked to use methods that their therapists firmly insist upon to reduce or eliminate its occurrence. Especially with patients who had inadequate limit-setting or guidance as children, therapists serve a parental function in this regard. I say, for example, to the aggressor:

> Pete, your abuse of Sylvia *must* stop and it must stop *now*. What I want you to do is to keep very careful track of your anger. When you feel it building, stop the argument. Take a time-out. Go to your shop and work with your wood for a while, or take a walk. Do *not* get close to Sylvia again until you have cooled off. And don't discuss that issue with her again. Bring it to our next session so that I can help you both resolve it without your actions getting out of hand.

And to the recipient of the abuse I might say:

> Sylvia, you have to help yourself avoid being hurt and also help Pete to stop abusing you. We have identified the things that tell you the situation is about to get out of hand between you. You also have to take a time-out at that point. Tell Pete that you have to leave for a few minutes and tell him exactly where he can find you when he cools down. But *don't* resume arguing about that issue. As I said to Pete, bring it here.

Using Persuasion, Advice, Suggestion, and Behavioral Prescriptions

Some of these tactics must be used judiciously! We do not persuade or advise people about important life decisions. We do offer advice about the decision-making process. We often warn patients against precipitous action. With excessively indecisive patients, I often find myself saying things like the following:

> It's important for you to make a decision about that; get it off your agenda. I realize that your conflict about it is not totally resolved and may never be. However, we have to learn to make and to live with choices even when we have some mixed feelings about them. So give yourself a deadline: I'll make up my mind about that no later than . . . you fill in the blank. I think it would be a good idea for you to set it for no later than two weeks from now.

We should use direct advice sparingly. The danger of fostering dependency and weakening patients is substantial. So when a patient says, "I'm so confused, what should I do, Doctor?" it's important to reply without actually answering the question:

> At this moment it may seem to you that the best way I could relieve your distress would be to tell you what to do. I don't think so. I believe you have the capacity to answer your own question. If I answer, I would be depriving you of the opportunity to use your own good intelligence. What alternatives can *you* think of?

Most of the time it is not supportive to encourage weakness, even if this is a strength for this patient in the sense that it has been one of the successful adaptive strategies previously described.

Although I never follow a strictly behavioral therapy protocol, I have made certain behavioral techniques my own and worked them into my supportive therapy. It's not that I don't believe in the efficacy of behavior treatment for certain conditions, such as phobias. I do. But carrying out any procedure in a repetitive, step-by-step way doesn't fit my personality; I feel bored. I do find certain behavioral style prescriptions very useful, however. Recently I gave a directionless, immature 18-year-old the following task:

> Okay, you have identified selecting a career as important to do at your stage of life. I agree with that. It will make no difference which road you take if you don't have any idea where you're going. So between now and our next appointment in two weeks I want you to go to the library and research any careers that you have even the slightest interest in. Ask the librarian for help if you need it. Of all that you read about, pick three and write out what's in favor of and what's against each of them. That's what we'll talk about next time. Will you do it? . . . No; trying isn't good enough! Either say you will or won't. . . . Very good! Then we'll have a firm agenda for our next meeting.

In this case, allowing the patient to drift in therapy as he was drifting in life would have been a disservice to him.

Correcting Faulty Thinking

Beck and other creative cognitive therapists have made the correction of faulty thinking into a therapeutic system (Beck 1976). Having been trained in logic by Jesuit philosophers, I have always been sensitive to thinking that is logically flawed. I have used what is now called a cognitive approach in several different ways. Remember the insecure woman I described who misinterpreted her husband's early morning behavior? In a session with both present, I would invite her to ask him about the meaning of his behavior. In an individual session with her I would say:

> So Jack left in what looked to you like a bad mood on Wednesday morning and you thought he was angry with you. Could Jack have been upset and angry about something else? We both know that he keeps a lot of things to himself because of his pride. How could you have found out for sure what was bugging him, rather than using your imagination? We also know in what direction your imagination is likely to lead you astray. So how do you think you could save yourself from a day of worry next time?

With somewhat obtuse patients, I use the following story under similar circumstances:

> Ten-year-old Johnny cheated a little bit on a test in school. The next morning the teacher seemed to look at Johnny and make a "mean" face. Johnny thought that she knew about his cheating and that she would punish him; she would tell his parents. Actually, the teacher and her husband had had a row that morning and she arrived with a headache and in a bad mood. Now, can you apply that example to yourself and Jack?

Delusions are extreme instances of faulty thinking. Even in supportive therapy, explanations can be used effectively to help patients understand the circumstances and feelings that are likely to make them experience delusions more intensely (Fromm-Reichmann 1959). We may be able to say, for example:

> So before you became fearful that you would be caught and punished by your enemies, you were feeling very guilty because of your daydream of having an affair with Joe. Could it be that you believe that you deserve to be punished?

Although we do not argue with patients about the reality or unreality of their delusions, we can urge patients to examine their beliefs very carefully, as follows:

> A man stood across the street from your house and you thought he took a picture of your house. Was the camera aimed at your house and only your house? Could it have been a real estate salesman talking a picture of a house that's for sale? Are there any houses close to yours that are for sale?

Even if none of these speculations is accurate, what we model for the patient is logical, analytic thinking of the sort most of us do automatically to evaluate situations like the one the patient described. Again and again, we subject the patient's delusional thinking to this kind of scrutiny. We speak our thoughts for the patient's benefit. Patients then do this for themselves and, in time, they often say:

> Well, I got into my psychotic thinking again last week. Then I thought of the questions you would raise and I got myself out. This time I didn't even have to take an extra Stelazine.

The same approach can be used with the hallucinations of patients suffering from schizophrenia and with the bizarre ideation of patients with schizotypal personality disorder.

Diminishing Guilt and Shame

Therapists function in some measure like food blenders. We take in patients' negative feelings and attitudes toward themselves, grind them up, blend them, and give them back, attenuated. We are continuously curious, questioning, and challenging. When the patient says, "Isn't that terrible, Doctor?" we ask, "According to whom?" or "Where did you learn that?" When patients block, blush, or look down and act ashamed, we say:

> What happened just now? What stopped you from saying what you started to say? Perhaps you got concerned about how I would react. Please tell me what got in your way.

Our empathy toward the patient and our understanding of his or her dilemma counteracts the guilt or shame. As we listen quietly and tolerantly to patients as they confess their "crimes" or stand "naked" before us, they gain a new perspective on their behaviors. Sometimes we express our attitudes more loudly and powerfully. For instance, I might declare, "But you were *only* 10 years old!" Or, in some cases, I might say:

> At times, most kids hate their parents and wish them ill or dead; at that age we think magically and believe that our wishes can actually do harm. Deep down somewhere, we continue to think in that magical way as adults. So we punish ourselves for wishes as if they were actions.

Sometimes I say, "Welcome to the human race; it's very reassuring to learn how human you are!"

In one way or another, we take in our patients' guilt and shame, reprocess them, and return them wrapped in gentleness.

Enhancing Self-esteem

A by-product of reducing inappropriate and excessive guilt and shame is enhanced self-esteem. Self-esteem can be damaged or fail to thrive for many reasons, however. Commonly in our society, worth is too closely tied to performance. The popular football coach Vince Lombardi said it very well: "Winning isn't everything, it's the only thing!" Explaining to patients how difficult it is to feel worthwhile in our highly competitive world can be very helpful. Therapists must be alert, noticing and *openly acknowledging* patients' meritorious qualities, their little successes, their valiant efforts, and the swift streams they often swim against to keep up with or not fall too far behind the more fortunate. Humility, and a sense of the concatenation of events that lead one person to be famous and another ignoble, should help us genuinely believe, "There, but for the grace of God, go I." Whatever we believe, we project silently or seize every opportunity to assert. I say to the patient whose self-esteem needs bolstering:

> But of course you can't keep up with Joe. You have had this terrible anxiety to contend with for a very long time through no fault of your own. It's as though you were running into a strong wind while Joe has the wind at his back. He will reach the finish line first, but you have run the harder race.

Or, I might say something like this:

> I notice that you fault yourself whenever you don't measure up to your overweening standards, but you never give yourself credit for reaching your goals.

In this process, analogous to the reworking of guilt and shame, patients give us their disfigured images of self, which we polish up and return to them in better shape. When patients fail or have made a mistake, I ask:

What can you learn from that? Don't compare yourself with anyone. Compete only against yourself. How do you plan to do better next time?

And so gradually and inexorably, patients come to feel better about themselves.

Reinforcing More Adaptive Defenses and Behaviors

By eschewing long silences, by answering most questions patients raise, and by actively engaging in supportive treatment, we deliberately discourage the dismantling of suppressions or the lifting of repressions. In more uncovering therapy, we would note and mention examples of patients' cruelty or facilitate their becoming aware of their hostile intentions. In very supportive treatment, we do not do so. I might say, "That was, as usual for you, a very kind and generous thing to have done." Or I might say, "Your need to be helpful to others is very strong. Have you thought of doing any volunteer work, like for the Big Brothers (or Sisters)?" The latter also suggests a behavior that is a better coping strategy than, for example, sleeping to escape from dysphoric feelings.

Most mental health professionals are very good at intellectualizing, and we sometimes become impatient with patients who do likewise. We complain that getting beneath their intellectual defenses is like peeling an onion; there's always one more layer. In very supportive therapy, however, we welcome patients' intellectualizing, especially if it is one of their most reliable defenses. How do we buttress this defense? By being ourselves and joining with the patient by stating such things as the following:

I agree with you. Motivation is frequently impossible to determine. We can speculate, but we're usually wrong. Have you read Camus's *The Stranger?* The ending makes that point when the protagonist says that he killed because the sun was in his eyes.

Therapists use their creative imagination to accomplish this important therapeutic job in many different ways.

With couples who need a more adaptive behavior to replace constant bickering and to stay in touch, I would maintain:

You've fallen into a rut. What did you used to do together years ago to pass the time and have fun? If you can't reactivate a former interest, you'll have to use your heads to find a project or activity that neither of you currently does, something new and different that you can enjoy together.

Titrating Frustration

I have said that in very supportive therapy, therapists avoid long silences, talk a lot, and answer most questions. However, as patients make progress and grow in strength, we frequently change *very* supportive therapy to make it a little less so. Most of the time it is not advisable to change the format of the treatment without explaining the change to the patient. So I say:

You have made good progress and are now stronger in many ways than when we started together. Now it's time to change the form of your therapy a little. I need to listen to you for longer than I have been without replying. This will probably be more difficult for you at times.

Putting that change into practice builds into the treatment a way of helping patients tolerate progressively increasing amounts of frustration without regressing in dangerous ways. Some manageable degree of anger toward the therapist now usually develops. When it does, we can mute it by increasing our responsiveness temporarily or exploring and explaining the negative feelings to the patient. As I have emphasized previously, we handle negative transferences promptly in this mode of therapy.

Discouraging Patients Acting Up and Acting Out

Certain patients act up, that is, act in ways that decrease tension or ward off something threatening; this behavior reflects the way their personality is organized. For example, prior to treatment one patient frequently punched holes in the walls of his home in reaction to his wife's thwarting him. When patients act instead of verbalizing to deal with an issue in therapy, we call their behavior "acting out." By means of the therapeutic contract and alliance and other "holding" tactics we employ, we discourage both forms of acting when we structure treatment according to the individual needs of each patient. When patients act out, we need to act promptly to contain it, by saying, for instance:

> When you broke the speed limit on the expressway, you were violating our agreement. Remember that you agreed to refrain from any kind of hazardous behavior and to get most of your feelings out here. I strongly suspect that you have some anger or resentment that would be better and more safely dealt with here. What feelings can you find within yourself?

Or, if I am reasonably sure of what led to the patient's acting out, I may say so:

> [First two sentences as above] I think I know what happened. At our last session, I said some things that bothered you more than you were able to say at the time. You left the session hurting and angry with me besides. If I am correct, it would be much better next time to tell me your feelings promptly. Let's try to understand now what made that impossible for you to do last week.

With more sensitive patients, I might take some of the responsibility myself by adding, "And I'll have to work on telling you about my sensing of your feelings more promptly next time as well." When patients do indeed respond to these interventions by ventilating their feelings or talking issues through, I will reinforce these more adaptive behaviors immediately by stating emphatically, "Very good! Now that you've discharged your feelings, it won't be necessary for you to do something that might hurt you or your treatment."

Using Interpretation Supportively

Interpretation is the hallmark of psychoanalytically informed or dynamic, insight-oriented psychotherapy. Interpretation can and should be used in supportive work as it is indicated. How it should be used is the question (Pine 1986). The less acceptable an explanation we have to give to a patient, the stronger the patient has to be to receive it. Therefore we can use palatable interpretations of patients' dynamics, motivations, behaviors, and transferences more freely than those that go against the grain. "You seem to get a kick out of humiliating her" is typically more difficult for someone to take than, "You seem extremely sensitive to anything that you perceive as the slightest bit critical." So we must be sure that patients are strong enough to withstand the content of the interpretation. However, if we err in any direction, we are more likely to underestimate rather than overestimate patients' toughness or their ability to ignore or deny an unacceptable interpretation. Recently a patient told me that what had helped her most was an explanation that I had delayed making for quite some time because of my concern about her fragility. I told her that she was equally responsible for the ménage à trois that her husband had persuaded her to engage in. True, she felt dependent upon him and fearful of opposing him, but nevertheless the decision was a bilateral one. The patient accepted this insight, something she needed to do before she could arrive at self-acceptance and self-forgiveness.

If the therapist delivers interpretations in a tentative way and prepares patients to hear something difficult, it is easier for them to consider, retain, and make use of the interpretation. Therefore I say:

> Now I have something to explain to you that may be difficult for you to hear about yourself. I'm not very sure of it. Would you rather I wait for a while until it's clearer or would you rather hear it now?

Note that I also gave the patient a choice and some measure of control. Additionally, it's helpful to wait until patients are relatively calm. Even if we understand something at a time when patients are wrought up about the matter, we wait until later to share this understanding. We strike when the iron is cold (Pine 1986). Also we instruct patients *not* to respond to the interpretation immediately, but rather instruct them as follows:

Because, as I said, this is something I'm very unsure of, it will be better if you spend a good bit of time thinking about this notion. Go on to the next thing that's on your mind now. You can tell me what your reaction to my impression is at our next session.

Systemic Interventions

Inpatient care is currently in deep trouble. Many state mental health systems are cutting back on or eliminating inpatient care. Also third-party payers (especially those with "managed care") are severely restricting payment for inpatient psychiatric treatment. Very disturbed patients are being treated by clinicians working in community mental health centers, by outpatient clinics affiliated with hospitals and with departments of psychiatry in medical colleges, by family agencies, and by private practitioners. It's like working in a mental institution without walls. It has become imperative for therapists to learn how to work with spouses, mates, and parents of patients who are or could become seriously upset (depressed, suicidal, withdrawn, manic, paranoid, noncompliant with urgently needed treatment, psychotic) (Atwood 1990). Whatever resources in the patient's social network or in the community that can be mobilized on the patient's behalf should be, as needed (Tolsdorf 1976).

For patients whose medical condition is complicated by psychological factors or who are experiencing somatization or somatoform disorders, hospitalization can be extremely stressful. Because these patients commonly have little or no insight into their emotional issues and the connection between these and their symptoms, they are very frustrating to care for in the hospital or out. In-hospital management of such patients is made more difficult by the large number of staff (residents, interns, nurses, aides, primary care physicians) who are responsible for their care. Staff toleration for patients' defensiveness may be limited. Distortions of messages and information among staff, families, and patient further confuse and frustrate all. The task of mental health consultants, usually psychiatrists, is to understand what is going on within this system and to clarify the situation for all. Clinicians offer as much care and attention to staff and family as they give the patients themselves (Peteet 1982, Pinney 1981). It is usually unwise to suggest to patients some connection between even an obvious psychosocial stressor and their symptomatology. Therapists build trust and coordinate the efforts of all caretakers so that patients' stays can be as smooth and comfortable as possible. Promoting minimal insight to make it possible for patients to address their psychosocial issues can wait until later—sometimes much later!

Family Interviews

In family interviews, in contrast to family *therapy,* the symptomatic patient is the focus of the treatment. I use the term *family* here loosely; it could also include any close associate of the patient who does not live with or have meaningful connections with a spouse or other family members.

At times, depending upon the information the therapist elicits at the first telephone contact, it is important to ask patients to bring to the first consultation the person(s) they identify as important. Most of the time, this is the family or a part of the family with whom the patient is living. We can elicit information, indispensable to making an accurate diagnosis and effective treatment plan, from families when patients are unable to do so (e.g., patients may not realize that they had a psychotic episode). If such is necessary, these people are incorporated as collaborators in patients' continuing therapy at regularly scheduled sessions.

Therapists establish a clear contract with patients and their families about the way these others will participate. Most communication between therapist and family members will take place in the patient's presence. Under critical circumstances, it is understood and agreed to by all that spouses, mates, or parents may inform the clinician of their concerns about the patient. The therapist in need of the assistance of the patient's alter ego in an emergency (e.g., high risk of suicidal behavior) may contact this person.

We need to keep in mind that these affiliates of patients are themselves often confused, frustrated, fearful, resentful, or angry. Also, how they and patients treat each other becomes a matter that deserves therapeutic attention. For example, schizophrenic patients have been observed to have a higher recidivism rate when they live in a family atmosphere of high "expressed emotion" (Brown et al. 1972). Psychoeducational family treatment may be indicated for these patients and their families (Anderson et al, 1980). Or family interviews, under the subtle or more

direct guidance of therapists, may be converted into that
or some other form of family therapy. But first we have to
ensure and contract for regular family interviews as follows, addressing patient and family member(s):

> This has been our first meeting as a team; what has it been
> like for you? . . . Well, that's fine; we're off to a good start
> then. I would like to have meetings like this at regular
> intervals. Do you all think that meetings of this sort could
> be useful to you? . . . How often would you, Eric and
> Martha, be able and wish to attend? Perhaps you could
> take turns. . . . Is that okay with you, Phyllis? . . . Now,
> Phyllis, we have already established that sometimes you
> have slipped into an upset state without being aware that
> it's happening; it gets ahead of you. And then you've
> ended up in the hospital. We want to avoid that, if
> possible. Is it all right with you if Eric or Martha calls me if
> either notices the warning signs which we've reviewed
> today?. . . . Great, that will make your therapy go much
> more smoothly. And I'd like your permission, also, to call
> Martha or Eric if I become concerned about something that
> we need their help with, if you're not able to tell them or
> if you're too upset to think clearly. . . . Is that clear to
> everyone? Any questions?

These agreements will be revised appropriately if the
family interviews become family therapy.

Family Therapy

Most forms of family psychotherapy are supportive,
regardless of whether therapists regard the patient to be a
family member or the family unit. Psychoeducational
family treatment is one of the most supportive of all; it
was designed for use with schizophrenic patients and

their families but can be adapted to fit the needs of other seriously disturbed patients as well. I will consider several ways of conceptualizing family pathology and of conducting supportive family therapy in Chapter 6.

Coordinating and Engaging Patients' Social Network

Most people have meaningful connections with many others in various positions in their social network. Supportive therapists help patients make use of these people to the maximum degree possible. I regard it to be part of my function to intervene directly with a person who has the capacity to be helpful to a patient in some way. My intervention may be either necessary or more powerful than the patient's because of my role as psychiatrist and physician.

Some patients have spiritual or religious concerns that are beyond my training and expertise. Furthermore, how I think about religion will usually be different from the way my patient does. I will be alert to the possibility that the patient is classifying an issue as "religious" in order to avoid therapeutic scrutiny, but I will not automatically assume so. To the patient who expresses a sincere religious concern, I explain:

> Well that's out of my department and I do not hold the same views about religious matters that you do. It would be better for you to consult your priest (minister, rabbi) about that. Let me know what he or she has to say and we can discuss it further then.

For many therapeutic reasons, a patient might have to be relieved from responsibilities in school or at work. It then becomes necessary for therapists to write letters to or have personal contact with school counselors or advisors, personnel managers, and union representatives. There are times when these kinds of interventions require therapists to be tough-minded. I was working recently with a young teenager and her family. She was on probation under "house arrest" because of delinquent behavior and was not cooperating with her parents or with me. When the parents reported that her probation officer was about to end her probation, I said:

> Although you have not broken your probation, Tina, you have not been cooperating with your parents. If you believe that it's the correct way to proceed here, Mr. and Mrs. Jones, I would urge you to talk with the probation officer; tell him what's going on with Tina and ask him to extend the probationary time. If you need my help with that, let me know and I'll give him a call too.

Bolstered by my authority and firmness, the parents were able to take this action aimed at showing Tina their determination to discipline her properly.

There are sometimes potential sources of support that patients do not know about or have been reluctant to seek out. For example, it is common for therapists to have to prod patients who live with an alcoholic spouse to attend Al-Anon meetings. Because it is usually indicated and because I do not want to be called by an intoxicated patient at midnight, I strongly push alcoholic patients to join Alcoholics Anonymous and even, in some cases, make their treatment with me contingent upon their doing so.

Most of these examples seem self-evident. Others require therapists to use their creative imagination. Divorced and widowed women often have extreme difficulty in meeting acceptable men and they are usually diffident about pursuing men openly. I persuaded two such patients, one divorced and one widowed, to insert notices about their wanting to meet suitable men in the Personals section of their local newspaper. Both made contact with several eligible men who fit their strict standards. Both women eventually married men they met in this way.

Therapists' Use of Language

I have already commented upon therapists' talking with patients in language tailored to the level of their comprehension. Therapists speak in ordinary and colloquial English unless there is some reason to do otherwise. And there often is. To unblock a patient's anger, the use of expletives is sometimes in order. For example, I might ask, "So, how do you feel about what that son-of-a-bitch did to you?" And then, using another technique to promote the expression of emotion, I press the patient with, "Now say that louder. That's better, and now even louder!" And so on, until the patient sounds very angry.

I have found myself being too careful about my use of language. Once I was working with a minister's wife, and, thinking about her in a stereotypical way, was watching myself so I wouldn't use any "inappropriate" language with her. One day I forgot myself and said, "If somebody treated *me* that way, I'd certainly be pissed off. Were you?"

And she replied, "Thank God! Finally someone is treating me as if I'm something other than just a minister's wife. That feels good!" Actually my excessive caution with this woman had inhibited her from expressing herself with me. I had assumed, incorrectly, that her delicate manner was natural rather than defensive. We should always keep in mind the probability that patients clean up their language for our sake, because of assumptions they have made about us or prohibitions they have projected onto us. In a very expressive or analytically oriented therapy, patients' defensiveness would be handled with interpretation as opposed to the therapeutic use of self exemplified here. This caveat also applies to the use of humor in therapy.

Therapeutic Use of Humor

In my book on marital (or couples') psychotherapy I describe the use of humor, especially sexually tinged humor, to diminish guilt, shame, and inhibitions about sexuality (Fitzgerald 1990). Humor serves to strengthen the alliance, lighten up the therapy, and teach or reinforce a very adaptive defense.

Recently a patient I was treating with very supportive psychotherapy and medication for his major depression with psychotic features was talking about getting his house painted. He expressed his frustration about the estimates he received from several contractors. I suggested that he might look in a neighborhood weekly newspaper to find a painter to do the job more cheaply. He did so and was pleased that the estimate was very reasonable. Several weeks later the patient told me that most of the paint had washed off his house in a heavy rain; he sounded very angry, in part at me. So I said:

> So much for my advice! Next time you should get a second opinion. And I'll bet the painter didn't give you any psychiatric advice.

This drew forth a weak smile from the patient. Part of his difficulty was his deadly seriousness.

Note that in this example I am laughing at myself. We laugh *with* patients, never *at* them. It is fine to join in if patients are laughing at themselves and using humor to get through something difficult. If this is a new behavior, congratulate the patient for it.

Stages of Supportive Therapy

Early

It is customary to divide psychotherapy into early, middle, and late stages. As with most things, the early phase is usually the most difficult. It is the time when therapists introduce patients to therapy, teach them how to go about it, and focus intensely on the housekeeping tasks of conducting therapy properly (contract, alliance, boundaries, limits, etc.). Later on, after patients settle in, these matters become more ordinary and automatic. The early phase is a time also when patients test all the parameters set forth by therapists, and therefore a time when we need to focus intensely on them. If the therapy survives the first phase, we have won at least half the battle.

Middle

Now therapists can relax and attend more to understanding patients and their complex and changing needs. During this middle phase, we accomplish much of the substantive work of therapy. With the various kinds of sustenance we give patients, they are able to consider their emotional issues, make up for lost time, learn more about themselves, and get beyond the blocks and fixations in their psychological development.

Late

The late phase is the time of separation of patients—be they individuals, couples, or families—from their therapists. If therapists kept the intensity of the transference at tolerable levels and allowed only minimal dependency to continue, separation issues are not as difficult as they otherwise could be. Naturally, to whatever degree they are present, we must handle them in a sustaining way. I have already talked of the use of the term *interruption* as opposed to termination; it is comforting for patients to know that they can return if they wish and it makes parting that much easier. Some patients, of course, will need to be seen at widely spaced intervals for continued, intermittent support or long-term medication management. Other patients will go as far as they can in a first treatment experience and return for one or more experiences as required over a period of many years.

Therapists also encounter some difficulty letting patients go. When, at last, we look forward to a patient's session because it's so easy, even fun, that's one sure sign the treatment is over. Now we must steel ourselves to bid the patient goodbye, and, what's worse, prepare ourselves to go through all those difficult times with a new patient, couple, or family.

5

More Expressive Psychotherapy

This chapter will discuss the indications for and the strategies and tactics used in more expressive or psychoanalytically informed psychotherapy. I have already described the procedure involved in formulating a dynamic, as opposed to a nosologic, diagnosis. The methods described in this chapter will help therapists expand and amend their dynamic formulations as required by the material flowing from patients' response to therapeutic interventions. I will also further describe and give examples of planning for treatment or of changing the plan. In addition I will discuss how to use silence, how to examine and soften defenses, how to clarify the often confusing mass of information furnished by patients, and how to respond in specific ways under various circumstances. I will also consider the function and use of corrective emotional experiences, and ways in which a therapist can work with dreams, manage various typical therapeutic problems, and conclude sessions. Finally, I will explain how to bring therapy to a close smoothly.

Indications for Expressive Psychotherapy

Robust Personality Organization

Patients with fragile personality organizations are described in the chapter on supportive psychotherapy. We can characterize those patients for whom more expressive therapies are indicated by using all the antonyms of the words used to describe fragile patients (Perry et al. 1983). Again, the DSM diagnosis gives us only the roughest sort of guidance. Usually these patients will meet the criteria for DSM-III-R diagnoses other than the psychoses and severe personality disorders. These are bright, curious, high-functioning, attractive people who have some fight and determination. They are capable of sustaining long-term relationships and are able to maintain meaningful emotional ties with others (including therapists), often in spite of great ambivalence toward them. Other characteristics include some measure of self-control; the ability to modulate affect, tolerate some frustration, and delay gratification; some aptitude for introspection and self-observation; a sense of humor; and, last but not least, the motivation for expressive therapy along with the practical resources to afford it (time, money, and energy).

It may seem that the kind of person described above would be quite exceptional. Not at all! However, few people possess *all* the characteristics noted above. And some seemingly quite ordinary people meet the criteria for the use of expressive psychotherapy. Let me give you an example:

A woman who consulted me came dressed in her work clothes. Mrs. K. was the working manager of a medium-sized farm. To keep her appointment, she had had to interrupt her farm chores. Although she possessed attractive features, her moderate obesity obscured them. For eight years she had been suffering from symptoms typical of "atypical" depression, that is, with considerable anxiety and reverse neurovegetative signs (hypersomnia, hyperphagia, weight gain). In spite of her depressed mood, she displayed a sense of humor and quickly grasped the implications of questions I raised. For example, she said, "Yes, I'm often like a child with my mother. I get to feeling so small and helpless and get so angry I can't get my point across to her. It's only afterward that I think of all the things I should have said." Mrs. K. had dropped out of high school to marry after she became pregnant. She explained, "I got pregnant so we'd have to get married and I could get away from my mother; I couldn't stand her domination. My rebellious feelings ruled my head then." She had obtained her high school diploma by means of the GED test. Her knowledge of farming had been acquired through reading and taking a few college courses. When I explained the dietary restrictions necessary for her taking a monoamine oxidase inhibitor (MAOI) she said, "Most of those foods and drinks are fermented or changed some way by aging.'' I felt empathic with the patient easily and had the impression that she was emotionally connected with me.

Although I had much more information about the patient than I have summarized here, what I do note above suggests that the patient was a candidate for some degree of expressiveness in her treatment. In my treatment planning I assigned her to number 6 or 7 on the supportive–expressive continuum. I decided to wait until she was beginning to respond positively to the medication before implementing the more expressive aspects of her psychotherapy.

Testing Our Initial Assessments

In the expressive mode of psychotherapy, we plan to be less active and give less direction. We do offer directions to the patient as to how to proceed and what to expect from us:

> Now it's time for me to turn the floor over to you. It's your responsibility to bring material for us to consider together to these sessions. Anything goes, so long as it's put only into words. We may have to sift through a lot of dust in this gold-mining operation before we find a nugget, so everything that's on your mind is important; don't leave anything out. I may have to listen to paragraphs, maybe even pages, of what you have to say, before I have anything useful to say back to you.

Note that I've given myself some leeway. I can respond in a shorter or longer time. At first I want to test patients' reaction to their free associating and to the anxiety, frustration, and regressive pull that will result from prolonged therapist silence.

It is difficult to describe all the danger signs that tell us to go more slowly. Certainly if hidden symptoms of a psychotic process surface, like delusions or a thought disorder, or if patients' potential for suicide proves to be more dangerous than we first estimated, we must rethink the treatment plan. If we cannot elicit a no self-harm contract (see Chapter 4) when we believe that suicide is an imminent danger, we must persuade patients or their families to institute hospitalization.

Intense transferences of any kind that develop too quickly, or evidence of excessive use of primitive defenses (splitting, denial, projection, introjection) will also give us qualms. Let's assume that all goes reasonably well, so that we can continue with our exemplification of expressive treatment.

More about Planning

In addition to those aspects of treatment planning covered in Chapter 2, there are other important elements to consider (Alexander and French 1946). One of these is the frequency of therapy sessions. For effective psychotherapy, in the more expressive mode, I have found weekly sessions to be most common; twice per week, infrequent; three times, very rare; and more than that, never. There are several compelling reasons for limiting the frequency of interviews. Most of the time we wish to keep the patients' transference feelings and the degree of regression at manageable levels. Increasing the frequency of interviews, all other things being equal, usually increases both. Definite indications should be present for planning a therapy at more than once per week. Usually patients who have experienced severe deprivations and losses in childhood require a more intense therapeutic experience.

For these patients we allow more dependency on us because a kind of re-rearing is necessary. Also we expect these treatments to last longer. However, reality is cruel and limiting for many people. We cannot plan a more intense and longer-term treatment for those patients who cannot afford it. And we would be foolish to plan such a therapy for those who can afford it but will not.

There are other factors under our control that influence the nature and intensity of the feelings aroused and ventilated by patients within the therapy. The more we focus on family of origin or so-called genetic issues, the more intense and/or childlike the feelings will be. Therefore, one way to moderate both feelings and regression is to keep our and patients' eyes on the present.

How active we are also influences the course of treatment in many ways. The less active we are, the longer we remain silent, the more ambiguity and frustration we build into the therapy. And the more frustration and ambiguity we create by our deliberate inactivity, the stronger and more regressed patients' feelings become.

To summarize this complicated subject, the following tactics usually foster regression with its associated increased intensity of the transference and heightened awareness and expression of emotions: (1) less activity on our part, (2) less use of specifically supportive measures, (3) more use of interpretation, (4) fewer revelations about ourselves, and (5) more interference with defenses.

Relatively Silent Listening

After we have given proper directions to patients, we shift out of the rational–active mode and into the sensuous–receptive one and begin our silent listening. At first patients need affirmations that they are proceeding correctly, that we are hearing them, and that we understand their anxiety about being in unfamiliar territory. I am reminded of the story of the child who was asked if he was afraid of the dark and replied, "Whose dark?" We remember that the patient is in our dark; thus we say, if necessary:

> You're doing fine. Of course you're apprehensive; almost everyone is. It's risky to open up so freely to a relative stranger. You will feel easier about it as you gain experience. Every new thing in life is like this for us to some degree.

When Patients Ask Personal Questions

How to answer questions, especially those of a more personal kind, is a vexatious problem in both expressive and supportive therapy (see Chapter 4). Less experienced therapists inevitably express concern about how to respond properly. Perforce, we reveal a great deal about ourselves to observant patients. We do or do not wear a wedding ring. We may or may not have pictures of our spouse and children in our office. For those of us who have an office in our home, even more of ourselves is there for all to see. Many of these opportunities to learn something about therapists are missing for patients of trainees who use common interview rooms with their homogenized, institutional appearance. When I use one of these rooms, I dim the lights to diminish the police station interrogation room feeling. In any event, while speaking freely, the patient asks, "Are you married, Doctor?" or "I'm Methodist, what is your religion?" This type of question can be handled in one of several ways.

In very expressive therapy, 8 or 9 on the continuum, we might reply:

> In this kind of psychotherapy, it's much better if I don't reply to your questions as questions. Rather, it's better to view the questions as thoughts and for me to listen for your next thoughts. That way I can understand how the curiosity about me, which is understandable and natural, fits into the picture of all the other thoughts and feelings you have today.

Alternately, with a more sensitive patient or with a therapy planned to provide more support, I might say:

> Let's consider that question two ways. What would it mean to you if I am married and what would it mean to

you if I am not? Once we thoroughly understand what your interest is all about, then I'll answer your question, if it continues to be important for you to know. I know how unbalanced and difficult it is that I learn so much about you and that you know so little about me. But that's the way this therapy works best.

After a time of testing, patients accommodate to the more analytic stance of therapists. Blocks to the revelation of material become more direct and more clearly associated with feelings about the material itself and are also related to those distorted perceptions and feelings about therapists, which we call transferences.

Intuitive Sensitivity

While therapists are listening to patients, they are also listening to themselves and looking at the images and fantasies that occur to them. For example, a young woman was describing her memories of some terrifying experiences she had had as a child, mostly connected with bedtime separation from her parents. Meanwhile, I heard the melody of Brahms's "Lullaby" playing in my head and began to sing inside, "Lullaby and good night, and may angels attend thee. . . ." In this way I got in touch with what this woman had missed as a child, the warm reassurance and comfort of a loving parent. Theodor Reik called this "listening with the third ear" and wrote a beautiful book with that name (Reik 1983).

Listening in the sensuous–receptive mode leads to understandings of patients that we fit into some respectable conceptual framework (Pine 1987). We hear thinking that calls for correction and shift into a cognitive therapy mode. We hear of conflicts that lead to compromise formations, note defenses at work, and seek to make patients aware of and able to gain more conscious control over these less conscious processes. With other patients we tune in to their repetition of interpersonal scenarios and intervene at this level. Nor are we unmindful of patients seriously damaged by early parental empathic failures: we borrow from self psychology to attend these extremely sensitive souls and their serious ego deficits. The ways of responding to what we think we understand are legion, and I will consider examples of many of these later in this chapter.

Examining Defenses

In expressive psychotherapy a clear dynamic picture does not emerge spontaneously from the material the patient offers. The preceding section on silent listening does *not* mean to say that the patient talks, we listen and understand, convey what we understand back to the patient, then settle back and listen more. We need to guide our patients, teach them analytic methods, so that we and they become genuine partners in deed as well as in word. Spoon-feeding them turns out patients who *need* spoon-feeding; it stifles growth.

Tact and Timing

I have chosen the term *examining defenses* with a purpose. It's not us against them. We don't hammer at defenses or take a meat cleaver to them. At times we may have to be bold and confrontational; usually this occurs later rather than earlier. Timing and tact are important considerations. Remember that the more sensitive patients are, the more likely they are to take *anything* we say as a critical attack. How do we know when patients are ready or almost ready to hear something unpleasant about themselves? We know it when they themselves are about to reach an unpleasant (ego dystonic) conclusion and need only a little help to get there. Perhaps we have already done a little leading or have passed some test the patient has set up. The latter might take the form of the patients' telling us about how mean certain friends have been and ask, "Isn't that awful, Doctor?" And we were wise enough to reply, if we spoke to the content at all. "Well it sounds like your friend may be hurting or has some kind of a problem that shows in that way." I trust that you recognize that patients often use the defense of displacement in this way. After we pass a test of this nature, patients are then more ready to own their hostility and now say that something they did was mean, which gives us the opportunity to say:

> It's favorable that you can acknowledge your own difficult side in that. Every relationship has its share of both love and hate. It's helpful for us to know about both sets of feelings in ourselves. The hatred will be less feared and less powerful, the better we understand it!

Had this patient previously protested her or his peacefulness, the defense we would identify is reaction formation. Note that in both cases I did *not* advocate an interpretation like, "I suspect that the meanness you're seeing in John is, in part, some of your own that you have put off onto him." With a patient further along in therapy who has been over this ground several times but has slipped back, I might ask, with light ridicule in my voice, eyebrows raised, and head tilted: "*Whose* meanness?" In talking with patients in these ways, I am also, by example, chipping away at their defense of intellectualization.

Silence as a Tool

We can use silence as a tool to further patients' productive work. They come close to some meaningful truth or insight and then veer away to reduce their anxiety and lead us astray, if possible. At these times it is better to remain silently bored and to become alive and responsive only when the patient returns to the central theme. Some analytically oriented therapists would claim that they eschew behavioral theory and practice entirely, but I doubt this. We may negatively reinforce with silence and positively reinforce with our responsiveness, depending upon how patients experience each. If patients spend too much time lost in the woods in spite of our silence, we get out the therapeutic compass and say:

> You seem to be off the main trail and lost in the woods. I thought I heard you say that maybe Joe's passivity got to you because you yourself— then you paused and changed the subject. What blocked you at that point? It seemed that you became quite distressed.

What threatens patients at the point where they are about to become aware of or reveal something to therapists is far more important than what the content of that something is. More often than not, patients' difficulty here involves the reenactment of what they once experienced as struggles between them and their parents. Patients project the internalized images of their parent(s) onto us and now the conflict that had a limiting or symptomatic outcome can have a different, more adaptive, outcome. Technically, what patients manifest in this regard is called *transference resistance*. Giving patients corrective emotional experiences is a powerful tool to preempt or counteract this complication.

Out of Confusion, Clarity

Focus on Changes for the Worse

Information that patients relate about their lives, past and current, has been drastically altered by selective perception and recording, repression, and other distorting influences. Patients lose the connections between events, symptoms, feelings, and behaviors. Listen to a couple or several different family members recount the same incident and you will hear the effect of all of these errors of processing and memory of each and of the alliances among them. Sorting all this out is difficult. In family therapy, therapists direct those present to reconsider the issue here and now, as opposed to repeating how it went several days ago or last night. In individual therapy, we ask patients to take it from the beginning:

> Begin with your arrival home and let's look at it step by step. What time did you arrive? What door did you enter

159

by? Where was Dave? How did you greet each other? What did you say to each other? Then what did you do next?

Or, if the circumstance we are exploring is not an inter-personal one, we raise the following kind of questions:

Before you became aware of that change in your mood, exactly where were you? Which chair were you sitting in? What news item in the morning paper were you reading? Can you quote exactly what it was that you had read immediately before you put the paper down and started weeping?

Focus on Changes for the Better

Although therapists usually focus on what leads to a change for the worse or an increase in whatever symptom is under consideration, it is equally important to study changes in the opposite direction:

It's very helpful for us to identify what made that go better for you. If we shoot the ball far and straight down the fairway [the patient is a golfer—I'm not, but can speak the language], it's nice to know what we did right so we can repeat it. Go back over that evening with Jennifer carefully and see if you can find what you did that was different.

It's constructive to raise similar questions when patients report diminished symptoms or better control over prob-lematic behaviors.

What is most effective is to trap change as it occurs within sessions. For example, we become familiar with the range of affect each patient displays during therapy hours. When patients depart from that "normal" range, something significant has happened and we want them to know what it was. If we know, we could tell them, but telling them would lose the opportunity to teach them a piece of self-analysis. *How* to understand themselves is more important than any particular thing patients come to grasp. So I say:

> You seemed to relax and have some fun just then. What helped that happen? . . . So, you felt better when it seemed to you that I changed from neutral toward you to approving. Can you connect that with any earlier experience in your life related to someone's approval and disapproval of you?

My suggestion here of a connection between what's happening now and what patients experienced during their developmental years is designed to lead them toward insight of a special kind. It will ultimately lead, if all goes well, to the conclusion that behavior (ideas, feelings, attitudes, prohibitions, and the like) that was once necessary is now anachronistic and not needed. What is most important is that patients muster the courage to take the risks involved in behaving differently with us and with important people in their current lives. But how important is insight in promoting change in psychotherapy?

Insight and Change

The importance of insight is controversial (Alexander and French 1946, Marmor 1979a). In all the years that I have been asking patients at their final session what they learned in therapy that has been useful and meaningful for them, few have named insight or understanding as such. What patients have mentioned is what they have *experienced* with me personally, how they have learned to solve

problems in living, and how they have come to commu-
nicate their needs better and get those needs met. Therefore I regard insight as frosting on the cake; it's good to
have and is useful for some patients, but I very much
doubt that it is the most powerful mutative component of
psychotherapy.

Various Ways in Which Therapists Respond

Many of the ways that therapists respond to what patients bring to therapy have already been exemplified. Therapy constitutes a repetitive process of listening and responding, listening and responding. How long we listen and exactly how we respond determines the often subtle difference between more expressive and more supportive methods. Therapists should always display empathy, kindness, and warmth. Right? *Wrong!* Most of the time, yes, but not all the time. Frieda Fromm-Reichmann said to her plaintive patient, "I never promised you a rose garden"—a statement that became the title of a beautiful little book that I highly recommend to all of you (Greenberg 1989). Note that I said "display empathy," not "be empathic," that is, be able to walk in your patients' shoes. To respond correctly, we draw back, objectify what we have learned about the patient's plight from our empathic stance, and plan our response accordingly.

Toughness and Empathy

Many depressed patients with certain psychosocial symptoms are likely to feel worse when therapists treat them too kindly or with insufficient firmness. Think of the kind of circularity involved here, say between spouses. The symptomatic spouse elicits attention and care from the asymptomatic spouse when, and *only* when, the former exhibits sadness or pessimism. Having gotten a response based on this "shameful weakness," the patient experiences a further drop in feelings of self-esteem and feels worse later. Therapists must avoid playing into this situation by exercising restraint in responding to patients' plaintiveness. We could wait until patients show more positive attitudes, or we may say:

> Yes, life is often very rough. But so long as you think of yourself as a helpless victim of fate or of what others do, you are powerless—as though you were just standing there and the tornado hit. If we figure out what in *your* attitudes or behavior you could change to better your position, you will be more in charge of your life. Then, and only then, will you feel better.

To the patient who repeatedly manifests a combination of pathetic and cynical attitudes, I have been bold enough to say, sardonically, if I'm convinced that the patient can take it, "Right! Life's a bitch and then we die."

What has worked for the patient to elicit sympathy or reassurance from others has totally failed to impress us, and this kind of intervention opens up opportunities for patients to examine and alter these behaviors.

Judging Behavior, Not Patients

Therapists should refrain from judgmental responses that speak to their patients' essence or to their fundamental worth as human beings. However, it is not possible or even desirable for therapists to avoid making judgments about *behaviors* that hurt others or violate their rights. If we are *that* detached, we are not in touch with patients at all! We should be fully aware of the negative judgments we make, avoid self-deception, and not claim that we are as neutral as stones. Also we should not give patients further justification to continue behaving in asocial or antisocial ways. In the extreme circumstance of patients' being in danger of doing great bodily harm to other people, our concern for the welfare of patients and others might justify our throwing privileged communication and confidentiality to the wind and doing whatever is necessary to prevent this disaster. In less extreme circumstances, I say:

> You know exactly how to hurt Lynne's feelings badly and that's what you did. We will have to understand what leads you to do things like that and what makes it impossible for you to treat another person decently under those circumstances.

I think that it's important to call a spade a spade. This is not to say that as therapists we can appropriately vent our anger toward patients, however justified doing so may be. First, as was discussed under the heading of countertransference, we understand and get our feelings under control; then we respond aseptically to patients. And we can do our jobs very gently and firmly, speaking to the patient in words like the following:

> Let's examine what your desire to tell Larry about your sexual involvement with Jim means. How do you think Larry will react? And then, how will you feel about Larry's humiliation? That's very forthright of you to admit that

you'll get a kick out of Larry's being so hurt. It's under-standable that you feel hurt by Larry and vengeful toward him. But do you think it will accomplish your overall goals in treatment to keep this negative tit-for-tat going between you and Larry?

In this case it's possible that, if we're too identified with our patient in individual therapy, we may feel that Larry has asked for punishment and has it coming. This is a countertransference feeling toward Larry that deserves to be analyzed and overcome; it would be much less likely to be a problem were the couple in psychotherapy together.

Making Connections and Clarifications

I have already discussed ways we help patients become more aware of the dynamics involved in the waxing and waning of their symptoms and other problematic behav-iors. Therapists spend much time and energy tying to-gether strands of information and feelings that patients have presented obscurely or disconnected from each other (known as the defense of isolation). Often we articulate what we think we have heard for patients in a way that is clear, concise, and meaningfully connected. What patients have said may span a longer or shorter time but is more often confined to the current session. Patients then can check our reformulations of what they have said and, if they agree, gain insight. For example, I might say to the mother of a 5-year-old:

> What I have put together out of all of that is that you felt exasperated with Jonathan and, like many mothers do, felt like pitching him into the sea or giving him away. In this mood, you punished him for his defying you. Your pun-

ishment was quite appropriate. However, you felt very guilty about your natural and harmless feelings. You then canceled your plans to have lunch with Hank, cuddled Jonathan, and, in his mind, wiped out your disapproval. And now, sadly, he's out of control again. Now you'll have to stand firm over time to regain the ground you lost. You might consider spending more time away from the constant burden that child-care is, so you can feel more relaxed and keep your balance in dealing with Jonathan. And this also demonstrates again how important it is for you to judge yourself on the basis of what you actually do and not on what you feel like doing.

Along with the clarification, this passage includes an interpretation and also a suggestion about how the patient might better cope with her dilemma.

Turning Questions into Statements

Questions we raise seek information, but frequently they also serve the function of leading patients gently toward confirmation of a hypothesis we have conceived. I led Larry's mate inexorably to her sadistic motive for "confessing" her sexual indiscretion. There are patients, chiefly early in treatment, who react to questions by becoming defensive. It's as if they read into every question something like, "Why did you do that [stupid, crass, evil] thing?" It will tax our ingenuity to do so, but it is possible to turn most questions into statements. I have tried this out and completed an initial session without asking a single question beyond the face sheet data. "What happened next?" becomes, "And then. . . ." "What led you to that conclusion?" becomes, "I'm not clear about your thinking that led you to arrive at that conclusion." This technique is a bit ponderous but worth the effort if it helps patients off to a better start with us. And note, again, that I never begin a question with the judgmental "Why."

Interpretations

In this section I will exemplify the use of several kinds of interpretations. I cannot overemphasize the principle of beginning with the defense. Surgeons do not wield the scalpel until they have anesthetized the operative site. For instance, suppose a patient states that he fears speaking up in a group. Our first probe will be to inquire about how he pictures that the people will react. *We* strongly suspect that this patient projects his own aggression onto the group members. Only after we have thoroughly discussed the content of the projections and defused them with our understanding and accepting attitudes will the patient be ready for an explanation that includes his aggression. So first we make interpretations that soften the defenses by making the wishes more acceptable. Suppose the patient says that Joan is a very critical person, that Joan has criticized others and made fools of them and is sure to do the same to the patient if the patient expresses his opinions in Joan's presence. So we say:

> Might it be possible that Joan herself experienced a lot of criticism as she was growing up? Maybe the kids in school teased her a lot because of her weight, her acne, or whatever, so she expects to be criticized and hurt. To protect herself from that, she lashes out first. She fights fire with fire.

What I am explaining here vis-à-vis Joan will help make the patient's unacceptable wish–defense admixture more acceptable to him. This defense, which I explained in ordinary language, we call identification with the aggressor.

Much later I would be able to make an interpretation of this same patient's transference expectations of me:

> But, of course you expect me to be critical of you. Throughout all the very impressionable years of your childhood, that's the way you experienced your father most of the time. It has been very courageous of you to take all the risks you have with me, telling me about many things that you were convinced deserved to be disapproved of.

Note that instead of being critical, I have taken pains to find a way to praise the patient at the very moment he is aware that he is anticipating the opposite.

This next example is from a marital session during which the husband attempts to convince his highly emotional wife that she should control her self-pity by relegating the past to the past and focusing on the pleasures of the present. In defense of herself, the wife mentions her husband's mother's incessant complaining, and her death by suicide. The husband became visibly upset so I asked him, softly, "Jack, what bothered you most about your mother's suicide?" In reaction to that, he began to weep openly and blurted out that his mother didn't wait to see their son. About this I was able to comment, with empathy:

> That's a very painful and real thing you have to feel sorry about and it's something that will be very difficult for you to put in the past and keep there. When Susan feels sad and sorry for herself, it reminds you of your feelings about how your mother hurt you.

This diminished the husband's need to keep his wife's emotionality under wraps or to escape from it and her into many activities (e.g., compulsive running) which, of course, had only increased her emotionality. This kind of interpretation is founded on object relations concepts.

Several years ago, before I had read any of Kohut's work (see Appendix A), I was interviewing a young man at his first consultation. During that session, seemingly out of the blue, he said, "You're probably thinking what a handsome guy I am." He sounded and looked embarrassed. I then became alarmed enough to support his reality testing. He proved to be seriously personality-disordered but not psychotic. Later I came to understand that it might have been more helpful to the patient to have said, "Perhaps you have needed to have someone find you attractive and tell you so, and would now be comforted if I did." I was not then sensitive to this dynamism and was off to a bad start in my treatment of this patient, having committed what those knowledgeable about self psychology would call "an empathic failure on the part of the therapist."

Confrontations

Confrontations that therapists employ are kinds of explanations that go against the grain and are difficult for patients to hear. The word "confrontation" has an adversarial connotation; I do not mean it in that sense. In Chapter 4 on supportive psychotherapy, I explained how to offer interpretations along with support. We can make a gentle confronting critique of patients' behaviors in the expressive mode as well. A potentially attractive young woman expressed extreme frustration about not being able to find a better job, in spite of having obtained a master's degree in her profession. It was obvious to me that she made an unfavorable impression on interviewers because she dressed in such a careless, haphazard way. Because of my desire to be tactful, I had not mentioned to her my observation about her personal appearance. After several painful rejections by prospective employers (who didn't give her an honest reason), I decided I had to tell her. So I said:

> I have an observation to tell you that will be painful for you to hear. However, I believe that it will be less painful than for you to continue to get rejections from prospective employers. I've noticed that you often look like you have thrown your clothes on and seem not to know how you look to others. Your stockings often have runs in them, or the hem of your dress is unraveled, or you wear colors that clash. Please examine yourself carefully in the mirror before you leave for work or for an interview. Maybe you'll need to take a class in fashion, or look at pictures in women's magazines, or ask a close girlfriend for help with this problem.

There was more to this patient's problem than simply missing pieces of information about personal grooming. However, approaching it in this straightforward manner was effective and made it possible for her to obtain a job commensurate with her level of training. Her fear of making herself attractive lest she attract a sexually avaricious male could wait for consideration later.

Other confrontations are applied to overcome seemingly persistent defensiveness, as follows;

> For as long as I have known you, you have talked about your feelings and have never shown any. That's making your therapy much less helpful to you than it could be. We're going to have to find a way for you to dare to show me your feelings.

Corrective Emotional Experiences

As I have already noted several times, the concept of the corrective emotional experience has great utility in the practice of both expressive and supportive psychotherapies. In explaining this notion, Alexander cited the story of Jean Valjean and the bishop from Victor Hugo's *Les Misérables* (Alexander and French 1946). Jean Valjean had become a hardened criminal. Most of us would consider him to be beyond the reach of our therapeutic efforts. He stole from the bishop repeatedly and, as often as he did, the bishop forgave him and treated him with exceptional kindness. Later Valjean, clinging desperately to his familiar behavior, stole a coin from a small child. Afterward guilt overwhelmed him, and then he reformed and became a law-abiding citizen. The bishop's forgiveness and kindness constituted the corrective emotional experience that penetrated Jean Valjean's callousness and galvanized his latent sense of decent behavior.

All the methods, attitudes, and therapist behaviors discussed here provide a generally corrective experience with a caretaker and a person in authority upon whom patients rely. Therapists behave in these ways as a matter of course. A "corrective emotional experience" is one that is specifically tailored to powerfully overcome rigid roles into which patients cast their therapists. Patients' inner templates of these expectations are formed by injuries to their psychic development experienced in relationship to those who cared for them at earlier times. The dynamic rule of thumb is that the injurious element was too much of something, too little of something, or something—such as guidance or discipline—given very inconsistently. This "something" was not necessarily unpleasant or unwelcome at the time. A parent may have needed to keep our future patient too close and therefore encouraged dependency and forbade independence. Knowing this, we would await every opportunity to encourage independence and, contrariwise, allow only the minimal necessary dependence on us. In this way we would be providing a corrective emotional experience for this patient.

Functions of Corrective Experiences

What purposes do corrective emotional experiences serve in psychotherapy? They keep transferences at manageable levels, especially negative ones and those that lead patients to oppose the therapy and us. With the use of this strategy, therapists preclude patients' proclivity to regress further than is necessary and make it conducive to carrying out treatment with as few complications as possible. Also, in this way therapists can complete an analytically informed therapy over the course of far fewer sessions than would otherwise be possible.

In considering the salutary effect of corrective experiences, we also remind ourselves again of the adverse experiences that therapists can inadvertently create. Any intervention that would be unacceptable to patients because it comes too close to what they dread facing elicits a negative reaction toward the therapist. Having tuned into patients' particular sensitivities during the exploratory phase of treatment helps us to be respectful of them. In a very real sense, avoiding interventions that would injure patients unnecessarily provides a corrective climate for patients and fewer obstacles for us to combat.

Planning and Implementing Corrective Experiences

In planning for and executing corrective emotional experiences, it is imperative for us to make an accurate appraisal of patients' transference attitudes and expectations vis-à-vis us. Recently I interviewed a young woman who was experiencing considerable anxiety and depression associated with the birth of her first child, a girl. Earlier, at the opening of her first session, Mrs. J. had expressed considerable concern about whether I would find her a suitable patient "to work with." At the time I had no idea about the basis for her apprehension. In this later session I learned that she saw her father as a brilliant, admirable, successful, generous person, but one who was exceptionally critical, highly opinionated, demanding, and with very high standards. As a child she had experienced him as favoring and less demanding of her younger siblings. In some measure she compensated for the hurt associated with these perceptions of her father's attitudes by learning to "work with" him on various projects. As I was concluding this interview, Mrs. J. asked, "Do you feel all right about working with me, Doctor?" I replied;

> Of course! Please know that anything I explain to you at this point is very tentative; I've known you for a very short time. Also, I'm happy, in this complicated task of understanding people, to be right about half of the time. From what you've told me so far about your background, I suspect that you might expect to have to pass some rigorous test in order for another person—especially a man—to find you acceptable.

The patient then relaxed and said, "You're right. But now that I think about it, you seem more like my mother and brother, more laid back." So after I had averted one pitfall, the patient promptly handed me two more. I would now have to learn more about—and be careful to refrain from replicating—the injuries that the patient had experienced at the hands of her brother and mother. I had already elicited some information about them. However, my age and gender first brought to the surface the patient's thoughts and memories about her father rather than those relating to mother and brother. An alternative explanation is that her difficulties with her father were more readily available and therefore less important dynamically.

Fortunately, I had learned that Mrs. J.'s mother was an extremely ambitious lady who was often away pursuing her career. In an early memory Mrs. J. pictured herself looking out a window and crying as her mother was backing out of their driveway on the way to work. When she followed up her comment about my being more like her mother by asking if we could meet twice a week for a time because she was eager to tell me so many things, I replied:

That will be fine with me. Let me look at my appointment schedule and see if I can find two hours that fit both of our schedules. We'll try that out and see how it goes for you.

If I later find that this level of intensity leads to untoward developments, such as excessive regression, I can always gradually reduce the frequency of the sessions.

Fine-Tuning Corrective Experiences

Sensitivity to transference issues and making strenuous efforts to forestall complications arising from them by providing a corrective therapeutic atmosphere doesn't always work. I had been working for some time with a patient who had had to seek a disability retirement from his career as a special education teacher because he could not tolerate the stresses associated with children who were difficult to discipline. I knew that Joseph had been severely abused, both verbally and physically, by his tyrannical father, and thus I took care to be very considerate of him and to seize upon every opportunity to acknowledge his positive attributes, efforts, and successes. One day, when he seemed ready to consider seeking an alternate career, I talked with him about his skill in mathematics and the good market for employment in the field of computers. At his next session he told me that he had purchased a computer and intended to learn computer programming. But he also felt much more tense and anxious. Exploration of his overreaction (buying the computer) revealed a memory of his father standing over him wielding a two-by-four to force him to do some unpleasant job that the patient had mildly objected to. So I had to repair this damage promptly by saying:

When I talked with you about your considering the field of computers, I must have sounded to you like I was issuing orders. I certainly didn't mean to sound like that. Now that I have heard about that bitter memory, I understand your difficulties much better. I don't think we should consider your returning to *any* kind of work unless and until you can feel it is something you have freely chosen and can look forward to with pleasure.

I never again took the initiative in talking with Joseph about his considering another career. Whenever he brought the subject up, I'd ask something like the following:

Are you very clear that that's what you want for yourself? When you picture doing [that job], does it feel good and do you feel better about yourself?

About a year later Joseph enrolled in college classes to prepare himself for a new career. He did it first and told me about it later! Naturally, I congratulated him for taking action on his own without concern about my approval or disapproval.

How to Work with Dreams

Patients vary in their ability to recall and make use of dream material. More often than not, therapists' expressions of interest in dreams influence patients to remember them and bring them in for discussion. Most patients do not have any idea about how to translate dream images and plots into information that will be germane to their lives or contribute to a solution of their difficulties. When patients first bring a dream, I inquire about what they know about how to go about understanding them. Patients who have had previous therapy may or may not know how to proceed. I suggest the following approach:

> Dreams are like works of art. They resemble poems or plays or short stories and may consist mainly of images; most have some kind of a plot. Our minds continue thinking and attempting to solve problems or to see things in a different way while we are sleeping. Dreams are our productions. We write, direct, and act in them. However,

they should not be taken at face value. In our dreams we use symbols and a kind of thinking that is often more childlike in form. For example, an umbrella is not necessarily that specific object but stands for something else in our lives, like the need for protection from something other than rain. Or, in a play on words, "umbrella" may stand for a person we know or once knew by the name of Ella. I will guide you, especially at first, in your consideration of your dreams. After you get the hang of it, you'll be able to do your own translations of them. Remember that the symbols you use in your dreams are yours and some may be unique with you. We can't consult a dream book to find out what your symbols mean.

At first, the dreams that patients bring into therapy are relatively transparent to us. Later, as patients become more sophisticated about the process of analyzing them, their defenses go to work and camouflage them more. The fact that a patient's dynamics are readily understandable does not mean that it is timely, tactful, or safe to share immediately what we think we know. The principle here is the same as for all other kinds of information patients give us. Begin by considering with patients those painful feelings associated with their knowing about their troublesome impulses and wishes.

At her third session, Mrs. J., who was discussed earlier in the section on corrective emotional experiences, brought the following nightmare—from which she had awakened terrified. In it her house had caught on fire; there was a strange man downstairs. Although she was determined to save her baby, she ran into one obstacle after another but couldn't reach her, and awakened terrified. After explaining the approach to dreams outlined above, I asked:

> What do you think would lead you to dream that such a terrible thing had happened to you? In actuality, have you ever been in any fires?

Mrs. J. told of an instance of forgetting that the baby's formula was warming on the stove; it boiled away, scorched the pan, and filled the kitchen with smoke. She blamed herself and felt very bad about this. Her thoughts about her fear of little Lisa's getting sick and dying led to memories about her fear that her parents would die when they left her alone to go on vacation together. She remembered feeling very angry with her parents for leaving without her and then feared that they would be killed in an auto crash. I remarked on the connection she had discovered between anger and fear and explained:

> Children think in a very magical way; they think their feelings are very powerful. As children, we believe that our perfectly normal and harmless anger can cause harm, even kill those we're mad at. And that magical part of us lives on. Somewhere deep down in all of us, we still believe those fantastic things.

Mrs. J. quickly grasped the significance of what I had illustrated and said that "good parents" shouldn't be angry with their children. So I asked:

> How's that again? Good parents don't get mad at their kids? Where did you learn that? I think that child-care is very onerous at times and that getting mad is inevitable! You're a quick study to have put children's and parent's anger together so quickly.

Note that I generalized about anger, gave the patient a psychologically accurate picture linking her anger and her childhood fears, and remarked that she understood most of this. It was not necessary for me to mention the obvious anger she wrote into her dream in the form of a fire (or my presence in the dream as a strange man she was allowing to see her rage and fear). Had the patient not gotten to her anger or close to it, I would not have interpreted her dream any further. I was surprised that she was ready, within three sessions, to face her repressed rage. Perhaps she had profited in this way from her previous therapy.

Bringing Sessions to a Close

In order for clinicians themselves to adhere to the therapy contract, they begin and end consultations and therapy meetings on time, except under exceptional circumstances. Therapists need to know the difference between firmly keeping one's word and rejecting patients. Some patients will feel rejected regardless of the reality of time constraints; we must address reactions of this sort as we would any other irrational behaviors patients manifest. The clock speaks and we too must obey. Also, extending a session for one patient, couple, or family does a disservice to the people waiting to be seen next. Therapists should also give themselves a break. We need a few minutes between sessions to relieve our bladders and minds and prepare ourselves for the next session. And we must avoid starting our 5:00 P.M. patient at 5:30 or 6:00 so that we are less stressed, do not keep our spouses and families waiting, and don't have to deal with one justifiably hostile patient after another all day long. Why do I make this long apologia for doing what should come naturally? Because I have seen trainees and less experienced therapists fight this battle and lose it too often. Patients have a way of holding on to us and, often, playing upon our proclivity for guilt or our responsiveness to pain to get us to prolong sessions unduly.

Tactics to Employ

What antidotes can we put into effect? We should have one or more clocks strategically placed in our offices so that we can do some unobtrusive clock watching. Ten to fifteen minutes before the time runs out we begin to end the session. Our nonverbal signals, to which patients will become conditioned, are important at this point. We may, for example, look at the clock obtrusively, or shift in our seat in a certain way. At the end of a diagnostic interview we close our folder and put it aside. And we do not encourage patients to start on new material at this point, say, by raising a question that will require a long explanation. Rather, we begin to think of what to say by way of closure, a summary perhaps, or ways to counter patients' predictable moves to prolong their time with us. As you may have already noted, some patients save a really juicy piece of bait to hook our therapeutic curiosity during these last moments. To counter this practice, I will make a comment acknowledging the importance of the patient's message but bridging it over to the next appointment:

> That's too important to try to cover in the few minutes we have left. You can start to tell me about it, if you wish, but

we'll have to put a consideration of [that matter] at the top
of our agenda for next Tuesday's meeting.

If patients get into a pattern of bringing significant things
up at the last minute and do *not* respond to my invitation
to start there next time, I will remind them or ask:

> I notice that you frequently bring up things that seem
> important at the end of your sessions, then don't pursue
> them in the following sessions as I have invited you to do.
> What's that all about?

Alternately, I may say at the end of sessions that patients
have tried to prolong:

> You seem to have difficulty with endings. That's a very
> common thing. Parting can be difficult for us and espe-
> cially difficult for some of us. Next time we'll explore
> what happens inside of you as you notice that our time is
> running out. If you don't remember to start there, I'll
> remind you.

At the other end of the extreme, there are patients who
must beat us to the punch and end the sessions themselves
a few moments before we would. This is the other side of
the same coin, and therapists address this problem in the
same ways.

Exceptions and Additional Comments

Sometimes we make the mistake of exploring new
material or making an intervention too late in the session.
Our doing this may stir up feelings in the patients that we
then have to deal with. We must prolong the interview to

allow them time to regain their composure or allow us to give appropriate support to help them regain control. We should take care not to make this kind of mistake often; experience will help us with this.

Be alert to comments that patients drop as they are leaving. They may say very poignant things, especially regarding their feelings toward us, at a time when we are in no position to respond fully. We can say, "I heard that! And we'll have to talk more about that later, after I've had some time to think on it."

These are the kinds of things we train ourselves to remember from session to session. Doing so is much better than relying on notes unless we regularly set aside time to read them beforehand. Information buried in a progress note is not of much use to us if it needs to be used, for instance, to open the interview:

> Last time as you were leaving you sounded upset and angry with me. What did I do or say that hurt or annoyed you? I went over it and couldn't locate anything; perhaps I stepped on a corn of yours I didn't know about.

At first, I want to know what the patient experienced. It is possible that I did say something insensitive and was not aware of it. We should not assume that every negative reaction to us that patients manifest is transference.

Stages of Expressive Therapy

Early

Early during therapeutic contacts with patients, clinicians do the following things (to summarize what I have already described):

1. Establish a nosologic diagnosis.
2. Determine the degree of support that is indicated, including the use of medication.
3. Make and write out a dynamic formulation, including the complications we anticipate and possible ways to avert or deal with them.
4. Include in the dynamic formulation what corrective experiences may be helpful for patients to experience in their relationship with us and others in their current lives.

5. Revise all of these hypotheses and plans as indicated by fresh insights we gain as therapy proceeds.
6. Teach patients about the process of psychotherapy.

Patients learn about and accommodate to this new and strange situation, and test out many aspects of the therapy and the character of therapists. I must again emphasize the critical importance of our behaviors' matching the precepts about therapy we have explained to patients. At the same time, we must be sensitive enough to be flexible. For example, if patients' financial situations change because of factors beyond their control, we can adjust the fee accordingly or agree to extend credit.

Middle

We continue to learn more about patients and to revise and enlarge upon our earlier dynamic formulations and plans. Patients change, we change, and the therapeutic relationship changes. Therapy is itself a dynamic, evolving process. It is commonplace for patients' transference feelings to alter. When all goes well, for example, trust gradually replaces mistrust as therapists demonstrate trustworthiness. The transference that patients experience at first characteristically changes, sometimes becoming more difficult, and then requires different interventions. To cite a common circumstance, patients may first react to us as potentially abusive fathers, but their deeper hurt and rage emerge later in association with their mothers' failure to protect them. Unless we are prepared to deal with transference promptly and effectively, it can turn very nasty at that point. An intervention framed in the following way might then be in order:

What I have to say to you now could be somewhat hurtful. Often anything I say may hurt somewhat. I hope that a short-term pain will pay off for you in a longer-term benefit. If you're not feeling up to absorbing something painful today, this can wait till later. I want to be very careful not to exceed your tolerance, so I need your guidance. Please tell me how you wish me to proceed.

This interpretation is very supportive, although given within the context of a more expressive mode of psychotherapy. At tender times for patients, we are commensurately soft.

Much of the substantive work of therapy is accomplished during the middle phase. As I have emphasized, patients learn the tools of therapy that they can use profitably throughout the rest of their lives. We never resolve problems once and for all. The same ones recur or others replace them contingent upon the patient's entry into another phase of the life cycle or the occurrence of a crisis. This is why the tools are so much more important than any particular dynamic, however important it may be.

Late

A carefully planned and executed treatment has prepared for the patient's interruption of it from the very beginning. We deal with dependency issues continuously and vigorously. Like a good coach, we expect patients to go that extra mile in the race, using their own muscles to a maximal degree. If patients typically become so dependent upon us that they have great difficulty declaring their independence, we need to look at what we have done or failed to do to set them free.

We can, of course, expect some difficulty. Graduations and parting are, to borrow from Shakespeare, such sweet but sorrowful events. Be not dismayed by a temporary upsurge of symptoms and reassure patients that such an occurrence is to be expected as treatment ends. Again, note that in helping patients to consider and overcome their difficulties in ending sessions, we have already prepared them for the final separation and loss. And we remind ourselves that the loss is bilateral. We must be able to bear our grief over the repeated loss of our patients if we are to help them bear the loss of us. In this way, we strengthen patients to better endure existential pain.

We reassure patients that further therapy may be necessary and warn them of the twin dangers here:

> If you find yourself tempted to return for more of this therapy too soon—in less than three to six months—remember that you have not given yourself a fair chance. Therapy does not end when therapy ends. You must give yourself a chance to use the tools you have learned to help yourself out of jams. My own treatment ended formally years ago and I still get into trouble I have to work my way out of. And I sometimes get into bad moods that I never come to understand; time alone takes care of them. The other danger is that, out of pride or feelings of embarrassment or humiliation, you would wait too long before returning to address again some difficult issue you have worked on diligently here. You might use the methods you learned here for a reasonable length of time but its resolution might elude you. So there are two pitfalls for you to avoid—returning too soon or not soon enough. I realize how hard that may be to sort out. I'd rather you erred in the former direction. If we determine in a single

meeting that further treatment is or is not necessary, that will be fine either way!

And now we are ready to say, "All that remains now is for me to say that I wish you well and goodbye. It's been a pleasure working with you."

6

Brief Time-Limited Dynamic Psychotherapies

Expectations and Actualities
of Therapy Length
Definition and Patient Selection
Technical Considerations

There are necessary and respectable forms of psychotherapy that are customarily very brief. They range on a
continuum from *crisis support* or *emergency treatment*
that deals only with the immediate situation, to *crisis
intervention* that also enhances patients' coping skills to
deal with future difficulties and thus shades over into
brief psychotherapy (Sifneos and Greenberg 1988). This
chapter will discuss brief *time-limited* dynamic psychotherapy, which should be distinguished from brief dynamic psychotherapy that occurs without a time limit's
being set by the therapist (Flegenheimer 1982, Flegenheimer and Pollack 1989, Malan 1976, Rasmussen and
Messer 1986, Sifneos 1979). For the trainee and the less
experienced therapist I must underscore that brief therapy
is much more difficult than longer therapies and requires
the most skill to carry out. Give yourself time during your
years in training or early in your career to work intensively and over a long time with several patients. You
might just as well fill some of those empty hours with
patients even if you must charge a discounted fee. *Really*

get to know people and your craft. Then you will be ready, fast enough on your feet, and skillful enough to do shorter-term treatments. Because I do not personally conduct this form of therapy, I cannot provide case examples in this chapter.

I would be remiss if I did not mention that Freud's therapy of Gustav Mahler (Austrian musician, composer, and conductor) was very brief. Freud walked the streets of Leyden with his famous patient for one session, lasting four hours, and purportedly relieved Mahler's impotence (Jones 1955). However, no one claims that Freud put a time limit on this brief psychoanalytic treatment. Ferenczi and Rank both experimented with shorter and more active psychoanalytic treatments. Rank was the first to make setting a time limit a central aspect of his analytic therapy. I previously discussed Alexander's work in other contexts. These psychoanalysts did not advise setting a time limit at the outset but did impose interruptions of analytic therapy under certain conditions, especially when progress slowed or stopped (Alexander and French 1946). Recently Strupp has raised questions about the purported advantage of setting a time limit at the outset and recommends instead that therapists adopt a brief therapy attitude and apply it in a flexible manner (Binder et al. 1987).

What about expressive therapy that turns out to be brief without necessarily having overtly been planned as such?

Expectations and Actualities
of Therapy Length

Expectations

Most therapists have personal needs and inclinations. Some prefer to work less intensely with a greater number of patients, others prefer to work more intensely with fewer patients. Different therapists have had different training experiences and develop values, beliefs, and attitudes about the efficacy of different modes of psychotherapy. We work within communities consisting of consumers of our services and peers, and we are influenced by the standards and attitudes of these groups. For example, Toledo, Ohio, and Ann Arbor, Michigan, are only 45 miles apart geographically, but significantly more long-term analytic therapy is practiced in Ann Arbor. The attitudinal gap between the two cities is large. The number of people in any community who can personally afford long-term intensive psychotherapy (more than two hours per week) is quite limited (except for places like Beverly Hills). Therefore, payment allowed by third-party payers is also a limiting factor in therapy length and intensity. As has already been discussed, patients vary in their motivations and in the emotional and other resources available to them. Very well-motivated patients will pay for whatever treatment is necessary, even at great financial sacrifice. Therapists should be flexible in their arrangements for payment of fees, and realistic in their predictions about length of therapy. Obviously, clinicians would not predict a long therapy for patients with strong egos presenting with acute, uncomplicated disorders such as Adjustment Disorders. On the other hand, long therapies *would* be predicted for most schizophrenic patients. All of these variable factors lead therapists to present different expectations or recommendations to patients concerning the form and length of psychotherapy.

Actualities

In most settings in the public sector, the number of sessions is surprisingly low, a median of five to six (Garfield 1978). For private psychiatrists, the average was 12.8 patient visits (Langsley 1978). I recently reviewed the therapy length data on the last seventy-two patients of mine who terminated their therapies. For all patients the average was fourteen visits and the median was twenty-three. When I excluded the two patients whose therapies exceeded forty sessions, the average was eleven. I cannot speak to how the typical or average psychiatrist in private practice goes about talking with patients about therapy length. I can speak only for myself, and what I say most of the time is something like the following:

> So far as how long your therapy will last is concerned, all I can do is give you a statistic, that is, the median number of sessions my patients have required—the middle between the extremes. And that is twenty-four sessions or about six months. Some patients will finish in ten sessions or less, others will continue for two years or more. Exactly where you will fit, I cannot predict. Much depends upon how much you want to accomplish and what rate of change you are comfortable with. There's a big individual difference in these things.

I will have to give a less favorable prognosis to some patients and tell them that they may have to be under someone's care for life or at intervals throughout their lives (patients with affective disorders, schizophrenic disorders, and some serious character disorders).

Without my deliberate imposition of a brief time limit, my therapies *are* relatively brief and well within the parameters set by many therapists who do brief time-limited dynamic therapy. Much of what these therapists emphasize about the characteristics and techniques of and the criteria for patient selection is similar to what I have already discussed in regard to the more expressive psychotherapy that I practice. Perhaps this is why my therapies are also usually brief without my setting a time limit. Keep this overlap in mind as you read the following. Much of this material has been discussed earlier in other contexts and it is repeated here because it has been underscored by authors who practice this system of therapy.

Definition and Patient Selection

Definition

At the outset, the therapist must set and adhere to a time limit that is part of the treatment contract. The length varies from twelve to forty sessions, depending upon the school of brief therapy employed (Marmor 1979b). Mann (1973) imposes a limit of twelve sessions. Other proponents of brief dynamic psychotherapy individualize the time limit according to the severity of patients' disorders and their ego strength, but they name up to forty sessions. In my view, however, forty sessions is within the *medium* range of therapy duration.

Central Problem and Realistic Goals

Therapist and patient working together must identify a primary problem, and they must formulate it clearly and concretely. For example, a patient says, "My need to please others causes me great difficulty and often leads me to avoid getting involved with other people. This limits my social life and I spend too much time alone." Both therapist and patient must agree on realistic and attainable goals germane to the fundamental trouble. I say both therapist *and* patient to stress that therapists, who may be used to more ambitious goals, often must lower their sights and accept more limited objectives. These criteria apply to some degree in other forms of psychotherapy but are of critical importance in brief therapy.

Motivation and Level of Functioning

Patients' motivation for change must be strong and reasonable. Patients therefore must *not* be so infantile that they are seeking in the therapist an omniscient and omnipotent parent who will magically cure them, or so childlike that they wish for a parent surrogate to depend on who will do all the work. Patients must be willing and ready to cooperate with and learn from the clinician and assume their share of the responsibility for changing. These are characteristics that reflect aspects of emotional maturity and ego strength.

If clinicians cannot find one important area of living in which patients are highly functional and have achieved success commensurate with their abilities, grave doubts would be cast on patients' ego strength and brief dynamic therapy would probably be ruled out. Again, this is another variable we take into account in assessing how robust or fragile patients' personality organizations are.

Interpersonal Relationships

In the first interviews of a trial therapy, therapists have the opportunity to experience directly how patients relate to them. Without some evidence that the patient is capable of forming a durable, positive bond with the therapist rather quickly, brief time-limited dynamic therapy may not be possible. From a historical perspective, it must be possible for clinicians to elicit from patients memories of at least one meaningful, beneficial early relationship and the capacity in the present to form and maintain at least one similar affiliation. Therapists cannot just sit and wait for the patient to form such a relationship with them; they actively promote it in ways that will be discussed in the section on technique.

Communication Skills and Expression of Affect

Patients selected for time-limited brief dynamic psychotherapy possess a reasonably good ability to articulate their problems in a distinct and incisive manner. At the same time, intellectual and other defenses must be soft and flexible enough to allow for the expression of powerful emotions. Obviously, patients have to be able to identify, name, and express their feelings; they cannot be alexithymic.

Thinking Style

Patients must have enough intelligence to be able to grasp the significance of our explanations. They need not be very well educated but must have the potential for understanding the way we think dynamically. Much of the responsibility with respect to patients understanding us rests with us. If we speak in abstruse, obfuscating, technical language, no one except some of our colleagues may be able to understand us. My test of whether *I* understand one of our concepts is my ability to explain it to Mr. and Mrs. Average Citizen in ordinary language so that most of them understand it. This can be tested in the first interview by our making a tentative interpretation of what we believe we understand. For example:

> Something seems to be blocking you from expressing your feelings. You have talked of things that would arouse fear and anger in most people as if you were talking about a change in the weather. Perhaps the fact that I'm a stranger and you don't know how I would react is inhibiting you. Or this could be a long-term problem of yours. What do you think?

Patients who are able to respond intelligently to this kind of statement probably will be able to comprehend dynamic concepts.

Reverse Indications for Selection

By reverse indications I mean that for some good reason, longer-term therapy would be hazardous or beyond the reach of certain patients because of their limited resources (personal plus a supportive and flexible environment). The resource variable has already been mentioned. Certain kinds of patients pose a risk for long-term therapy—especially those with underlying, relatively serious character pathology who are in acute crisis. Time-limited dynamic therapy, with its persistent focus on a single presenting problem, may avoid the potential of these patients for regression and their development of a difficult dependent or hostile–dependent transference relationship or other untoward complications.

It is tempting for us to rationalize the use of long-term therapy for such patients by telling ourselves, "I might just as well treat this very dependent patient for as long as she feels the need to continue, because if I don't, she will find another therapist to do so." This is tantamount to a surgeon doing an appendectomy on a hysterical patient. However, our situation is not as clear-cut as that of the surgeon. There are indeed dependent patients who cannot recover from their dependency without a longer-term corrective treatment relationship; they must first be allowed to become dependent before they can become more independent. It is a judgment call. We should keep this in mind as we weigh the pros and cons of time-limited treatment. My use of the female pronoun in the example above is not sexist. Dependent men often do far more destructive things in denying their dependency needs than dependent women do in seeking and sometimes achieving overly long therapies. We cannot fairly place the responsibility on the patients for staying in treatment too long. Therapists must avail themselves of all strategies that reduce and contain excessive dependence on them. Using a time limit at the outset is one way of doing this in a very powerful way.

Technical Considerations

Rapid Engagement

Photographers learn that, to get an excellent picture, they must use f8 and *be there*. Those who do brief therapy are with patients and stay with patients intensely. They get very personal with patients very quickly. Each therapist works in his or her own way and you will have to find what suits you best. It is easy to become confused if you are looking for the best way to do brief time-limited psychotherapy. The similarities among this relatively small group of therapists may be more important than their particular styles or the content areas they focus on. The fact that Mann (1973), for example, sets a time limit of twelve sessions after the first two or three evaluation sessions will perforce, for many patients, tap into separation–individuation issues immediately. That he listens attentively and mirrors or joins with the patient is evident in his precise use of the patient's words in his questions and comments. Further, he is gentle, empathic, and overtly accepting of patients as they present themselves.

Reading the verbatim interviews or sections of them from sessions conducted by Sifneos and Davenloo (1988), or watching videotapes of them, demonstrates that their intense demeanor, quick grasp of dynamic issues and rapid-fire confrontational interventions compel patients to interact meaningfully with them. It seems that patients have only two choices: to depart or to participate in a meaningful way. There is great contrast between the way these representatives of brief dynamic therapy work and the way Mann does. What they all have in common is that the therapists and patients join together in a purposeful and poignant endeavor (Rasmussen and Messer 1986). Other therapists who practice brief time-limited psycho-therapy—Wolberg, Marmor, Gustafson—describe or ex-plicate in their writings equally incisive methods to stim-ulate patients' rapid emotional engagement with them (Gustafson 1984, Marmor 1979, Wolberg 1965). Wolberg emphasizes sympathetic listening, communicating under-standing, confidence in one's approach, and combatting patient hopelessness.

Ameliorating Symptoms

For most of these therapists, the selection process weeds out patients with symptoms severe enough to require medication. Sifneos even refers to his technique as "anxiety-provoking," because his confrontational style and tenacity in blocking defensiveness does indeed keep the therapy at a high level of tension. Most of the patients selected are tough enough to tolerate a classical psychoanalysis, were such indicated and feasible. Those patients for whom a brief regimen is selected by means of what I have called *reverse indications* represent the exceptions. In these situations therapists usually employ longer term psychotherapy combined with pharmacotherapy or refer their clients or patients to a colleague for the latter.

Timely Dynamic Formulation

One of the reasons that only seasoned therapists should apply time-limited dynamic psychotherapy is the necessity for making a correct and usable dynamic diagnosis quickly. Therapists cannot internalize this knowledge except by clocking a certain number of hours doing therapy, in much the same way that a pilot must solo for a minimum number of hours to qualify for a license. To review how we go about eliciting the requisite data and formulating a tentative dynamic diagnosis, see Chapters 2 and 3.

Sustained Focus

Intimately associated with making a rapid and accurate dynamic formulation is the necessity in this mode of therapy of identifying a central area to treat. With more time, therapists and patients have the luxury of exploring branching paths of the main presenting difficulty, but in brief time-limited therapy they must stay focused on understanding and changing the central personality problems. Usually these are connected with the presenting distress and the precipitating stress that led to it.

Obviously, patients are not aware of the connections between their suffering and its context and their personality vulnerabilities and conflicts. It is up to therapists to diagnose these hidden connections. Next, therapists must convincingly demonstrate these correlations to patients. Therapists who practice time-limited dynamic psychotherapy emphasize, as I have, the importance of raising questions, clarifying underlying themes, and explicating these interrelations in detail.

It is also therapists' responsibility to sustain the focus on the central area selected unless further experience with the patient indicates that a different area should have been selected. In most time-limited psychotherapy, the patients are tough enough to bear a high level of tension and anxiety with only brief periods of respite. Therefore therapists must not allow patients to wander far from the main path marked for therapeutic attention and correction.

Although none of the author-therapists I read expressed any concern about how arduous this form of therapy is for them, I assume that they experience some wish to wander down a more restful branch of the difficult mainstream from time to time. As with countertransference, therapists must get themselves in hand when they tire in order to have any chance of getting patients back on the difficult track.

Sensitivity to and Resolution of Resistance

Therapists must promptly detect subtle forms of difficulties that patients have in adhering to the therapy program. Blatant resistance is easy to spot; however, imagine that the patient is drifting from the central area of focus by small increments. This would be easy for therapists to miss, so they must be very alert and sensitive to any deviations from the therapy plan and must keep the initiative in maintaining the pace of the therapy.

This group of therapists is very interested in keeping the therapy in close touch with patients' everyday lives. They teach patients how to improve their important relationships by using what they have learned in therapy, and encourage them to do so without delay. The force of the time limit will exert this kind of pressure as well. I am reminded of the cartoon, probably in *Playboy,* which depicted a man lying in bed next to a voluptuous lady and saying, "Be patient, dear, just one more visit to the analyst!"

Detecting and Handling Transference

I have already discussed many of the varieties of transference, especially those of a negative sort that interfere with patients' progress in treatment. Therapists who practice time-limited dynamic psychotherapy take a similar position, namely, that negative transference must be detected and handled right away. They regard the development of a transference neurosis as contraindicated. A high degree of activity (not direction) preempts regression and the unfolding of a transference neurosis. Immediate and skillful handling of negative transference is imperative according to these psychotherapists. None except Marmor mentions the use of the corrective emotional experience to deal with negative transference. This style of therapy also accents the importance of maintaining an optimal level of positive transference throughout the therapy and uses some of the tactics already discussed to do so.

Addressing Destructive Systemic Issues

Only Wolberg discusses the environmental troubles patients experience that interfere with their progress in therapy. Mainly he discusses ways to clarify and interpret the role of patients in provoking or failing to resolve these systemic impediments. Further, Wolberg considers the need to support patients more directly in dealing with them. For example, he advises giving patients information about community resources or referring them to a social worker or agency. Wolberg also mentions interviewing family members to gain their help, referring relatives for therapy themselves, and recommending family therapy. How the latter would fit into the time-limited protocol, Wolberg does not expand upon.

Therapists as Mentors

Although the term *time-limited dynamic psycho-therapy* may suggest the exclusive use of uncovering or expressive techniques, you may have noticed that some supportive measures are practiced. Most of these therapists describe the educational facet of this system of treatment. They particularly highlight the necessity for the patients themselves to learn a method or to acquire tools (examples have been given in this book) so that what therapists teach by precept and example becomes a continuing positive factor in patients' lives. It is partly for this reason that these therapists and their patients seem to have little difficulty in sticking to the agreed-upon time limit.

Countertransference

Therapists must keep careful track of how much of a drain it is to see many patients for short spans of time. Also, this way of doing psychotherapy is associated with rapid turnover and increased time and effort in processing new patients. Just as it is not wise to treat too many terminally ill or suicidal patients, we need to know our limits in doing brief time-limited psychotherapy. Refreshed therapists are more able to note and deal with their countertransferences. If we have difficulty, for example, in quickly confronting patients' hostility about our prescription of a time limit because of our own discomfort or guilt about it, the treatment will be endangered. We ought to feel comfortable enough about this form of therapy that we feel free to confront patients' difficulty in keeping focused on the central problem. If we allow patients to sabotage the intent of the treatment plan, our countertransference problem may be the cause. This is a prolix way of saying that we very much need to believe in whatever treatment we apply. Because I have trouble with the notion of setting a time limit, I don't conduct time-limited psychotherapy.

Concluding Treatment

When using time-limited psychotherapy, therapists end treatment at the appointed time regardless of whether all the objectives of the treatment seem to have been attained then. These therapists believe, as do I, that therapy does not end when therapists and patients stop meeting. If it has been an efficacious therapy at all, the benefits are cumulative and must continue after patients stop meeting with therapists. Brief time-limited therapists vary in the importance they attach to scheduling follow-up appointments. Marmor offers a visit after three or six months but says that patients rarely need one; Wolberg schedules a visit for a year after termination.

Whether we like it or not, for many reasons already elucidated, current trends seem to favor briefer treatments. Although their efficacy over the long term remains to be tested, most therapists should learn the principles of brief therapy.

Part III

COUPLE
AND FAMILY
PSYCHO-
THERAPIES

Couples

More often than not, couples who come for psycho-therapy are a subunit of a nuclear family and have children. These couples have identified the family problem as a marital one. Typically, the relationship between the couple is the most intense and meaningful one in their current lives. Because of this and the fact that the marital pair, in concert, care for and prepare their children for life in the wider world, the nature and quality of the relationship is of crucial importance to them and their children and to the surrounding society. And their mental and emotional well-being as individuals is a decisive factor in the quality of their relationship. Clinicians diagnose the difficulties brought to them by these couples so that they can employ the most accurate treatment. Although relationship problems are bilateral, this statement may or may not say much about causality and about what treatment is indicated. For example, in the presence of a psychosis or affective disorder in one spouse, treating the relationship as the primary problem would be a grave mistake. On the other hand, excluding the healthier spouse from the treatment could be an equally grave mistake. It is easy for us to underestimate the pain and frustration experienced by the healthier mates, the education and support they need, and the helpful contributions they can make to the therapy. Although there might be more of an indication for individual therapy than for couples therapy in cases of this sort, we should be ever mindful of these concerns about the healthier mate. As was discussed in the section on individual therapy, therapists may have to take the initiative in involving spouses in the treatment when they do not present as a couple for it. Here, concepts derived from general systems theory, such as feedback loops, help us understand the effect of the behavior of one member of the family or group on all other members and, in turn, the effect of the group, singly or together, on each member.

Other couples who present for treatment of their relationship are engaged couples (this is rare—smoke is in their eyes), couples who are living together but not formally married (including homosexual affiliations), and divorcing couples (rarely). As they do with married couples, clinicians must make accurate diagnoses of these couples' trouble. Very few of these couples have children, but some will have children later. Even some homosexual couples will acquire children through adoption. So, as with the married, more may be at stake in the treatment of these couples than their personal well-being.

Families

The most common way in which families present for help is by bringing a child to be helped by the mental health professional or team. Many of these families do not have the slightest interest in treatment for themselves and commonly react to a recommendation for family therapy as if they were being blamed for their child's difficulty. As therapists we are not interested in blame; we advocate family therapy because we appreciate the need for the parents or the whole family to be involved in some way with the treatment of the troubled child. Therefore, we must apply the notions gleaned from systems theory to ease the families of disturbed children into therapy in such a way that they can feel proud and courageous about taking this action and we can avoid activating their guilt. Mental health professionals and clinicians are *very* clear about the difference between responsibility and guilt. We all know that what I do may influence you in certain ways and that we must both take our share of the responsibility for these consequences. Clarifying the difference to others is always difficult and sometimes impossible!

Thoughtful, introspective, and less defensive parents identify their children's problems as family problems. Although one or more of their children manifest symptoms or problematic behaviors, these parents present the family as patient. Obviously, these families are easier to work with because of their readiness to look at their group dynamics.

Regardless of families' readiness for family psychotherapy, therapists should know and emphasize the pain and grief parents of sick children suffer. They have sustained a serious loss, that of the healthy, well-adjusted child they had hoped for.

7

Psychotherapy for Couples

Conceptual Considerations
Presenting Problems
Indications
Diagnosis
Treatment Planning
Beginning Therapy
Strategies and Tactics
Bringing Sessions to a Close
Stages of Therapy

The aim throughout this book is to present therapies from my own eclectic and integrative perspective. With psychotherapies for couples I will discuss the common problems that couples present with and my methods of treating them. As with individual treatment, I picture a continuum of support and expression and use methods garnered from other theoretical orientations—analytic (especially object relations), systems, and behavioral (especially cognitive). However, I will not describe each school of therapy separately; those who wish to do so may read books, articles, or manuals that describe and explicate the procedures of specific schools. Because I know of no brief, succinct, and clinically relevant summary of the application of psychoanalytic and systems thinking to the marital relationship, I will offer one here. I have also included books and articles on these topics in the Reading List, Appendix A.

Conceptual Considerations

Psychoanalytic

Certainly a basic premise in working with couples is that mate selection is not a haphazard, random process. I view it as determined by the needs and individual dynamics of both participants. Couples may make choices impulsively which, perforce, reflect the impulsiveness and/or immaturity of one or, more likely, both. We can neatly integrate individual dynamic thinking and systemic thinking. Imagine looking at a cell under the high-power magnification of a microscope and perceiving something of its internal structure and function. Now imagine shifting to medium magnification and examining the structure and function of the tissue and how the cell that you have just minutely studied fits into this picture. Now you can imagine how the cells work together to perform the functions of the organ you are studying.

When a man and a woman invest emotional energy (cathect) in each other, they set in motion their pleasure-seeking and aggressive drive derivatives. Ego functions and defenses determine the outcome of these drives, taking into account the reality of the situation and the constraints imposed by the superego (conscious and unconscious conscience). Each partner perceives the other through memories (mainly unconscious) of experiences with past important people in their lives; including parents, siblings, and other important people from the near or distant past, portrayed as the subject perceived them. Internally, subjects have recorded themselves and all these people with their feelings and their behaviors and the relationships among them. The mate is then perceived through this mélange. In her first meeting with Joe, Joan makes the following "choice" (I infer the following unconscious inner dialogue):

> When I was playing with my brother, we were having fun; it was exciting. Mom and Dad applauded and joined in our game. Joe reminds me a little of my brother. Not only will I be able to protect him when he's vulnerable, I'll also be able to enjoy him. He's someone I can have fun with. I'm even feeling sexually aroused and that's okay.

This young lady is ready to form a relationship with this man that promises to be very positive and enduring. However, the young man, Joe, "decides":

> My father said he'd kill me if I ever fooled around with my sisters and he meant it. And my mother was no help. I couldn't count on her to protect me from him. He punished me severely for trivial things. Joan has green eyes, just like my sister Pat. But she's attractive and sexy. I feel myself getting aroused. I'd better get out of here fast.

So the relationship between Joan and Joe ends abruptly. Joe fled and experienced a drop in self-esteem. Joan felt disappointed that she never had the opportunity to know Joe better or have fun with him. Had Joe's reaction been of the same nature but less intense, the couple might have formed a long-term but sexually dysfunctional relationship and entered marital therapy to correct it. I have oversimplified this example to make it easier to understand. The ideas expressed here are based upon object relations analysis, and will be expanded upon.

Another way of putting together what happened between Joan and Joe is to think in terms of each having projected into the other aspects of themselves. What Joan projected into Joe was part of her own freedom to enjoy intimacy and some vulnerability, and she would be able to approve of and nurture these qualities in him. Joe, on the other hand, projected an internalized forbidden object (his sister) into Joan and rejected and fled from it. Technically, this process has a terrible and difficult name, *projective identification.* We deal with those aspects of ourselves that we project into others in many different ways, depending on our dynamics as seen from an object relations viewpoint. We may take good care of these aspects of ourselves in the other person, attempt to change or control them, reject and punish them, or flee from them. This is not to say that the qualities we project are not also present to some degree in the recipient. Projections can be like iron filings going to the magnet that draws them to itself.

Redundant repetition is also present in these relationship dynamics. We tend to repeat past relationships. Sometimes we recapitulate a relationship because it is the only way we know how to be in one. Or we may need to master or undo the hurt of a former relationship. At times it seems that couples enact the tale about kissing a toad:

> Oh, what a triumph it will be if I pick someone who resembles my internalized mother or father and, out of love of me, he or she changes into the parent I wished for. All my pain will magically disappear, as if I had kissed a toad and it changed into my prince or princess.

Again I have simplified and dramatized a complicated and commonplace circumstance. You may have noticed the similarity of these processes between intimates to the transferences that analytic therapy stirs up.

Yet another way of viewing marital relationships within an analytic framework is the concept of reciprocal or complementary patterns. For example, for every caretaker there is one who needs to be taken care of, and for every person who needs to suffer there is a partner predisposed to cruelty. Mittleman (1956) has written beautifully and in detail about these dynamics and I urge you to read his chapter (See Appendix A).

The marital bond does not consist mainly of pathological ties, however. There are almost always healthy, adaptive features to intimate relationships. What, in part, determines the viability of the relationship is the balance between the adaptive and maladaptive sides of it. Sadly, there are couples who are locked together in a painful, pathological yoke, unable to leave it or change it in a positive direction.

Systemic

Here we think in terms of circularity referred to in Chapter 5. In the vernacular we would say, "One good (or bad) turn deserves another." More technically, we think also of negative and positive feedback loops. Negative ones conserve the status quo and thus maintain homeostatic balance in a system. This is like the thermostat that keeps the temperature of a room within a narrow range. When a new adaptation is required in a human system because of a natural life cycle change (such as the, birth of a child) or a crisis (like the serious illness of a young mother), a too-powerful negative feedback mechanism is maladaptive; it blocks the necessary accommodation to the changed circumstances. Positive feedback loops are deviation-amplifying ones. Imagine the police chasing a felon: both of them are in automobiles, and the closer the police get, the faster the felon goes; the faster the felon goes, the faster the police chase. Usually these kinds of processes escalate. In this example, both cars get to a rate of speed at which one or both go out of control and crash. Now imagine that a love-sick wife is pursuing her husband to get her needs for closeness and warmth met, and that her husband is threatened by closeness and warmth. The faster she goes in pursuit, the greater distance he puts between them. Ironically, the deviation-amplifying feedback mechanism also preserves the status quo because the distance–closeness issue between the couple is rarely resolved. Out of guilt or the pressure of passion, the husband moves closer, but now the wife is too hurt to respond or she perceives her husband as sexually rapacious, so she rejects his overtures.

A group of three or more interdependent people involves even more complicated systemic dynamics, so that we have to think of boundaries, alliances, triangulation, and other concepts derived from systems and communication theory. These will be discussed in the chapter on family therapy.

Presenting Problems

Before describing common problems that couples present with, I should make it clear that complementary patterns are universal features of most relationships. This fitting together works smoothly and efficiently for a couple if the balance or ratio of each other's qualities is acceptable, even gratifying to both. Each one must, however, be flexible enough to modify his or her role if necessary. If the person in a leadership role becomes temporarily or chronically disabled, both leader and follower in this relationship must trade places. Doing so will entail a period of adjustment in which both may suffer "normal" symptoms, but adapt they will or must. The arrangements described below, which cause great distress to one or both parties, either begin as unbalanced or escalate and become increasingly extreme, as often occurs when one person grows and the other stagnates.

Communication

People who have very limited intelligence, speak a foreign language, have thought disorders, or are manic find it difficult or impossible to be understood by others. I am not talking about these types of problems, but rather the type that couples often refer to as a "communication problems." Often the partners exhibit abundant misunderstandings between themselves, each feeling deprived and unloved by the other. First the therapist must find out what the couple means when they name this as their central concern.

When part of the problem consists of messages getting lost or distorted between them, there are common underlying causes that we must attend to. The following are some common ones:

1. Neither listens because each is so defensively preoccupied.
2. Each blames the other equally, so that their arguments go in circles, without resolution.
3. They go from issue to issue so rapidly that they consider none in depth.
4. They are embroiled in a power struggle so that each must win and both therefore lose.
5. They don't know how to debate in a civil way and their argument deteriorates into an ad hominem one.
6. They don't know how to compromise or take turns conceding points and thereby fail to solve problems.

Manifestly, we must discern the more basic issue(s) before we can make effective interventions. This approach applies to every presenting problem.

Distance and Closeness

In the previous section on systems concepts I gave an example of what happens between couples whose needs for closeness and distance differ. Males tend to press for more distance, while females seek more closeness. Each takes the other's need as a personal affront or as a sign of inconsiderateness or insufficient love.

Emotional Expressiveness

Again, I must note a gender difference. Many men, perhaps most, are less emotionally expressive than women, except for anger. A few men have alexithymia, but in all my years of clinical experience I have yet to meet an alexithymic female. I have come to believe it's in the hard wiring of some men. Many women expect more emotional expressiveness from men than some are able to manage. It is sometimes a mystery why a couple with these personalities picked each other in the first place. The woman may have been enamored by the myth of the "strong, silent type," and the man by the woman's lavish emotional expressiveness toward him.

Most of these unexpressive men are not alexithymic. Rather, they are blocked in their expression of emotions by defensiveness, some of which is culture-bound. These men are often amenable to treatment. Alexithymia may be an intractable condition to which the spouse may have to adapt by lowering her expectations and appreciating that her mate has a genuine disability akin to color-blindness. On the other hand, some of these men respond to some degree to the proper therapy; they must be taught the language of feelings and how to identify them in themselves and others.

Competitiveness

We think of certain kinds of couplings as symmetrical, ideally, two people working together for a common goal. However, although the increasing number of two-career mates of approximately equal income, status, and prestige has increased, many such relationship are damaged by excessive competition. When one partner becomes considerably more successful in some way than the other, or receives more notoriety, the other overreacts.

Parent–Child

There are many varieties of parent–child combinations represented by married couples. Ibsen, in his play *A Doll's House* depicts one such couple. Visualize a continuum (a scale of 1 to 10) with, for example, extreme helplessness located at the far right (10) and extreme independence at the far left (1). Now imagine that you can pick up the line representing the continuum and make it into a circle. The two opposite qualities are at the same point on the circle. In some sense, then, blatant helplessness and uncompromising independence are homologous. This fact accounts for both the fit and the instability in these combinations. Some other species of this pattern are the following extremes:

1. Disciplinarian–rebel.
2. Responsible–irresponsible.
3. Frugal–wasteful.
4. Cautious–reckless.
5. Repressed–liberated.

The precipitating event that brings some of these couples to treatment may be a well-advertised extramarital affair—similar to the marijuana hidden in a teenager's sock drawer.

Dominance and Submission

Not so many years ago I would have had to say that most "traditional" marriages were male-dominant/female-submissive. Much of this "tradition" is, of course, culture-bound. A North American mental health professional would have to consider this context in the evaluation of, say, a Saudi Arabian couple. With the feminist movement, the question of male dominance has become a more sensitive issue. Both men and women have difficulty adapting to this new cultural climate. Some men don't have a language for it. As hard as they try, they continue to say, "I help my wife with . . ." rather than, "We share the responsibility for. . . ." Some women who work or pursue an avocation while their mates attend to the children or household tasks cannot enjoy their freedom to do so because of guilt about or inability to let go of their more traditional roles.

Even before the recent societal change, the extremes of dominance and submission contributed to serious trouble between mates. As might be expected, the female usually sought assistance, with the reluctant male in tow. Husbands occasionally complain of feeling burdened by carrying so much of the family responsibility and are unaware of how they have helped bring it on themselves.

Abuser–Victim

Unfortunately, one of the most common presentations is that of battered women. This is more common at family service agencies and community mental health centers than in private practice. It is, unfortunately, rare for the couple to present together or for the man to seek help for himself voluntarily. Alcohol abuse or dependence is often an associated or the primary problem. Instinctively, it is easier to feel empathy for the victimized woman than for the abusing male. It is even unpopular, although clinically accurate, to say that the victim frequently plays an important role in this bilateral transaction. Such a statement does not give justification to the abuser, nor does it denigrate the victim. It is simply a description of what takes place.

Substance Abuser or Addict and Co-Dependant or Enabler

The spouse of an alcoholic male or female partner used to be viewed as an unwitting victim of the alcoholic mate or of the society that permitted the purchase of alcohol or other drugs. Recently the role of the mate or intimate other has been identified and popularized. Now it is unusual for a therapist to refer a substance-abusing patient for treatment or to a self-help group without referring the partner or family as well. The patient with alcoholism is referred to Alcoholics Anonymous, the spouse to Al-Anon, and children to Alateen.

Dominance Conflict

After seeing the play *Who's Afraid of Virginia Woolf?* I came away with the sense that, in spite of their vicious cruelty to each other, deep down the couple cared about each other. It may be more accurate to say that they desperately needed each other. There are many couples like this. Each partner anticipates that exposing tenderness to the other would make him or her extremely vulnerable. They avoid expressing their tenderness. Instead, they assure themselves of their importance to the other through their ability to get a reaction with painful insults. Other couples seem to be mostly sadistic and hateful and seem to have no loving side at all.

Sexual Dysfunction

Ever since the work of Masters and Johnson, clinicians have regarded sexual dysfunction as a condition whose treatment requires the participation of both partners. Therapists consider the sexual relationship as an integral part of the total relationship pattern. While it is true that one person can have a sexual dysfunction without any help from a partner, once this person enters into a relationship the dysfunction becomes a significant part of it.

An accurate diagnosis of the nature of the sexual problem, however, continues to be very important. A significant percentage of cases, especially in the older patient, entail an organic factor, so that the dysfunction, such as impotence or dyspareunia, may turn out to be 60 percent organic and 40 percent psychological. Diagnosis is equally important for prognostic purposes. Primary impotence— wherein the man has never under any circumstances had a functional erection—carries a very poor prognosis regardless of the quality of the relationship. Such is also the case with the woman who has never experienced orgasm under any circumstances and proves unable to climax with masturbation prescribed by the therapist.

Indications

Couple therapy is usually indicated when couples apply for it at their own initiative. Earlier I discussed the significance of motivation in determining the indications for psychotherapy. Poor or devious motivation, which may not be evident at the outset, is a contraindication. A partner may, for example, enter therapy with the hidden agenda of appearing to be making an effort to change while planning to continue the behavior that is grieving the mate. We should not take at face value the couple's diagnosis that the relationship is the *primary* problem. Rather, we should evaluate each partner thoroughly to establish accurate diagnoses that can be woven together to determine how the disorders (Axis I and/or II) contribute to the relationship pathology. Therapists should urge individuals who ask for treatment for relationship problems to persuade their partners to attend. Further, we should warn them about the possible untoward consequences of individual therapy when their intimate relationship is in trouble. These include separation or divorce, diminished efficiency of the treatment, distress in the other if the patient makes a pivotal change, and strenuous efforts on the part of the other to sabotage the treatment.

This is not to say that individual therapy aimed at improving a patient's marital relationship cannot be successful. To explain how such therapy can take place, we invoke an aspect of systems theory. When one person in an intimate relationship makes a significant change in the nature of her or his transactions with the other, the two-person system is thrown into disequilibrium. The other must respond in some way to this change. First the other reacts with strong opposition to the change, then he or she must either make a complementary change or leave the relationship.

Diagnosis

For couple therapy the diagnostic process proceeds as follows. First, therapists see the couple together to elicit history, goals, and expectations from both. Therapists also observe how the couple relate to each other and to them. It is usually possible to estimate the quality and strength of the motivation of both in this initial session. Therapists begin to establish a therapeutic alliance with each patient—including their relationship—and make the contract for the first few sessions.

Next, clinicians conduct evaluation interviews with each patient, covering the same ground that has been outlined in Chapters 2 and 3. Doing this may require as many as three sessions with each. In a sense, this represents a trial at therapy as well as a diagnostic procedure. If therapist and patients agree to continue with the marital therapy, or with some combination of individual and couples' therapy, the therapist explains the terms of the therapy contract. When we decide that individual treatment for one spouse is the treatment of choice, a useful rule of thumb is that the more disturbed this mate is, the more useful it is to involve the spouse with regularly scheduled joint sessions.

Nosologic

The method of arriving at a nosologic diagnosis for each spouse does not differ from that described for individuals. Because couples are apt to come for therapy after some crisis has brought matters to a head, we commonly diagnose adjustment disorders. Often, personality disorders contribute to or are associated with marital problems, so we can correctly diagnose each spouse within the framework of DSM-III-R. Earlier in this book I emphasized the value of diagnosing a psychiatric disorder requiring specific treatment such as medication.

Dynamic

We use the usual procedure in formulating a dynamic diagnosis for each spouse. We must, however, fit together the dynamic formulation of each in order to comprehend their relationship dynamics. Having done so, we might arrive at the following, as an example:

> Jerry and Trish went together during most of their college years and married just before Jerry entered medical school. His parents' marriage was the "traditional" type to an extreme. His mother was apparently comfortable with her submissive role as housewife-mother and waited on her husband and children hand and foot. The father's chief

roles were those of breadwinner, decision-maker, and disciplinarian. He ruled with an iron hand and overtly used the threat, "It's my way or the highway." Jerry therefore was overindulged by his mother as her only son and her favorite "little prince," while at the same time internalizing a rigid, punitive superego based on the way he experienced his father. Trish also grew up within a "traditional" parental relationship. However, she perceived her mother as unhappy and resentful of her position; Trish herself found it impossible to please her mother or her demanding father.

During the early years of Trish and Jerry's marriage, while he completed medical school and residency, she worked to help support them. Trish devoted herself to taking care of Jerry's every need and he basked in the glow of her nurture. Jerry had identified with his father in every respect. He became a very successful, affluent physician and believed that he was demonstrating his love for Trish through the material things he provided. This arrangement worked well until their children were at an age that permitted Trish to go to graduate school to pursue the career that she had put aside when she married. At the university she obtained an additional education from her contact with the younger, more liberated female students. She became aware of how much she resented the role she had "freely" adopted and had deceived herself into believing she was happy with. She also began to resent Jerry for appreciating her only for her skills in keeping a beautifully appointed house, cooking, entertaining, and tending to the children. During all of their years together, she now realized, Jerry had failed to acknowledge her most precious asset, her intelligent mind.

After Trish obtained her Ph.D. in business administration, she went to work. Although Jerry supported her return to school and now her working, he continued to ignore Trish's intellectual accomplishments and failed to take her opinions seriously. She found in an attractive colleague the affirmation she needed and soon entered into an extramarital affair.

Jerry soon learned of this circumstance, because Trish took few precautions to hide it, and it was a profound blow to his pride. He became outraged, depressed, and punitively moralistic toward Trish. The more he used guilt-inducing ploys to get her back, the more Trish justified her behavior. After several months of their being caught up in this vicious circularity, they sought therapy.

In the above case description I have woven in history with dynamic formulation so that it will make more sense to you. During the early years of this marriage, the dynamics of each of the partners meshed like the mechanism of a fine watch. It was only after Trish made substantial changes in her attitudes and behavior that trouble ensued, because Jerry was unable to accommodate to the "new" Trish. Note also the systems concepts incorporated in this formulation.

Treatment Planning

Degree of Support and Expression

In planning for degrees of support versus uncovering strategies in the treatment of couples, the guidelines that I have already discussed pertain. The old expression, "A chain is as strong as its weakest link," also applies. We provide the degree of support that will meet the needs of the more disturbed partner. For example, in the treatment of a bipolar woman (referred to here as Judith) with pronounced dependent and histrionic traits, I was very careful to offer abundant support and, early on, to meet some of her dependent needs by offering her suggestions about how to reduce her stress. After a time, I discerned that the husband had been doing likewise and that we were both playing into her "helplessness." Our "helpfulness" thus reinforced her pathology.

Early in one session, Judith summarized what she had learned at a previous session about her lack of self-confidence leading her to solicit too much outside affirmation. Later she asked me how to handle a problematic situation and I replied:

> Earlier you neatly summarized one of your most difficult problems, your lack of confidence in yourself. I understand that you now feel a strong need for me to help you with another problem and previously I have done so. But now I believe that by helping you with the second problem, I'll make the first one worse. How can you learn to believe in yourself if you don't consider what *you think* is the right way to proceed? Even if it doesn't work out in exactly the best way, it will give you experience in thinking things through and solving problems, and next time you'll do better. That way you'll build confidence in yourself!

This intervention does two things: It gives this patient a chance to take credit for her own growth, and it also models for her husband a change he needs to make so that he, in his sincere efforts to be helpful, will not continue to reinforce her dependency.

Use of the Dynamic Formulation

In dealing with a couple, we have to keep in mind three things: (1) both sets of dynamics and how they mesh or clash, (2) two sets of transferences to us, and (3) our countertransferences to both. Planning is more complicated and the treatment is fraught with more potential complications, which we must anticipate and plan to avoid or deal with. Because most of the transferences run between the two partners, and the therapist maintains a central, mediating, and active empathic presence, transferences toward us are fortunately attenuated, so they are easier to manage than in individual psychotherapy.

Beginning Therapy

The Contract

One element of the contract that we have to stress with couples is that both must attend the scheduled joint sessions. I state this requirement as follows:

> From now on, this will be a joint endeavor. Unless the three of us agree to a change in the plan, we will be meeting together as a team. I will not be meeting with either of you alone unless we change the plan to include individual sessions for one or both of you.

It is difficult to do but we have to keep our word about this aspect of the contract, and if one of the couple arrives alone, he or she must be sent away after a brief exploratory conversation about what happened. Unless the absent partner has a very good reason for not attending, such as a sudden onset of serious illness, I explain:

> This represents a violation of our agreement about these meetings, so we won't be able to continue today. I will see you both at our regular time next week and we can discuss it more then, so that we can understand what this is all about.

What if Trish arrived alone because her physician husband, Jerry, had been delayed at the office but "will be here soon"? My beginning the session in this case would parallel how they behaved in their lives. Now, while Jerry has his "affair" with his practice, she would have a symbolic one with me. So I would leave the door open and we would talk about the weather, the end of summer, and other trivial matters as we waited to begin the session when Jerry arrived. After a few minutes of this, I would ask Trish to call Jerry at his office and check whether he had left yet. If he had not, I would abort the session as described above. This maneuver also preserves the alliance with both equally.

The Alliance

Picture yourself as the therapist seated at the apex of an isosceles triangle with the couple positioned equidistant from you and at varying distances from each other. This is the stance we bend every effort to sustain. We are equally empathic to each member of the couple. When we make a painful confrontation to one, we await an early opportunity to balance it with a similar intervention directed toward the other. This balance is the essential difference between building and sustaining the therapeutic alliance with couples as opposed to individuals. We also regard the couples' relationship as our patient and can use this conviction to avoid taking sides. When couples attempt to get me to take one side or the other, I respond:

> I am aware that each of you would be comforted by someone taking your side; that would feel good to one of you, bad to the other. It wouldn't help for me to take sides. Besides, I have to consider that *side* (I point at a spot halfway between them)—that of your relationship.

In taking this approach in such a situation, I attend to both transference and systematic issues in making my intervention.

Transference and Countertransference

Although in couple therapy the transferences are muted and the type of interventions that are made keep regression and transference to a minimum, we must be alert to certain hazards. I considered one above in the case of Jerry and Trish's apparent collusion to have her arrive alone. Another common hazard is the way couples vie to be better than or at least not as bad as the other in the eyes of the therapist. Having listened to enough of this, I state lightly:

> Now that I know how wicked you both are and how important it is to each of you to have me believe that the other one is worse, perhaps we can get started on working out those problems you said you want to solve. Who would like to begin?

You may have noticed my discouraging the couple's efforts to invite me to disapprove of one of them more than the other and my urging them to get to work on the treatment objectives they selected. This is an example of operant conditioning discussed more generally in Chapter 1. Interventions of this sort usually work eventually. Sometimes we have to be repeat them several times until patients have sufficiently tested our resolve.

When we are less active and are using more uncovering tactics in couples' therapy, we anticipate that all the usual transferences will take place. Patients may project onto us what they have experienced with their parents or siblings. We must watch for these reactions to us and talk about them as they occur. As we explore these transference reactions with one patient while the partner listens, the latter's sensitivity to the former's difficulties often deepens. For example, had Joe and Joan (described at the beginning of this chapter) made it into a marriage and into therapy with me, I can imagine making the following interpretation:

> Joe, when you began to speak of feeling some beginning sexual interest in Joan [after six months, there had been no intercourse], you flushed, looked at me, and seemed very apprehensive. What happened there? . . . Well, what might *I* think? . . . Have I ever said or done anything to suggest to you that I have an anti-sexual attitude or would disapprove of your enjoying yourself sexually? . . . We know who *would* have disapproved, don't we? . . . That's correct, and it's very important that you not get my feelings about and attitudes toward you confused with those of your father!

Here I made a more classical analytic transference interpretation. It might have been more parsimonious, as well as a powerful corrective emotional experience for Joe, had I said simply, with applause, in response to his speaking of his sexual impulses: "Hooray! That's a welcome sign of progress!"

Incidentally, it was fanciful of me to put Joe and Joan together. Had Joan's dynamics been exactly as I depicted them, she would not have been likely to have picked Joe in the first place.

Older male therapists would have to be alert against feeling an avuncular countertransference toward Joan. They might feel overprotective of her as an "innocent little girl, not yet ready to experience sex." This view could also conveniently mask such a therapist's envy of youthful male sexual prowess.

Strategies and Tactics

More Supportive

All the supportive strategies and tactics described in the chapter on the more supportive psychotherapies can be used in work with couples. We are usually more active in work with couples and families, because it is important for us to take charge of the sessions. I find more expressive interventions less effective here. Certainly, free association, like total honesty, is usually contraindicated in couples and family therapy. Interpersonal tact requires us to censor some of what freely comes to our minds.

With couples and families, I am likely to prescribe straightforward tasks. Recently a couple described in detail what the husband's homecoming entailed. Usually, when Eugene arrived, Mona was on the phone with one of her many close lady-friends. He walked by her, sat down in their family room, became resentful about her being on the phone, and left for his regular daily exercise. Only when Mona got off the phone did she become aware that Gene had left without greeting her, and then *she* felt resentful. This kind of interaction exemplified how they often treated each other, like ships passing in the night. I prescribed as follows:

> You two have got to find a way to get out of that rut. It's very painful for both of you. Gene, from now on, when you pass Mona, bend down and give her a kiss on the cheek or the back of her neck. When you notice Gene's kiss, Mona, end your conversation and join him in the family room. Then spend just five minutes, no more at first, talking with each other. Tell each other what your day was like.

I based this intervention on my dynamic understanding of the couple, but I used behavioral reciprocity training in my prescription. Notice that I didn't ask for too much and deliberately specified five minutes as the time they should spend with each other. Fortunately, this change began a process of modifying the hard feelings between them, gradually making it possible for them to become more intimate. Behavioral clinicians often direct patients to practice these prescribed tasks within therapy sessions. Doing this lends further power to the assignments. I often advise nonverbal ways of sending some important messages. At tense times, when we open our mouths we often shoot ourselves in the foot—to mix metaphors purposefully.

I also use supportive cognitive approaches with couples as follows:

> I hear you sounding as if what you're saying is, "Either he loves me totally, completely, all the time, or not at all."

Human nature just isn't like that. We love our mates more at some times and less at others. It is certainly easier to think of it that way than in the all-or-none way that you typically do!

Another way in which I might attempt to undermine an analogous way of thinking that's all too common is with the following words:

I'm hearing you say, in effect, "Either I'm totally free or totally bound, an unfettered man or one in chains." The world isn't like that. All of us are only relatively free. I might have felt like going for a walk in the woods on this beautiful fall day, but because I made a deal with you to be here, I am.

In this intervention I have exemplified the therapist as mentor, offering patients a better, more accurate philosophy of life or way of thinking. Cognitive therapists have developed a system of cognitive marital therapy. Material about cognitive couples psychotherapy can be found in the Reading List, Appendix A.

More Expressive

For patients who are tough enough and well enough motivated for it, we can employ more uncovering, expressive methods in therapy with couples. The same general guidelines apply as with individual therapy, including the use of corrective emotional experiences. A more analytic approach to material offered by one spouse could be stated as follows:

So, what you're saying is that in your family, throughout your developmental years, it was a family rule, enforced by your mother [what the patient said is repeated for emphasis], that no one could openly express anger. But you learned to get away with showing yours by accidentally on purpose dropping and breaking your mother's favorite dish, and doing other clever things like that to get back at her. You told of some other examples a couple of weeks ago.

Now the partner as well as the patient will be on to the latter's passive–aggressive ways. Therefore I say to this patient's mate:

It will be important for you to remind him, in a nice way, of this difficulty he has in expressing irritation openly. When he says that he forgot something important, ask him what he was mad about. That will be helpful for both of you. Eventually, it will avoid the usual trouble with his anger seeping out in some indirect way.

In this type of intervention I combine analytic, systemic, and behavioral styles. They are not in conflict; rather, they augment each other.

Bringing Sessions to a Close

It seems easier to bring sessions with couples to an end than sessions with individuals. Probably this is because couples leave together whereas the single patient feels thrust into an interpersonal void. I often see couples talking for a while before getting into their cars to go to different places. They're doing a wrap-up without me. People who drive together some distance for their appointments tell me they spend a good bit of their traveling time talking in a more personal way than has been usual for them. As interruption of therapy approaches for these people, I say, in a humorous vein:

> You'll save a good bit of money soon, provided you get into the habit of taking a thirty-mile drive, stopping for a cup of coffee, and driving back home again once a week. You can pretend you've had a session with me and buy each other treats with the leftover money.

Customarily I keep in mind the same plans about ending couple sessions as I do individual ones. For example, I block patients from breaking new ground when we're within fifteen minutes from the end of a session. I say:

> That sounds like a very important topic. You can get started on it, if you wish, but I'm sure it will require more time than we have left today. We can begin next time where you leave off today.

To bring a session to a smooth and productive end I often review for my patients, in summary form, the substantive material of that session. A former patient of mine, the president of a large corporation, did this as a matter of routine at the end of every session. He taught me the value of this procedure. It is also a neat way to prevent patients from starting to discuss new material at the end of sessions.

Stages of Therapy

Essentially, couples therapy follows a course analogous to individual therapy. I will state briefly only the special features of this type of therapy.

Early

Early, patients are anxious. They are defensive with each other and in reaction to the presence of the therapist. Few people like to wash their dirty linen in public. Therefore patients often require ample reassurance and support at the beginning. Therapists should explore the compelling adverse influence of shame and guilt. Therefore, we should vigorously probe patients' anticipations about our untoward judgments about them. Blaming and other futile and destructive, redundant circularities de-

249

mand strong, determined, and repeated interventions. If patients are unable to move away from these transactions within a reasonable time, couples therapy may have to be abandoned, at least temporarily. A period of preparatory individual therapy for both may prove to be necessary.

Middle

This phase of therapy is essentially the same as with individual treatment; there are no differences worth noting here.

Late

Like individuals, couples consolidate and integrate their gains during the last phase of their psychotherapy. Because the most compelling feelings and attachments are to each other and because I have sought to deflect transference toward me, the process of separation from the therapist is easier for couples. Rarely do I encounter a prolonged leave-taking.

If all has gone as planned, each mate is ready to terminate therapy at the same time. When we first discuss discontinuing treatment, I make it clear that the decision must be a consensus. Unless I have very strong feelings to the contrary or clear evidence that the couple is interrupting therapy prematurely, I leave the decision to them. Most of the time I require that all three of us agree that the time has come to decrease the frequency of visits, to taper off and then interrupt them, or to name a date to interrupt.

In deciding whether or not to advise an interruption, I assess transference issues and the status of the defensiveness of each spouse. For example, as a couple was beginning to deal with their avoidance of intimacy, Bill—who had a problem with his sexual potency—pressed for a reduction of the frequency of visits. Laura would have deferred to him resentfully. During her developmental years, she had experienced extremely painful parental rejection and abandonment. I therefore took the position that it was critical that Laura state her feelings forthrightly, and I indicated that Bill and I would join in supporting her feelings. I also explained how important it was for Laura to feel that she had a clear choice in the matter in order to avoid a repetition of her childhood trauma. Bill understood this and then put aside his need for comfortable avoidance. We were able to understand and Bill was able to overcome his fear of ridicule of his sexual dysfunction. Shortly after the couple resumed their earlier gratifying sexual activity, Laura took the initiative in suggesting that she was ready to reduce the frequency of sessions and begin to disengage from treatment. Under this circumstance I concurred.

8

Psychotherapy for Families

Conceptual Considerations
Presenting Problems
Indications
Diagnosis
Treatment Planning
Beginning Therapy
Strategies and Tactics
Strategies and Tactics of Other Family
    Psychotherapies for Case Study
Stages of Therapy

This discussion of the family psychotherapies will continue the format used in the previous chapters. Because there are distinctive schools of family therapy, I will elaborate on the conceptual models and methods of the main ones. In an introductory book such as this, it is necessary to summarize. I hope that I can be succinct and, at the same time, clear enough so that you will understand this material with relative ease.

Conceptual Considerations

Psychoanalytic Concepts

Some authors see a conflict between classical psycho-analytic theory and the use of psychoanalytic thinking in family therapy. I have no problem integrating the two. As I have already said, psychoanalysis includes within its purview a general psychological theory, a developmental psychology, a method of treatment, and a research tool. Typically analytic thinking is linear. Most family therapists have studied systems theory and apply circular logic in conducting family therapy. I find no inherent conflict in applying psychoanalytic understanding in family psychotherapy. I modify it to encompass circularity. Remember the way that Joe—discussed in Chapter 7—projected an image of his triangular relationship with his father and sister onto Joan and his relationship with her.

An analogous maladaptive process may occur between parents and their children. For example, parents expect certain behaviors of a child because they project the image (within the parent) of another person into that child (Stierlin et al. 1980). This phenomenon is also called *delegation.* Suppose the image of a special and gifted child who died at an early age falls on and distorts the actuality of a child born subsequently. This dynamic is not rare. Parents then expect of this child accomplishments that are beyond the child's talents. When this child fails to live up to the likeness of the deceased one, the parents convey their disappointment and disapproval, which lead the child to feel anxious and disloyal. Consequently, the child accomplishes still less and the parents increase their pressure, leading the child to achieve even less, and so on.

Analytic and systems thinking fit together smoothly. In other forms of delegation or projection, the content consists of aspects of the parent(s). For example, a father recounts the story of his 10-year-old son burning down a neighbor's barn; when he gets to the end and says, "Burnt to the ground, it did!" he smiles broadly and is not aware of his smiling (Johnson and Szurek 1952).

Other concepts derived from psychoanalysis that are valuable in our comprehension of family dynamics include differentiation of self from other, separation-individuation, splitting, projective identification, mourning, identification, collusion, and boundaries. Freud used the oedipal myth as the paradigm for the Oedipus complex, a very significant family dynamic. In the version of this story that Sophocles wrote in *Oedipus the King,* King Laius of Thebes was told by an oracle that his unborn son, the future Oedipus, would kill him. Laius therefore ordered that this child be killed soon after his birth. The servant entrusted with this awful responsibility disobeyed the king's order and gave Oedipus to Polybus, king of

Corinth, to rear. Oedipus did ultimately kill Laius in a confrontation years later about which of them had the right of way on a road. Later, Oedipus married Laius's widow, Queen Jocasta, and became King of Thebes, none of them realizing that she was his mother and Laius had been his father. When the truth came to light, Jocasta committed suicide and Oedipus blinded himself and was sent into exile, at his own behest, by the king who succeeded him. In early Greek drama, authors did not account for human behavior on the basis of internal motivations. Rather, they accounted for all behavior as dependent upon fate, which it was believed the gods ordained. Freud stood Greek cosmology on its head by basing the Oedipus complex on the instinctual drives, fantasies, and distorted perceptions of children. The Greeks made external forces primary whereas Freud made *internal* ones primary. A more measured and contemporary view grants importance to the interaction among all of the participants in the drama and to their individual internal states. For example, well-adjusted parents will not allow their child to split them. The father will claim his husbandly rights without displaying excessive jealousy, anger, or punitiveness toward a son who presses his claim for possession of the mother. Family therapists observe and intervene in dysfunctional family triangles *in vivo*. For example, in a mother–father–son triangle in which mother and son are very close and father is antagonistic toward the son, family therapists will intervene to modify the triangle. The therapist helps the father and son heal the rift between them and get on better terms, and will also assist the mother and father, as husband and wife, to move closer together. Because they will then need each other less, the mother and son move a little farther apart.

In our efforts to clarify family dynamics, we can apply

a combination of Freud's (1905) and Erikson's (1959) models of development of the individual to delineate the various stages of the family life cycle. The family with infants and toddlers and relatively healthy and supportive grandparents is a very different family than one further along in the family life cycle. Later on the children will be teenagers or young adults. The parents' parents may be in failing health and one or more of them may have become a responsibility and/or a burden. In conducting family assessment and treatment, we must keep these family life cycle differences in mind.

Our cognizance of how children behave at various developmental levels and what their needs and vulnerabilities are deepens our empathy for them. It also hones our empathy for their parents who must, somehow, get them through all these developmental hazards without irreparable damage. Our grasp of what the parents have experienced during their developmental years also deepens our compassion for the difficulties they have in being parents. It is extremely difficult to empathize with abusive, incestuous, or neglectful parents, but less difficult the better we know them and their histories. Boszormenyi-Nagy and Spark (1973) characterized the process of transmission of pathological parent–child relationships as the "revolving slate." Without question, these are unconscious processes, fairly easily discerned by us but not so easily imparted to and changed in the family (Ackerman 1962, Boszormenyi-Nagy and Spark 1973, Bowen 1978, Lidz 1963, Paul 1967).

To look at this from yet another angle, "incest" in families exists in varying ways. When the husband does not adequately meet his wife's need for closeness, she may turn to their son to get this need met. The husband, angry with his wife, may allow or provoke their daughter to rebel against the mother. These are instances of misalliances which we can view as emotionally incestuous (Lidz 1963).

To conduct psychoanalytically oriented family therapy, we first determine a family's dynamic diagnosis, akin to the kind we make with couples. However, the larger the family, the more difficult and complicated this is. Hence it is advisable to have a co-therapist in the practice of family psychotherapy, although because of financial constraints, a co-therapist is not very often feasible.

Concepts about Communication

Two prominent schools of family therapy that have incorporated theories of those who originated or enlarged upon human communication concepts are the *strategic* school and the *structural*. These will be discussed separately.

Strategic. I have mentioned the idea of cybernetic feedback loops, which can maintain homeostasis in systems or contribute to escalating deviation. Strategic theorists think of change in families in terms of the balance between negative (homeostatic) and positive (deviation-amplifying) feedback loops. Strategic therapy is also based on the concept that symptoms and problematic behaviors in the "identified patient" in a family serve the function of solving a family problem. This problem results from a need to change because of a natural life cycle event (youngest child leaves home) or a crisis (father's myocardial infarction, as in the J. family described in Chapter 3). Formulating a hypothesis about what function the problem performs in the family system, why it has failed to do so effectively, and what more adaptive solutions would be possible for the family is the equivalent of a dynamic formulation. Strategic theory does not concern itself with the internal dynamics of any individual family member. Its central focus is on the here-and-now difficulty and family goals (Haley 1976, Madanes 1981, Stanton 1981).

Structural.   Structural family therapy concentrates on the hierarchy, power structure, boundaries, and triangles within the family system. In the optimally functioning family, the united parents are clearly in charge of the administration of the family group. The boundary between the marital domain and the parental one is neither too permeable nor impermeable. Mates resolve marital conflicts and meet each other's individual emotional needs within the marital orbit. The degree of closeness and other emotional dimensions between parents and children in the one or more father–mother–child triangle(s) is balanced and appropriate. Structural family therapists diagnose maladaptive family patterns in these terms, and they plan their therapies to correct pathology of family structure and function understood along these lines.

Experiential Theory

According to experiential clinicians, growth of the family and its individual members will take place through poignant experience between family and therapists (they highly recommend a co-therapy team for this form of therapy). The experience provided by the therapists is on a symbolic, primary-process level, similar to play therapy with children. Therapists use their intuition and their countertransference reactions openly and playfully in a type of spontaneous therapeutic use of self. Whitaker, the most prominent teacher of this form of family therapy, believes that therapists should trust what they can learn by being in touch with their own unconscious selves and should impart this to families (Whitaker and Bumberry 1988). He does not believe in learning-specific techniques. Others in this school use the experiences their patients had with their own parents in their families of origin to understand how they function as parents in the present. These latter views are similar to analytic object relations theory.

Behavioral Theory

Theorists and therapists of the behavioral persuasion use concepts derived from operant conditioning, social learning theory, and social exchange theory. Behaviorists apply their knowledge of operant conditioning to understand the problems parents have in their discipline of children with conduct disorders. In transactional situations, as between spouses, behavioral clinicians view the behaviors of each as reinforcing the behaviors and feelings of the other. Behavioral therapists also believe that behavior is associated with the context in which it occurs. They may have borrowed this idea from systems theory. Thinking in terms of social exchange theory, behaviorists see each member of a transaction as attempting to maximize gains and minimize losses. As intrafamily experience accumulates, the family or marital pair develops regular patterns (rules) in their interactions. To look at this from the behavioral perspective, couples and families who employ mainly positive reinforcement or use rewards for behavioral regulation and need gratification are functioning optimally. Couples and families who apply mainly punishment or negative reinforcement for these purposes are judged by behaviorists to be maladaptive. Behavioral therapists also believe that effective communication is an important interpersonal skill.

Psychoeducational Therapy

No theoretical superstructure preceded the implementation of the psychoeducational approach with families. Some clinicians believed that imparting information about schizophrenia and offering support to families of schizophrenic patients would have a beneficial effect for these patients and their families. Clinicians treating schizophrenic patients have struggled for years to find a way to reduce the acute exacerbations of the illness; medications alone were not entirely satisfactory. Various forms of family therapy seemed at times to make matters worse, because therapists implied or families inferred that therapists, seeking to understand, were blaming them. For emphasis, I will repeat what I said in the Introduction: As clinicians and therapists, we must be very careful not to confuse an association between one thing and another as having proven the etiology of one of them. One group of British clinicians first noted and published their finding of an association between exacerbations in schizophrenic patients and what they called high expressed emotions (EE) among the families of these patients (Brown et al. 1972). These and other clinicians applied these findings in their treatment of schizophrenic patients and their families, as I will now describe. When therapy was successful in lowering family EE, rates of subsequent psychotic episodes decreased *pari passu.* An excellent review of the subject of families in the treatment of schizophrenia appeared in a recent edition of a mental health letter (*Families in the Treatment of Schizophrenia,* 1989a, b).

Presenting Problems

The Adult-Identified or Index Patient

Having arrived at the conclusion that some family member—the identified or index patient—needs some type of psychotherapy or counseling, someone is appointed by the family or assumes the responsibility for making contact with a mental health professional. Least complicated are those calls made by identified patients for themselves. An older adolescent or young adult living at home or with strong emotional familial ties may call. A family member other than the identified patient may make the call. More often than not, the wife-mother is the spokesman for the group. How we handle this call is of the utmost importance. I have previously discussed the advisability of a clinician's taking personal responsibility for conducting a mini-intake before scheduling an appointment for *any* patient. Since this is of singular importance in the case of a family member making an appointment for a related adult, I will elaborate on the procedure here. In the mini-intake, the first thing we need to determine is whether the person whom the caller has identified as a prospective patient agrees with this depiction and is receptive to the proposed consultation.

It may come as a surprise to you to learn that occasionally a relative will call *without* having first talked with the prospective patient. Some carry this kind of maneuver to an extreme and attempt to get the clinician to see the patient under false pretenses. The caller might say, "Couldn't you tell my husband that you want to check his physical condition; he'll probably agree to come if he thinks you're a regular doctor." As you may have discerned, some of these calls are inappropriate; moreover, the process should be aborted at the time of the call or you'll have many unwelcome free hours. For beginning clinicians this can be a serious financial loss. You will probably want to suggest that the caller talk with the person whom he or she believes is in need of help and that the two of them come in together for a consultation. You might conclude, on the basis of this exploratory phone conversation, that several family members should attend. At this point it is better to be less than eager or enthusiastic and to purposefully say:

> My experience leads me to believe that if your [relative] does not feel the need for help, we're not very likely to get anywhere. So have a serious talk with him [or her] and then get back to me or have your [relative] give me a call. I'll set up one consultation for the three of us [or include additional family members] and at the end of that we can discuss where we go from there.

Frequently the matter will end there; you will not have wasted your time and energy on a case that is not a case!

The caller may be the family "ambassador" and mention that there is trouble in the family about which he or she would like to consult with you. Alternately, your probing questions may bring to light such a situation. When this is the case, I begin the process of setting up a contract for all implicated family members to attend a consultation:

> Because family problems are an important part of the picture you have described so clearly, it would be much better if all family members attended the first or first few consultations, if we have more than one. You seem to be the one who is most concerned, so have a serious-minded talk with everybody and persuade them all to come in. I'll put you in my card file of patients who have applied for treatment. Please get back to me about this as soon as you can.

When I meet objections to a total family meeting, I see the person who called or as many as will agree to come. During the early meetings I'll attempt to understand and counteract whatever is in the way of obtaining the cooperation of all family members embroiled in the family's predicament.

The inquirer may be the adult child of a parent whom the child believes to be in need of help. Commonly, son or daughter will express concern about "mother's memory" and wonder about Alzheimer's disease. Also, commonly the offspring will express worry about a parent's emotional status, such as "Dad's loneliness and depression since Mother died." Under these kinds of circumstances it is almost never difficult to gain the cooperation of the

caller to bring the parent for the interview and to participate in all or part of it.

I prefer not to deal with situations that require me to be
a part of a commitment process. Therefore, on the telephone I attempt to screen out cases of that sort and refer
them to the appropriate public agency (in Lucas County,
Ohio, for example, that is Rescue–Crisis). You would have
to know how to proceed in your region. Naturally, it is
not possible to avoid all of these cases, so it is expedient
for us to know how to accomplish this unpleasant task.

The Child-Identified or Index Patient

In the introduction to Part III I mentioned a parent
calling because of symptoms or problematic behaviors in
a child. It is not too difficult, even in cases of parents'
seeking to have the child or adolescent treated without
the child's participation, to convince the parents (and
sometimes the child's siblings) to come in for one or more
conferences, as follows:

> I treat children and adolescents with the help of their
> families. Most of the time this is what works best. If this
> would not be the best plan or is not what you're looking
> for, we'll have to make a different plan. At the outset,
> however, I need your help in giving history and back-
> ground information that Patrick wouldn't even know
> about. Parents know about their children's early develop-
> ment, illnesses, and other history that the children them-
> selves do not. I also like to meet *all* the kids and get their
> ideas about their brother's problems. So let's schedule one
> total family meeting, see how that goes, and then plan the
> next step in Pat's treatment.

I am not a child psychiatrist and do not treat children and very young adolescents in individual psychotherapy. If I run into intractable opposition to my recommendations for introductory family meetings, I tell the parent that it would be better to seek help elsewhere. I do not say where. I wouldn't want to stick a friend or colleague with this type of case.

Indications

In the section on "Treatment Considerations" in Chapter 2, I considered the indications for individual and family treatment. In that section and elsewhere I also discussed the indications for varying levels of family participation in the diagnostic and treatment process. For emphasis, I will summarize here the indications for family participation in the diagnosis and treatment of the index patient, and for family therapy.

Participation in Diagnosis

In most situations it is useful to obtain information from observers who are close to the index patient. For patients whose mental status is seriously disturbed, including those who are actively psychotic, who are deeply depressed, or who may be bipolar, it is sometimes absolutely necessary to get information from others. In these cases it is wise to invite the patient to bring a family member or close friend to one of the early evaluation sessions. Sometimes we do not become aware of the need for ancillary information until later on. When the diagnosis is in doubt or when patients are not responding to therapy as expected, obtaining additional data often solves the mystery. Perhaps patients have been unable to reveal some important piece of information; alcohol or other substance abuse is a common example.

Participation in Treatment

In the treatment of seriously disturbed patients, the regularly scheduled or intermittent participation of family members, as needed, is often of crucial importance. This topic has already been discussed in sufficient detail.

Family Therapy

Marital or couples psychotherapy is a form of family therapy; I have already discussed the indications for the former. Family group therapy is indicated in all cases associated with intrafamily issues or conflict. By thinking in the circular mode, we minimize the question of causality and magnify the objectives of relieving pain, solving problems, and enhancing function. There are many ways to convey this perspective to patients. Following are examples of three of my favorites:

> We are *not* here to determine who started the series of events that got you where you are now. It makes abso-

lutely no difference how that first stone came loose from the top of the mountain, or who kicked it, to start the avalanche. What we have to do, together, is find a way to slow it down, change its direction, or stop it and start something new and better for everyone concerned.

The second example is more sophisticated:

In his second inaugural address, Lincoln traced the history of the onset of our tragic Civil War. He ended with, "And the war came." They didn't start it, we didn't start it, this or that didn't cause it—*it came!* It is much better and more accurate, from a psychological point of view, for us to look at your family troubles in the same way.

The third example is more familiar and visual:

Think of a videotape spliced together so skillfully that we can't find where the splice is. Imagine it going round and round in your VCR. If we stop it at Mike's frame and watch what he does, we'll say, "It all starts with Mike." Let it go around some more and stop it at Jennifer's frame. Now we say, "No it didn't start with Mike, Jennifer caused it." And so on with Tim, with Sarah, and with Mom and Dad.

All of these make the more abstruse point in a relatively understandable and acceptable form. This is not evasive. It's what I believe. I hope to influence patients to see both the desirable and undesirable events in their lives this way.

At the outset, of course, we accept the family's view of their problem. If their consensus is, "Fix Johnny and everything will be fine in the family," we accept that statement and start to work to do just that. In some cases, families' diagnoses are correct. Relieving one member's symptoms or difficult behaviors can be enough. The support (including necessary medication) and guidance provided by the therapist can free up the natural healing forces and family strengths, so that fixing Johnny will make everything fine for that family. Most of the time, however, further change in the family as a group and in other family members will be mandatory.

Diagnosis

Nosologic

There is no systematic way to formulate a family diagnosis analogous to any nosology of individual pathology. We diagnose one or more family members using the current DSM system. Although it is important for us to think in systems terms in assessing family structure and function, it is equally important to be cognizant of individual psychopathology. I find no conflict between the individual evaluation and the family evaluation; they complement each other.

Dynamic

From the very moment an informant (family member or person making the referral) begins to tell us the story about the reason for seeking family consultation or therapy, we begin making hypotheses about what is happening in the family. Next we make a plan about how to proceed in the first family consultation. During this consultation and at its conclusion, we will revise our formulations and plans as determined by the way the family responds to our interventions. Mainly we will be eliciting data by using that list of journalistic questions with each family member. We will also observe their reactions to us, ours to them, and theirs to each other.

Case History: A Suicidal Father

Recently a therapist who had been working with patient Martin M. for some time called to ask for a family consultation. The sequence of events unfolded as follows:

> The patient's individual treatment was at an impasse and he was talking seriously of suicide. He was married, the father of four children ranging in age from 9 to 17. Both of his parents had been alcoholic and abusive to an extreme extent. Martin left home at an early age and lived on the streets. Several times he feigned illness, once a mental illness, to obtain admission to hospitals for care and respite. Later he was befriended by an elderly lady, who allowed him to live in her home and furnished him with food and clothing until he graduated from high school. In spite of his early deprivations, he functioned well at his long-term job. He was, however, miserable. When all treatment failed, including adequate trials of several antidepressants, he vowed that he would kill himself rather than continue to live in such misery. Martin lived at great emotional distance from his wife and children. He was convinced that he was no more than a meal ticket to them and that they did not really care whether he lived or died.

His therapist believed the risk of suicide was high, that further hospitalization would only delay the inevitable, and that family therapy might be helpful. Martin's therapist asked me to give family psychotherapy a try as soon as possible.

I agreed to see the family under the following nonnegotiable conditions: (1) All family members must attend, and (2) Martin's suicidal ideation had to be shared with the family. The patient's therapist told him about these terms, talked with his wife, and they agreed to attend and bring all the children.

Hypothesis and Plan.   In the case under discussion, because the patient's individual therapist had not seen the family, we had only fragmentary information about them. We knew that Martin had feigned illness in the past and that his manner was histrionic. We also knew that his father had been a brutal tyrant and that his mother had failed to protect him. Martin had been resourceful enough to survive on the streets and to cultivate a good relationship with a maternal surrogate, who had treated him with kindness and generosity. I speculated that Martin's suicidal threats represented a vigorous cry for help and that his therapist had correctly concluded that he wanted help with his family. I decided, in conducting the family consultation, to defer to Martin and give him as much control as possible. Also I would be *very* gentle.

The initial consultation proved to be therapeutic for Martin and his family and they decided to enter family therapy. This case will be used as an example of beginning family therapy later in the chapter.

Treatment Planning

Degree of Support or Expression

We apply the same principles in determining the degree of support or expression we will implement in family psychotherapy as we do in individual and couples therapy. Keep in mind the aphorism, "A chain is as strong as its weakest link," in arriving at this judgment. If the index patient or another family member is seriously disturbed or presents with a fragile personality organization, we plan for abundant support. We may conduct some sessions differently when the most vulnerable person is not present. For example, if that person is hospitalized and actively psychotic, her or his attendance would be contraindicated for that time. In addition, we base our judgment about the level of support indicated for a particular family on the information at hand about the nature, quality, and intensity of their feelings and conflicts. I remind you again of the importance of our providing structure as a means of support. Recently I provided written rules and an agenda for meetings with a family that required the utmost support. The family group consisted of S., who was the identified child patient, her older brother B., her divorced biological parents, and their present spouses. Here is what I wrote out and handed each family member to read at the beginning of their first session:

RULES AND AGENDA FOR FAMILY MEETING:
The _____ Family

I. *Objectives:*

    A. The adults *must* continue to provide a more supportive and less tense family life for B. and S.

    B. The adults must continue to agree upon future policies and plans to make the first objective happen.

    C. S. and B. must agree to reasonable policies and plans for them. They may express their opinions and feelings about these, and the adults will be open to revisions they believe to be proper.

    D. Different objectives may apply to any future meetings that the adults, including myself, agree upon. These objectives are open to negotiation; I must approve them beforehand.

II. *Rules:*

    A. Directions about speaking given to adults:

        1. As the chairperson of this meeting, I have the

responsibility for keeping order, ruling people out of order, or ruling an issue as inappropriate for this meeting.

2. Each person must speak only of her/himself; talking about another person is strictly forbidden.

3. Speak to each other about issues in the present and future only; you may not discuss the past.

4. Only one person, designated by me, may discipline the members of the younger generation during a session.

5. After the adults have agreed about a plan, one adult, again designated by me, will explain the plan to S. and B. If there are misunderstandings, I will state what I heard.

B. Directions about speaking given to younger generation (S. and B.):

1. The same rule about speaking to, rather than about others applies to you as does the rule of speaking only about yourselves.

2. When granted permission by the adult in charge of your discipline, you may talk according to the rules stated above. I reserve the right to veto the permission given you if it seems inappropriate at the time.

3. Your opinions and feelings about issues will be listened to and seriously considered by all adults.

III. *Agenda for Today's Session:*

A. Adults will acknowledge any mistakes they made during the past week, especially any words or deeds that have made it difficult for S. or B.

B. Adults will apologize to S. and B. for these
    mistakes.

C. Adults will agree upon any additional policies
    that involve S. and B.; they will focus on any
    issues that arose during the past week.

D. The designated adult will state these policies
    and, as soon as possible, put them in written
    form and provide copies to all participants.

E. A few minutes before the end of the session I will
    offer my prescription for future meetings, and
    the adults and I will agree upon a contract re-
    garding them.

Now you may ask what led me to take such drastic action
before I had even met the family. That's a fair question.
The clinician who made the referral described the family's
previous failed therapy. He told me that he had taken a
nondirective approach. Family sessions deteriorated into
verbal brawls that this therapist was never able to control.
Fortunately, the family's previous therapist was honest
and responsible enough to own up to his mistake, tell me
about it, and refer the family for another try at psychotherapy.

Use of the Dynamic Formulation

I have illustrated how I use the dynamic formulation or
my hypothesis about the family dynamics to plan the
initial consultation. As more is learned about the family by
eliciting their history and observing them and us interac-
tively, a more complete dynamic diagnosis is formulated
and the therapeutic approach is changed to reflect the

changes made in the dynamic formulations. For example, after the first family consultation with Martin and his family, discussed earlier, I revised the hypothesis and made plans for the next meeting accordingly. I will continue the discussion of this family's further treatment later on.

Beginning Therapy

The opening moves in family psychotherapy resemble those for individual and couples psychotherapy. I usually take great care to welcome each family member warmly and take enough time with small talk to set them all at ease. I give equal empathic attention to each family member, in what Boszormenyi-Nagy and Spark (1973) call "multilateral partiality." What this means is that therapists join and empathize with each person's position, even if it represents a minority of one. Where the family members sit in relation to each other is important. The therapist or co-therapy team sits last. Co-therapists sit side by side, even if doing so means moving a chair.

The Contract

For family group therapy the contract has special features. Therapists spell out which family members will attend. If we deliberately make the contract strict and tight, then we must adhere to it. However, judgment and flexibility in our use of the terms of the contract influence the alliance and transference greatly. If we have concluded that a particular family will profit from firmness and discipline, we must hold them precisely to the contract's terms. If permissiveness will provide a positive therapeutic experience, we allow more leeway. We must make this critical decision when part of a family arrives and tells us that one or more members can't make it. Whatever the reasons are, we will hold the family responsible and exploit the situation for therapeutic purposes.

Therapists charge larger fees for family therapy, usually based on the number who will attend. All or several family members will be registered as patients, diagnosed, and charged part of the total fee. Third-party payers always set a different UCR (Usual, Customary, and Reasonable) fee for family, as opposed to individual, psychotherapy. It is financially advantageous for patients when our fee per patient for family therapy is equal to or below the UCR.

We make our contracts with the adult(s) in the family. It is their responsibility to get the family to therapy sessions regularly and on time, to pay fees in a timely fashion, and to intervene if children or adolescents act up or act out during meetings. For older adolescents, it is expedient, with the cooperation of the parent(s), to require them to pay part of the fee above that paid by insurance. Most of them have jobs or receive pay from their parents for doing chores.

The Alliance

We employ the same concepts in forming and maintaining therapeutic alliances with each family member as we do in individual and couples therapy. Therapists must remember that, as in couples therapy, the many relationships within the family as well as the family itself are also our patients. Family members have usually formed alliances among themselves and may each attempt to induct us into his or her own particular camp. It is proper and therapeutic to acknowledge efforts to get us to take sides, but it is wrong to side with one intrafamily subgroup against another. Were we to do so, we would lose the family. However, it is good practice to side with one person or subgroup provided we promptly balance this planned intervention by siding subsequently with the others.

Transference and Countertransference

As they do in couples therapy, family members display many of their most intense feelings or transferences between and among themselves. We are careful to avoid or minimize drawing transferences to ourselves. Toward this end we do not assume parental responsibility for the younger generation in the family. For example, Martin's younger son did not sit with the family. I did not tell him where to sit; rather, I said to the parents:

> Does it bother you that Bill is sitting way over there? . . .
> No? Then, since it's okay with you, it's okay with me.

Had Bill's behavior been destructive or disruptive of the therapeutic process, I would have enjoined the parents to get his behavior under control. I would not have continued the interview until they had succeeded in doing so.

What transferences do develop, especially negative

ones that threaten the continuation of the treatment, must be dealt with promptly in the standard ways.

Example of Beginning Therapy: The Martin M. Family Consultation

After completing social amenities and making a separate contract for this first session, I said: "Dad, this is your show, you're the star. How do you want me to proceed? I would like to ask your family what they understand about this meeting. Is that all right with you?" Martin agreed to this, and all, including his wife, professed not to know what the interview was all about. I then invited Martin to tell them. He was not able to do so; he gave me his permission to tell them. I said: "Dad has been very sad, has been suffering a lot in his feelings, and has been thinking of suicide. That's why Dr. _____ [Martin's therapist] asked me to have this family meeting."

All reacted with strong emotions. Mrs. M. expressed intense anger, tearfully. She directed most of her anger toward me for telling about Martin's suicidal ideation in front of the children. The remainder of her anger she aimed at Martin. Later she said that she had known about his suicidal thoughts beforehand and was sure he wouldn't do it. Eighteen-year-old Dick was very empathic toward his father and told of his own struggles with alcohol, drugs, and sex. Dick deplored his need to deceive his parents about his activities and problems. He welcomed the opportunity to share his feelings with them and offered to talk with his father and help him in any way he could. The two daughters echoed their mother's anger toward their father but also said they'd be very sad if he died. Bill (age 16) acted truculent and said that he'd tell his father to go ahead and kill himself and that he wouldn't care. Earlier, when this son sat at the furthest possible distance from the rest of us, I remarked, "Looks like we have a chip off the old block here." Martin smiled and looked at Bill.

My interventions were empathic and supportive toward all. On questioning, Martin expressed relief and, with my gentle persuasion, reassured the family that he intended to live a long life. At the end of the consultation I told the family that I thought he should continue his individual therapy. I offered to meet with them all at regular intervals and told them that family therapy might be helpful. To Mrs. M. I said, "I'm sorry that I hurt you so much; I thought it was necessary and didn't know how important it is to you to protect your children from harm. If you're so angry with me that you never want to see me again, I will understand." To all, I declared, "Please don't make any decision now, one way or the other, about returning. Think it over. It's a parental decision, but I hope you'll both talk it over with the kids too and will consider their wishes. Give me a call and let me know."

Revised Hypothesis and Plan

During the course of this consultation, Martin's wife, Judy, expressed some disagreement with him about the children's discipline. I also noted and filed away Martin's seeming pleasure in Bill's rebellious behavior. I wondered whether the mother was allied with the children against Martin, because of her own grievances with him. She seemed somewhat controlling, apparently trying to control me through guilt induction, and I noticed that this irritated me. Was Martin expressing his rebelliousness toward his wife by projecting it into Bill? If so, one possible remedy would be to facilitate conflict resolution between them. If my suspicion was true that Martin was playing the role of a rebellious 16-year-old opposite Judy's controlling-parent role, couples therapy with or without the children present would be indicated. I thought that I would probably need to help Martin move closer to the children and find ways to participate in activities with them. Although interventions would continue to be mainly supportive, family-of-origin issues might have to be explored and interpreted. In view of the older son Dick's age and clear receptiveness to therapy, it might prove advisable to recommend individual psychotherapy for him if he asked for such help.

A few days later I talked with Martin's therapist. She reported that his suicidal ideation had been resolved and that he seemed much less depressed, and she believed that it had come as a welcome and needed surprise for Martin to find out how much his family cared about him. Within a week Martin called to arrange another visit. I reinforced the terms of the contract, but he indicated that they might not be able to get Bill to come back. So I replied:

> You probably can if you want to use the leverage you have. You control the use of the car and television and the amount of money he has. It's important for everyone to be here. Please do your best to make that happen.

If Bill does not attend, I'll work with his absence as an issue but will not demand that he be present as a condition of continuing family therapy. I elicited no new data that negated my judgment about the advisability of my avoiding an authoritarian stance. To exemplify techniques utilized subsequently in the therapy of this family, I will discuss the further course of their treatment later.

Strategies and Tactics

The examples that have been given and others provided later demonstrate my practice of eclectic family psychotherapy. These samples of the way I construct dynamic formulations and hypotheses exemplify how to understand material in psychoanalytic, mainly object relations, ways. I make some of the interpretations illustrated in a modified analytic style. A more extensive grounding in dynamic or analytic methods will be enlightening for most therapists and I strongly advise readers to pursue it (Skynner 1976, Slipp 1984). In the following discussions I will divide the family psychotherapies into the more supportive and the more expressive ones and then briefly describe the strategies and tactics of the major extant schools.

More Supportive Techniques

Measures that are supportive in other modes of psychotherapy are supportive in family work as well. I regard behavioral, structural, and strategic techniques as relatively supportive. None of these modes weakens defenses or is invasive or probing. These family therapists are active and directive, even prescriptive. I also regard them as supportive because of the extreme care that most of them take in joining families and in avoiding the arousal of defensiveness.

More Expressive Techniques

We reserve more expressive, psychodynamic interventions for a small number of highly motivated families whose members all function on a relatively high level and have robust personality organizations. I find it very useful to frame my findings about families in psychodynamic terms, regardless of the specific tactics I implement. In this regard, we can learn much from the way psychoanalytically oriented group therapists formulate group dynamics (Yalom 1975).

You have probably already noted that I formulated the case of Martin M. and his family in a blend of dynamic, structural, and systems terms. At the stage of their therapy related above, it was not yet clear how much of the analytic type of interpretation I would use with them. I did not know then if I would ever say to them something like this:

> I would like to share some of my impressions with you for your consideration. Martin, when you feel controlled by Judy, you get mad at her and signal Bill to get back at her for you. Bill, you're at an age when some rebellion is normal, even desirable. You have to make your declaration of independence—but you carry it too far when you also act against Mother for Dad. Judy, you seem to take too

much responsibility for Martin's actions, almost as if you feel they reflect on you and diminish you.

This interpretation illustrates a mixture of analytic object relations concepts and systems theory.

Strategies and Tactics of Other Family Psychotherapies

Behavioral Family Therapy

I previously indicated my belief that many, if not most, therapists on the firing line have borrowed freely from each other. I notice that I have come to use positive reinforcement more deliberately, and state my opinions to or criticisms of patients' behaviors in a more affirmative manner, under the influence of behaviorists. They have conditioned me to say, for instance, "I think it would be better for you to tell her how much you would appreciate her considering your wishes, rather than criticizing her when she does not." Also I teach parents who are having difficulty with the discipline of their children how to construct and actuate a behavioral modification program. Such parents must be on good enough terms with each other to be able to cooperate in putting the plan into effect. Single parents, who are at a disadvantage because they have to do all of the discipline alone, often find behavioral modification programs useful. Therapists offer these single parents the guidance and support they usually need.

Behavioral therapists attend to their relationships with patients. They are alert to transference and deal with it, even though they do not usually include any analytic words in their lexicon. These therapists evaluate families in terms of what happens before, during, and after problematic behaviors or symptoms occur. They scrutinize sequences of behaviors to determine the operative positive and negative reinforcers. The main thrust of behavioral family therapy is to effect changes in the consequences connected with desirable and undesirable behaviors, including the manifestation of symptoms. Specific techniques include *contingency contracting, communications training,* and *problem-solving exercises.* What *contingency contracting* involves is simply negotiating with the family to agree to a number of quid pro quo tradeoffs (Barton and Alexander 1981, Jacobson, 1980). To illustrate, a father agrees to read his 8-year-old child a bedtime story every night, provided she has laid out her school clothes for the next day. Behavior therapists usually prefer rewards to punishments. Characteristically, they give patients tasks to do at home. The family members, guided by the therapist, agree to act in certain mutually reinforcing ways, carrying out this series of behaviors a certain number of times between sessions. To prevent patients' distorting or "forgetting" agreements that were made, therapists may write them out, keep a copy, and give another to a family member who will act as secretary.

In one method of *communications training,* the clinician assigns each of two family members the roles of speaker and listener, in turn, and gives instructions as follows:

> In the role of speaker, John, you must be careful to make all of your statements so that you say what *you* believe or feel, or how *you* are reacting. You must avoid all blaming, accusing, and judging of the other person. In speaking of your observations of the other person, you must be subjective and very tentative. What you say, then, would be, for example: "When it *seems* to me that you have been critical of me, I get upset and angry, and before I can think it through I lash out at you. Later I feel sorry about that, but usually I can't bring myself to admit it." Remember to keep your messages as short as possible. Imagine that you're composing a radiogram and will have to pay by the word. In the role of listener, Mary, you must listen very carefully, because I'll ask you to repeat in your own words what you think you heard John say. You must *not* add any material that is your own, no inferences and no editorial comments. I'll monitor the exercise and tell you if either of you breaks the rules of your role. Also I'll add anything the listener seems to have missed and correct things the listener seems to have distorted.

After some practice, therapists assign other family members to the speaker and listener roles, and the therapist may give the monitor role to some family member but will continue to chair the exercise. The therapist tells the family to practice the exercise for a specified time at regular intervals between therapy sessions. To evaluate and critique their progress with their communication exercises, the family will tape-record their practice sessions.

During and between therapy sessions, families will also practice *problem-solving exercises* engineered and guided by the behavioral therapist. Therapists ask family members to name a problem, a desired outcome, and several alternative solutions. Then they try out the one solution they select. In this way they gain experience in a trial-and-error method of solving problems. As they accumulate experience, the solutions they devise become more effective. Because some practitioners of psychoeducational family therapy incorporate behavioral techniques in their therapies, I will describe this method next.

Psychoeducational

Clinicians who have incorporated structured education as an essential component of family psychotherapy with schizophrenic patients and their families seem to obtain better results along several outcome measures than with other forms of treatment (Anderson et al. 1980, Falloon et al. 1985). Patients have manifested fewer relapses, improved socialization, and reduced symptoms apparently associated with diminished expressed emotion (EE) in their families. These therapists work in several different ways, but all include an educational workshop or seminar; one group calls these ''survival skills'' workshops. Some use behavioral family management and others multiple family support groups.

Therapists guide problem-solving and communication exercises similar to those already described. In multiple family groups, therapists facilitate families' sharing with and helping each other. Member families support each other between sessions and sometimes after formal therapy has been concluded or interrupted. In these ways, families of schizophrenic patients learn how to help their disturbed members, elicit their cooperation, effectively interdict undesirable or hazardous behaviors, and, when it is appropriate or imperative to do so, call for help. These clinicians teach families the early warning signs of worsening of schizophrenic patients' conditions. When families forewarn therapists promptly, they can take steps to prevent relapses just as promptly.

Experiential

Dr. Carl Whitaker and his associates wrote two fascinating books about experiential family psychotherapy (Napier and Whitaker 1978, Whitaker and Bumberry 1988). Both read like suspenseful novels. It is extremely difficult to understand what he does, much less describe it. Although it's beautiful and apparently effective, I don't think it's teachable. Dr. Whitaker and his co-therapists make their intense involvement and dedication in their work with families very clear. There are many surprises. Dr. Whitaker, when in his late sixties or early seventies, tripped an arrogant teenaged boy and wrestled him to the ground, as the latter was attempting to flee from a family session. How many therapists would do that? How many of you would consider it? We might feel like doing it but probably would not. In one of Dr. Whitaker's videotaped interviews with a family, the young adult daughter seeks his advice about what she should do about a problem with her boyfriend. He replies, ''Merry Christmas!'' That makes some of my explanations about why I don't give that kind of advice seem prolix, if not stupid. What I advise you to do is read the two books and watch some of Whitaker's videotapes. You will learn something about doing therapy and about how to use yourself as a therapeutic tool, but you probably won't be able to put the method into words. Whitaker gives his patients the gifts of freedom and playfulness and, in some measure, he does the same for us if we can tune him in.

Strategic Family Therapy

Since strategic therapists follow plans that they execute in stages, it is relatively easy to describe how they conduct therapy. It takes work and practice to become proficient in the strategic method. Many therapists who specialize in this type of family psychotherapy work in teams. One or two therapists interview the family, weaving diagnosis and treatment intimately together. Several team members observe behind a one-way mirror and participate actively in the process, or they participate later in constructing formulations and planning for the next session (deShazer 1982, Papp 1980, Selvini Palazzoli et al. 1978).

In the first stage, strategic therapists make emotional contact with the family, elicit their view of one central problem, and find out their goals. In eliciting history, many strategic interviewers employ "circular" questioning, such as in the following:

> Marijo (the younger sister of the identified patient), what does Mother do when she sees Peggy eating too much? . . . Okay, then how does Peggy react to Mother's yelling? Does it slow her eating down any? . . . So, Peggy yells back and keeps eating and sometimes eats faster, eh? . . . And where is Dad while this is going on? . . . What is he doing? . . . How long before he stops watching TV and comes into the kitchen? . . . He orders Peggy to stop eating like that or he'll have her locked up in a place for crazy people? . . . And then does that slow Peggy's eating down? . . . Oh, she runs out of the kitchen, slams the door, and takes the food with her? . . . What happens then? . . . Mother cries and

Dad pats her and talks nice to her, huh? . . . And when Mom stops crying, Mom and Dad sit and talk for a while before Dad goes back to watching the baseball game on TV, is that right? Thanks, Marijo, you're a good little news reporter. John (Peggy's older brother), you were there at the time. I'd like to go over those same questions with you and check out what you saw and heard, okay? . . .

Then the therapists insist that the family members state objectives in explicit terms and describe their dipsticks for determining when their goals have been attained. For example, they might ask, "How will you know for sure that Peggy has been cured of her binge eating?"

The ways in which the family responds to these early interventions becomes a significant part of the assessment, and it influences the therapists in planning their next moves. With highly rigid families who display substantial reluctance to modify their attitudes or actions, these clinicians spend much time and energy in motivating them. With such families, they may elect to use so-called "paradoxical" tactics, such as saying something like this:

We must go *very* slowly here! We must be careful. To try something new to change your eating, Peggy, might cause more trouble for you and for all of you than you're already having. So, first I'd like to know how much your eating bothers you, Peggy, and how much it bothers each one of you. Who gets most worried?

On the other hand, with families who display a readiness to change, strategic therapists give straightforward directions. In their reactions to these directives, families reveal more about their structure, function, range of coping skills, and flexibility. Strategic practitioners set out to become part of the family cybernetic or feedback system in order to change it. After the family members have followed a series of directions, they change their transactions to the following posture:

> The mother observes Peggy starting to binge. She says nothing to Peggy. Instead she goes and gets the father, who has agreed to the plan, and says that she wants to go out with him for the rest of the day. They depart without telling anyone where they are going or when they will return. As you can see, there is now no reason for Peggy to binge. The family problem has been resolved.

Therapists warn patients that *nothing* works the first time. People must first note that there has been a change and then they must believe that the change will be consistent and enduring. Identified patients will usually increase their symptomatic behavior in order to restore the family balance, or some other family member will get anxious and do so. Therefore it is wise to predict this sequence before it happens, to forestall people's giving up prematurely on an important modification of their behavior.

Structural Family Therapy

Structural family therapists also plan for step-by-step interventions. Salvadore Minuchin originated this school of family therapy; interested therapists should read his book (see Appendix A). Becoming skilled in their method takes as much study and practice as it takes for strategic family treatment. In addition, we can learn much from these clinicians too about joining families and assuaging their defensiveness. Some of the effect of what we observe when we watch Minuchin's videotapes emanates from his personal charm; however, his skill and that of other structural family therapists can be learned and practiced. When we join families as they do, we make it clear, without question, that we can put ourselves in their place and that what the family or its members are doing is natural, expectable, and understandable. We also learn that we have to be tough enough to confront and challenge families.

The first step structural therapists take is to connect with the family's humanity. Next these therapists elicit a history of the family's view of their difficulty and observe how they interact with each other and the interviewer as they do so. The therapists quickly make formulations about the hierarchical structure and the distribution of power within the family. In their minds they diagram relationship dimensions such as close–distant, detached–enmeshed, and dominant–submissive. They visualize boundaries between the interpersonal domains of the family members. For the parents, there are both the marital and parental spheres. Ideally, partners in a marriage meet most of each other's appropriate adult needs within the spousal sphere. They are then free to cooperate in carrying out parental responsibilities. Within the parental sphere they obtain gratification of their appropriate emotional needs as parents.

Let's say that the structural therapist observes that a husband blocks his wife from taking care of him. Further, the therapist notes that porousness of the spousal and parental boundaries leads to a detouring into the parental domain of the wife's blocked need to take care of her husband. Consequently, she increases her mothering of their son. Husband-father feels excluded and withdraws, or withdraws and feels excluded. The son then gets too much of his mother's care and too little of his father's.

The mother might be described as "overprotective" but characterizing the problem only in these terms is near-sighted. So, the structural family therapist may elect to go to work first on strengthening the father–son relationship and giving the mother something else to do. Thus the therapist opens up the too rigid father–son boundary and fills up the too porous mother–son one. In this way the son is relieved of being the presenting problem, whatever that was, and the therapist, through the father, encourages the son's increased involvement with his peers. Without further work, however, the family balance would probably return to what it was. To finish their work, structural therapists now turn their attention to the disabled marital relationship and expedite its rehabilitation. Often they exclude the child or children from these marital sessions.

The Suicidal Father—Concluded

Because of real financial constraints and logistical difficulties, the treatment of the Martin M. family proved to be brief, a total of four sessions. Martin continued his individual psychotherapy at widely spaced intervals. Several aspects of my hypothesis proved to be incorrect or not germane to the therapy as it evolved. What did prove to be most significant was Martin's inability to serve a parental role because he lacked an effective model for it. Also, in his discipline of his children, he veered in the opposite direction from his experience of how his parents had treated him. Whenever Martin became even slightly irritated with his children, he withdrew from them out of his fear that his anger would lead him to assault them. As a consequence, he was unable to set appropriate limits for them. The younger generation of his family experienced Martin as indifferent, and Bill's acting up was motivated in part by a wish for his father to be more involved with him and to care enough to get tough with him. Earlier, Dick—the older son—also had acted up in an effort to provoke his father to action. When Dick matured and began to move out of the family, Bill took over this function. So I made interventions as follows:

> Martin, I understand how fearful you are of acting in the same way your father treated you, so one remedy for you and Judy to consider is to do it together. When any of the kids need to be brought back into line, have a conference, decide how you want to handle it. Then both of you have a serious talk with that child together. If you feel yourself getting mad and afraid you'll lose control, hold Judy's hand. Then, Judy, you hold his hand tightly and do whatever else you need to do to help him. This way, Martin, you'll learn how to assert yourself with your children and lose your fear. After enough practice, you'll be able to do it on your own.

Judy was frequently quite resentful about having to do all the discipline alone and about Martin's withdrawal from the family. To her I said:

> You have done a very good job with the kids. I realize how difficult it has been for you. I've noticed how open about their feelings they all are. They owe that to you and also to Martin's restraint. He carried it too far, but it was wise of him to take precautions against his becoming abusive. One of the reasons he picked you in the first place was because he knew how competent and effective you would be as a mother.

To the younger generation of this family I explained the family situation as follows:

> It seemed to you that Dad didn't care what you did.
> Dick and Bill, you tried very hard to pull him in. What
> you had no way of knowing was that Dad kept his
> distance because he cared about you so much that he
> felt he had to protect you from his anger.

Fortunately, Martin and Judy were able to follow my
therapeutic suggestions rapidly. At their own initiative
and with my encouragement, they attended meetings of a
self-help support group, Parents Helping Parents, and
they planned to continue doing so after discontinuing the
family therapy. Three months later Martin's therapist
reported that he and the family were doing well. Bill's
behavior had improved and was then within the range of
what is average and expectable for his age.

Bringing Sessions to a Close

I make the usual moves that I have stressed earlier in
bringing sessions gracefully and definitively to a close.
With families the final few minutes present us with an
opportunity to slow down the action by summing up or
by using the time to prescribe homework tasks. Also I
often like to end by asking:

> Please tell me your reactions to this session. What was it
> like for each of you? Feel free to express all of your
> feelings and thoughts about the session.

This method of sending the patients away encourages
them to ventilate any feelings they have about the session
or about my conduct of it that may have been lost in the
rapid exchanges that took place.

Stages of Therapy

For family therapy, the special features of the stages of therapy resemble those I have described for marital therapy. Again I will note, for emphasis, those elements that compel additional attention.

Early Stages

Many parents feel guilty and defensive as they await the dreaded appointment with us. The act of bringing their offspring for evaluation by a stranger implies, for them, putting their own parental worth on the line. Most of the time this anticipated blow to their narcissism is what leads to parents' reluctance to participate in therapy. It also leads to intense parental denial that takes the form of "Fix Johnny and that will solve all our family problems."

Experience with the extreme difficulties of successfully navigating the opening phase of family therapy has led family therapists to plan powerful strategies to overcome them. Whitaker has called the opening stage "the battle for structure," and I have described the time and effort most practitioners of family therapy put into joining families, displaying empathy with them, meeting families where they are, and combating their guilt. Accordingly, we must concentrate most of our attention during the first session on making contact with the family and assuaging their guilt and fear. Other significant elements of the family consultation may have to be deferred until later. Once we have engaged them and the family entrusts itself to our continuing care, at least half the battle is won.

Middle and Late Stages

These stages generally follow the pattern set forth for individual and couples therapy. Therapists should never lose sight of the import of continuing to individualize therapy to meet the updated needs of patients. If we discern an indication that it would be wise, in a particular case, to meet with the parents together, or with some family member alone, we should not hesitate to do so.

Part IV

QUESTIONS AND ANSWERS

9

"What If . . .?"

Assessment
The Therapeutic Contract
Countertransference
Ethical Considerations
Real Relationship
Technical Considerations
Transference

What problems in conducting psychotherapy most bother trainees and less experienced therapists? I wondered about this and asked my colleagues to furnish me with a list of questions that they were frequently asked.[1] This section will answer all the questions I have collected. The questions and answers are organized into categories that seemed to fit them best. You will find that some fit well in other categories too. Ethical and legal issues are often intimately intertwined, but I do not intend to discuss legal issues in depth here. All questions begin with, "What if. . . ." I will reply as if I were talking to a trainee, or to a less experienced therapist who consulted me. This analogy, of course, breaks down immediately, for if I were actually talking with the questioner I would seek detailed clarification about many facets of the questions

[1] I am grateful to the following colleagues, psychiatrists, social workers, and specialists in medical ethics who submitted questions or made helpful suggestions: P. Bair, W. Edinger, M. Engle, W. Faeth, M. Fitzgerald, M. Gottlieb, A. Hauser, I. Hauser, R. Kaufman, W. Kim, A. Mendel, M. Paluszny, N. Phillips, R. Shalvoy, J. Skeel, M. Tamburrino, and N. Yi.

before answering. Some of my questions might lead therapists to find their own answers, which often prove to be as fitting as or more fitting than mine; therapists' own answers best suit their style and personality.

Assessment

QUESTION: "What if you have evaluated an adolescent because of his academic underachievement and recommended therapy for him, but he says he's not interested? Would you advise his parents to bring him against his will?"

ANSWER: It is always better to avoid a power struggle with patients, particularly adolescents. Providing a good experience with a therapist for patients is more important than treating a relatively minor problem. Later, remembering the understanding and acceptance you offered, this adolescent may develop internal motivation for treatment. At the time, this adolescent's underachieving was probably more a concern to his parents than to him. His pride may have been in the way of his acknowledging any worries he did have.

If individual psychotherapy were indeed the treatment of choice, I wonder if you attended sufficiently to developing a therapeutic alliance with this adolescent during the evaluation. Sometimes it is imperative to interrupt the diagnostic process— after you have determined that the patient's condition does not entail a life-or-death matter—to make a meaningful emotional connection with the patient and establish the beginnings of a therapeutic alliance. I would certainly make it plain to adolescent patients that it is *not* my job as a therapist to fit them into parental molds. Further, I would make it equally plain that their grades are theirs and theirs alone and that I am totally unaffected by the level of their academic achievement.

I assume that this adolescent did not come at his own initiative in the first place. If I am correct that his parents were in more distress about the patient's difficulty than he was, family psychotherapy might be indicated. Did you consider family therapy? Did you evaluate the family as a group? If so, what did you learn and what hypothesis did you entertain about the dynamics of the patient's poor academic performance? Did the parents use effective, consistent discipline? What, if any, function did the adolescent's difficulty serve for the family? Did you detect any boundary problems in the family structure? I would want to know all of these things, and more, before recommending individual psychotherapy for a reluctant adolescent. Perhaps you could help the parents resolve any conflict they were having about this issue or teach them more effective methods to influence their son.

Were the adolescent's condition more serious—for example, if a major depression seemed imminent—it would be necessary to monitor the patient's condition at intervals. Perhaps the best way to do this would be to invite the parents and son to come together for follow-up visits. Also you should inform the parents about the symptoms and signs of a worsening of their son's condition. Thus you prepare them to take prompt and appropriate action, such as calling you to arrange for hospitalization, as determined by the further course of events. I would also make strenuous efforts to form a therapeutic alliance with any patient in such deep and potentially dangerous waters. To do so, I would carefully observe the way the parents deal with their adolescent child, and I would then behave differently. By offering a corrective emotional experience, I would hope to increase my chances of forming a relationship with this adolescent.

QUESTION: "What if the patient presents for treatment and is embroiled in an ongoing personal injury lawsuit, and improvement in the patient's condition might jeopardize the financial settlement?"

ANSWER: This is a time for a bit of educated paranoia! I would suspect that the patient's attorney might have sent her or him and that they were setting me up to be called to testify on behalf of a patient in treatment. We should bear in mind that the professional actually treating a patient enjoys more credibility in court than does an expert employed merely to examine the patient and offer an opinion about the cause of the symptoms. If this is part of the patient's or attorney's agenda, the therapist should be hired openly for that purpose. Before establishing a therapist–patient contract with this patient, I would definitely and clearly determine what part they wished me to play in the lawsuit. And I would explicate my conditions to act in the role of expert witness before accepting the patient for evaluation and treatment.

Once we have arrived at an agreement about our role, this kind of situation also calls for us to be forthcoming. I would address the issue of secondary gain honestly and directly:

> If you enter therapy and improve, it might decrease the amount of the settlement in your lawsuit. Under this circumstance, I doubt that any of us would have enough desire to get better. To improve would mean to lose money! Treatment would be more likely to be helpful after the court decides what the final settlement of your lawsuit will be. If you wish, I will continue with the complete diagnostic evaluation of your case so that I can write a report to your attorney. Later I may have to give a deposition or appear in court to offer my opinions, if your attorney concludes that what I have to say would advance the merits of your case.

If the patient fights me and insists that it is more important for her or him to feel better than to win the suit, I might take the patient into treatment. As part of the conditions of taking the case in the role of a potential expert witness, I would have already said that my opinion might be that there exists little or no connection between the injury and the symptoms the patient is experiencing. To avoid or to blunt the patient's probable disappointment and anger about an opinion that might harm the chances of a monetary benefit, I would emphasize this possibility again and would tell the patient my conclusions as soon as possible. Unless I know the attorney very well, I ask to be paid before I submit my report.

QUESTION: "What if during the evaluation I find that the patient is potentially dangerous vis-à-vis the therapist?" (Asked three times.)

ANSWER: It was very astute of you to pick this up during the assessment phase of your contact with the patient. I presume that you arrived at this opinion by eliciting a detailed social history or garnering data from an outside source, such as records detailing assaultive behavior. Past behavior is the best predictor of future behavior.

Therapists should be prudent and not take chances unnecessarily. A certain amount of risk comes with the territory, but it makes sense to take preventive measures when danger portends. This kind of case illustrates clinical and ethical concerns as well. It is not in the interests of the patient to allow her or him to harm us or anyone.

What type of protective measures might we plan? In the presence of grave and imminent danger, we treat the patient in a hospital and hold therapy sessions within sight of other staff members. Remember that patients on the verge of going out of control can be reassured and their controls bolstered by the *presence* of staff in large enough numbers. In a less hazardous outpatient circumstance, we could leave the office door open and sit near it. On the basis of personal experience, I advise therapists to avoid grandiosity of the "I can handle that patient'' sort. When I was a young and brash resident, I thought that I could handle a certain lady patient. Her physician had placed her in seclusion, and I went in to talk her down. She smiled fulsomely and proceeded to puff me up; I thought that she was responding to my charm. As we talked, the patient surreptitiously put her hands on the tops of my blazer side pockets. With one forceful pull she ripped both pockets from my jacket. *Sic transit gloria mundi!*

I work in a home office and sometimes am alone with patients. Therefore I exercise appropriate caution in regard to the patients I agree to see. This is another reason I have stressed the importance of therapists' doing their own telephone intake interviews before scheduling appointments for new patients. Such a precaution is especially important for therapists who work without an office staff or, say, with one nurse or receptionist on duty.

We should exercise caution as well under conditions other than the possibility of physical harm. Recently a female patient claimed, during a telephone intake interview, that her former psychiatrist had diagnosed her to be a multiple personality. Further, she said that he had verbally abused her and abruptly terminated her therapy. I decided not to see her in my home office. The current popularity of claims of physical and sexual abuse, and their use as ploys, strongly suggests that we must protect ourselves as best we can from false allegations.

The Therapeutic Contract

QUESTION: "What if the patient's insurance company refuses to cover therapy fees or has paid the allowable maximum? Should I continue the treatment?" (Asked twice.)

ANSWER: That depends upon the circumstances. Again, legal and ethical principles guide our actions. As a part of the initial contracting, I ask patients to check their insurance coverage so that we can agree upon a reasonable amount for them to pay. Except in the presence of financial hardship, I tell patients that I expect them to pay the full fee monthly, and the insurance carrier will reimburse them later (it may take three to four months for payments to start, and insurance companies typically solve their cash flow problems by delaying subsequent payments to patients or caretakers). Thus I determine, before making a final contract for treatment, whether patients can afford my regular fees. Then, if necessary and if I am able to offer their treatment at reduced fees, freely and without resentment, I do so. We must be realistic about the amount of income we require or want for ourselves. Therefore we ought to limit the number of patients we can see at reduced fee levels. When we are at or above this limit, it is wise to refer patients for treatment to public agencies or to private ones that have a sliding scale. By doing so, we avoid the inherent hazard of feeling resentful toward patients under our care. I find that I feel friendlier and warmer toward patients who pay the agreed-upon fee promptly, and consequently I can manage my countertransference more easily. With careful and honest self-examination, you may find that you feel the same way.

If patients' insurance coverage changes because of circumstances beyond their control after I have committed myself to treat them, I feel ethically bound to see the patient through the treatment. I will reduce the fee to what the patient can afford, or will spread payments out over a longer time span, or both. Therapists who believe that it is ethical to refer the patient elsewhere to continue treatment under this circumstance should proceed with caution, in order to avert legal action against them. These therapists should grant patients sufficient time to find another therapist or an agency to undertake their treatment, and should continue to treat them in the meantime.

State law dictates what we are required to do for psychiatric inpatients, especially those court-committed to our care, in cases of this sort. Because of the wide variability among states, I will not cover this matter here from a legal standpoint. I apply the same ethical principles equally to all inpatients, but the hospital administration ultimately makes the final decision about such cases or has formulated applicable policies.

To save ourselves trouble and serve patients well, it is wise for us to determine early on what their insurance status is regarding payment for mental health services. To accept a patient for treatment without this knowledge may lead to doing something harmful to patients and to ourselves. *Primum non nocere!*

QUESTION: "What if the patient acts out by lateness, failed appointments, and failure to pay fees?" (Asked twice.)

ANSWER: If the patient is irresponsible or personality-disordered and reenacting her or his usual behaviors in the therapy, acting *up* is the proper term. If, however, such behavior represents a reaction to the treatment, an avoidance of it, or an effort to provoke you to anger and rejection, the more proper term is acting *out*. Unquestionably, with these behaviors, patients violate the contract. If we tolerate these behaviors without comment, we are joining patients in a collusive denial of reality. The most common motivation for our failure to address these and other issues is our fear of arousing anger in patients. What we fear is that they will reject us, and certainly that is a very unpleasant prospect. It may be remedial for us to realize that continuing with a patient under these circumstances makes a mockery of the therapeutic relationship and treatment. With our lips, we say, "Tell me everything, no matter how difficult or embarrassing it may be." But by skirting an issue, we are in effect saying, "Do as I say, not as I do; some things we don't talk about in here." Which message do you think patients will read? In effect, we have lost patients by holding them!

So we have to bite the bullet and talk with the patient about these significant matters, using all the tools of psychotherapy discussed in this book to deal with them. As a last resort, I say:

> The next time you break our agreement about attending sessions regularly and on time or paying your fee within two weeks after I give you my statement, I will take that to mean you have dismissed me as your therapist, and your treatment with me will end at that time. I will not negotiate further with you about it, then or later.

QUESTION: "What if your patient asks you to be a reference for a job or a change-of-custody hearing and you have ambivalent feelings about the matter?"

ANSWER: This is an excellent question because it speaks to several therapy issues. I might classify this question as a matter of countertransference, ethical and legal considerations, technique, transference, or treatment planning. In my answer to the earlier question about the patient who was embroiled in a personal injury lawsuit at the time of the initial evaluation, I covered the question about what to do at that early stage of treatment. I presume that in the kind of case referred to here, you have been treating the patient for some time, that these exigencies were not issues at the outset and were not explicitly described in the contract. I will further assume that your ambivalent feelings do not arise from countertransference and that the patient's request is straightforward, adult patient to caretaker, rather than mainly transference. So, what to do?

If the patient's mental status is at issue in the change-of-custody hearing, you may have only a Hobson's choice. If your ambivalent feelings concern your patient's ability to function properly in a parental role, you will have to tell this to the patient and the patient's attorney. Unless the attorney is out of his mind, he or she will not call you to testify. In this case, you probably will be able to continue the treatment and deal with the patient's feelings about your explanations and actions.

If, however, the other side knows that your patient is in treatment with you, they may subpoena your presence, testimony, and records. Unfortunately, what you may have to say in court could destroy your relationship with the patient. What preventive measures you might have previously taken to avoid getting into this position, I do not know. Were the action initiated by the patient, you might have advised against it beforehand and explained your reasons.

The question of the job reference is another matter. Does your ambivalence arise from your concern that the patient might not be able to hold a job? Or does it arise from your acting as a reference and what that role might do to the patient's feelings about and toward you? If I believed that my acting as a reference might be harmful to the treatment, I would say, for example:

> I think I understand what it means to you to have someone on your side in this matter of a job. However, I am

concerned that my doing so would complicate your treatment. It is preferable for me to stay strictly in the role of therapist. I'd like to hear your feelings about this. I know this may seem like a rejection and hurt your feelings.

If, on the other hand, my treatment plan included my taking a very supportive role and acting as the patient's advocate if necessary, I would write the letter. Or, if I thought that the patient wasn't ready yet to handle the job in question, I would say so:

> My main concern now is that you get stronger so that we can be sure that you can handle a job with that much stress in it. You are making progress but it's important that you walk a longer distance before you try to run. I'll be happy to write a letter of recommendation for you later. For now, how about taking that course in accounting at the Acme Business College you've been thinking about? See how that goes and then apply again for that job or a better one.

Note that this is a very supportive rejection of the patient's request. While the patient may experience this as a hurtful rejection anyway, I provided a cushion which will make the feelings I have provoked easier to manage.

Countertransference

QUESTION: "What if the therapist feels intimidated by a patient perceived as more successful or more intelligent than the therapist?"

ANSWER: Regardless of how we define and measure success and education, some patients *will* be either more successful or brighter than most of us are. This concern may reflect your own lack of self-esteem, and I wonder if you are having a serious enough problem with this aspect of yourself to warrant personal therapy. Please don't feel as if that's a request for you to reveal personal things to me. You didn't consult me for that. I raise that question for you to consider privately. This question reminds me of a patient who challenged my wife's intelligence and financial success at a time when she was working in a state mental institution. He then asked her, "So what do you have that I don't?" She picked up her keys to the hospital, jangled them, and said simply, "These!" She then went on to have a

318

meaningful conversation with the patient about how he managed to get himself hospitalized in spite of his considerable intelligence and potential for financial success. Therapists have chosen fields in which the opportunity for income is limited. We cannot measure our self-esteem in dollars and cents.

QUESTION: "What if I do not like the patient for one reason or another (because of the patient's values, prejudices, or behaviors)?" (Asked four times.)

ANSWER: By putting this question under the heading of countertransference, I do not mean to imply that you and I are not entitled to our likes and dislikes. We have our prejudices, biases, and sensitivities too, and there is virtually no way for us to rid ourselves of all of them. Nevertheless, it doesn't hurt—and may help—to ask ourselves, "What is that characteristic of the patient's stirring up in me?" Successful self-analysis could resolve the problem. Most of the time, after we get through a patient's outer shell of defensiveness, we can get in touch with the commonality of humanness that binds us all together. And whatever is in any of us is somewhere in all of us! Having said these noble things, I can now say that if your dislike of the patient continues, it will probably be impossible for you to generate any warmth or empathy toward that patient. The most caring thing you can do for the patient and for yourself is therefore to refer her or him to a colleague. Tell your colleague about the patient first and about your feelings. It would not be fair to the therapist or to the patient to arrange a "blind date"; the patient should be spared the trauma of another rejection, and your colleague the unpleasant task of being the rejector.

A Jewish friend and colleague told me about the way he reacted when a patient who had been assigned to him for therapy told him that he was an active member of the American

Nazi Party.[2] The patient also said that he knew my friend was Jewish. The therapist responded:

> I'm your physician and I'm here to treat your illness as best I can. We'll leave politics and religion out of it and work together on getting you well, if you want to work with me.

How is that for maintaining a genuinely professional stance under extreme stress?

QUESTION: "What if I develop a special interest in the patient?"

ANSWER: Be very careful! Your special interest may already be, or may have some potential for becoming, an erotic interest. So long as your special investment in the patient remains contained within yourself, all is well. It makes no difference if you get sexually aroused in reaction to the patient, regardless of the patient's gender. We cannot control what our autonomic nervous system does. What counts is what we do with our *voluntary* musculature. If you believe that you are close to acting on your feelings in *any* inappropriate way, please talk your predicament over with a trusted colleague, or purchase a few hours of therapy from a therapist you do not know personally.

I have started at one end of a continuum. Sexual involvement with a patient or client is *off* the continuum and into unethical and illegal behavior. At the other end of the continuum are those ways in which we like some patients more than others. This is inevitable. We know that with the increase of distance between what we are like and patients are like, we may have

---

[2]Marvin Gottlieb, M.D., gave me permission to use this vignette of his. The patient continued under Dr. Gottlieb's care until he improved and was discharged from the hospital. Another therapist continued the patient's outpatient treatment.

increasing difficulty connecting with, understanding, and treating them. Dangers lurk as well when we treat patients who are too similar to ourselves, including other therapists or allied professionals. How can we be alert to overlapping blind spots? This is a difficult question and one I cannot answer, except to advise frequent peer supervision. We often talk about this but rarely do it! Only social worker therapists have continuous supervision built into their profession. So far as our own learning how to treat all patients equitably, I recommend good articles on cross-cultural psychiatry (Wohl 1989).

Less blatant kinds of special interest in patients are also problematic. These include very affluent patients, prestigious and powerful people, famous ones, and on and on. All we can do is be alert to these dangerous situations and take extra care in planning the treatments for these patients. If we ignore these perils, especially on an inpatient unit, we may conduct a chaotic treatment that does not help and may harm patients.

QUESTION: "What if I empathized so much with a patient that I broke down and cried?"

ANSWER: That's fine, just fine. Whatever the patient described must have moved you very deeply. Many therapists would feel very embarrassed about having "lost control." I would not. It is so much better than not being moved at all! Purists might insist that what you experienced was not empathy in a strict sense of that word, because you did not draw back quickly enough from identification with the patient to arrive at a more cognitive understanding of the patient. However, what you described does not contradict the dictionary definition of empathy: "Identification with and understanding of another's situation, feelings, and motives." I assume that after you dried your tears, you did understand what the patient reported. I hope your further training and experience does not toughen you up too much.

After you regain your balance, you might wish to say something to the patient to make a transition back to your more dispassionate therapist role. I might say:

> Your experience moved me very much, as you have seen. It touched me because it reminded me of a similar event in my life. Now I'm ready to continue listening to you.

QUESTION: "What if the patient seems to need to be touched?"

ANSWER: I have already given an example of a situation in which I believed it appropriate to hold a patient who was experiencing acute, severe grief (see Chapter 4). A touch on a patient's shoulder, arm, or hand is, at times, indicated. However, the rule of talking with patients about what they seem to need rather than doing it applies most of the time. Talking with patients about their leftover childish needs is usually more effective than meeting those needs directly. For example, I may say:

> I think I understand how intense your need to be held and comforted is right now. Were you a little girl (or boy) of 5 or so, I would feel like inviting you to crawl up into my lap, so I could hold and talk soothingly to you. That's a leftover need that no one can ever fill completely. Some hurt, some sense of having been cheated out of something you needed, may persist. It will be easier, because now you know its source.

In this situation, acting out this scenario would have been deceptive and harmful. It would have conveyed the idea that what was missing in childhood could be made up for now.

QUESTION: "What if two patients arrive for an appointment at the same hour; you find that you made a mistake and double-booked the hour?"

ANSWER: Let the therapist who has never double-booked throw the first countertransference stone! This calls for an apology, of course, and negotiation with the two patients so that they can determine an equitable solution. Offering half the hour to each is one solution. If one has traveled a much greater distance and the other lives close by, the latter could return at the time of your next opening that day. The choice could be based on which patient has the time to return later. It might have to be at your lunch hour or you might have to extend your day. If there is no compelling reason why one would generously agree to return later, have them flip a coin or draw straws. Your choosing one over the other would complicate the transference of both.

After the incident is over, we should make every effort to understand if anything has occurred beyond a mere slippage of our mental gears. We should do some careful self-scrutiny and answer such questions as: "Am I spread too thin?" "Do I need some time off?" "Is it time to cut back on my number of patient hours?" In my own practice, I have lopped off the 4:00 and 5:00 o'clock hours on Friday and I may soon begin to finish at noon.

Ethical Considerations

QUESTION: "What if I am unsure about whether or not I may break confidentiality?"

ANSWER: First it is important to distinguish between confidences that we keep on the basis of professional ethics and those that the law allows us to keep. The latter is called privileged communication. Usually, patients may waive their legal rights to privilege, and they do so automatically if they initiate a lawsuit in which their mental or emotional conditions are at issue. Patients may instruct us to release their records to named persons or institutions. They own their records and may have them at their request. Whenever we ourselves take the initiative to break confidentiality, we must have cogent reasons. Generally, we must judge that patients are dangerous to themselves or others or are unable to attend to their basic needs. In reply to a previous question I discussed how to anticipate and plan for such eventualities that might occur during psychotherapy. *How* dangerous or incapable of self-care a patient must be to allow a breach of confidentiality, we have to decide on a case-by-case basis. Different therapists may have different points at which they make this judgment in good faith. If, by acting ethically, we put ourselves in danger of a lawsuit, so be it! The questions that follow represent several different situations calling for judgments about violation of confidentiality.

Confidentiality is precious. It allows patients to share safely their thoughts and deeds. Without confidentiality, trust would be compromised and perhaps destroyed. In all my years of practice I have not had to violate it once. I have found that patients give their permission for us to act on their behalf when the therapeutic alliance is intact. For example, recently a patient called me to report that he feared he might not be able to resist his hallucinations that were commanding him to kill his father. He readily agreed to keep his distance from his father and welcomed my suggestion that I call his parents and tell them about his fear and distress.

QUESTION: "What if an attorney calls and asks about a patient's progress?"

ANSWER: Unless we have explicit permission beforehand, we cannot even confirm that the person the attorney asks us about is our patient. When we do not have that permission, the conversation ends before it begins. I say:

> I'm sorry but I can't either confirm or deny that the person you named is my patient. What I would advise is that you have your client complete a release of information form. If your client is my patient, I will be happy to talk with you with that form in hand and will call you promptly if and when it arrives.

Anyone can call and identify herself or himself as being connected to the patient in any number of ostensibly legitimate ways. Even when I have the patient's permission to talk with someone, I prefer to call that person to assure myself of her or his identity.

QUESTION: "What if a teenage patient reveals that he drives while dangerously intoxicated? What is my responsibility to try to protect this minor and his potential victims? What is my responsibility to his parents?"

ANSWER: To the extent that it is within their power to control, it is his parents' responsibility to put a stop to this adolescent's dangerous behavior. We should make it clear at the outset of treatment with a minor that confidentiality is not absolute. Under certain circumstances, the law or our ethics may require us to reveal what any person has told us. As I now think about this, I am remiss in not making this clear also with most adult patients. I do so selectively, and usually with minors, saying something like this:

> Most of what you tell me will be between you and me. Your parents are paying my fee and they deserve some feedback from me as to how things are going generally. Also at some times I may, or you may, want them to join us. Whatever I have to say to them I will say in your presence after I have first talked with you about it. I don't expect that you will become suicidal, but if you did and left my office with that intent, I would have to take whatever action would be necessary to stop you. The same holds true, for example, if you told me that you were going to burn down the school or endanger the life of another person in any way.

By framing it in this way, I hope to preclude restraining forthrightness on the patient's part.

QUESTION: "What if my patient threatens to kill a family member: What questions do I ask and what action do I take?"

ANSWER: We have to estimate the seriousness of homicidal intent in the same way we do suicidal intent. Because there is no sure way to predict either, we should take threats very seriously, especially if we believe patients are in imminent danger of acting on them. If I could not persuade the patient to enter a closed psychiatric unit, I would inform the potential victim. And I would do so on the spot, in the patient's presence. I would also tell the responsible family member that he or she should take steps to have the patient court-committed to a psychiatric facility. If none of these alternatives was possible for any reason, I would take steps to get an emergency commitment for the patient myself. I would take these actions out of personal moral or ethical considerations, not out of fear of legal action against me. It is our duty to protect our patients from suicide, and them and their likely victims from homicide or physical harm.

QUESTION: "What if my HIV positive patient reveals that he is having unprotected sex with others and not informing partners of his health status?"

ANSWER: Early in the AIDS epidemic, a psychiatric resident and I faced this question with regard to one of our patients. Fortunately for us, but unfortunately for this patient's partner (a bisexual married man in the child-bearing years), the patient refused to reveal the partner's name to us. He said, "If he knew, he'd kill me." The patient believed this to be probable. We made earnest efforts to convince him to reveal his HIV status to his sexual partner and confronted him with the possibility that his partner's wife and their future child or children could become infected. Our efforts failed and the patient did not continue long in treatment.

In some cases, the same ethical principle that applies to a patient who threatens homicide is also applied to HIV positive patients who conceal their status from their sexual partners. If the patient's sexual partners are other adults who know or have the opportunity of knowing the dangers inherent in unprotected sex, our responsibility is minimal. I would attempt to persuade the patient to use safer sexual practices. If an unsuspecting spouse is the victim of the patient's insouciant behavior (along with any actual or potential offspring), I would insist that the patient be forthright with the spouse in my presence. If the patient were unwilling to do so, I would invite the spouse in and tell her or him myself. In taking this course of action, I would place the patient's treatment at risk. But not to act would do the same. In that case the patient would know that I am a therapist who cannot be trusted, because I have joined her or him in a serious deception.

QUESTION: "What if a patient requests or demands to see charts, records, or letters? What should we put in records? Are *private* records ever indicated?"

ANSWER: As with anything that happens in therapy, we first deal with this question as part of the therapy process—that is, explore its meaning, address transference, and so on. When push comes to shove, patients own their records. To protect the patient from the consequences of their records somehow falling into the hands of others or being released for legal reasons, it is wise to write records as if the patient or others will read them. For research purposes or for our own instruction, it is certainly proper to keep private, unnamed records. Whether it would be ethically proper to withhold these records from patients who ask for them is questionable. I would exclude them from records requested by third parties.

QUESTION: "What if a patient reveals that he or she committed a serious crime many years ago and has not been prosecuted?"

ANSWER: This is a matter that is between patients' consciences and themselves. We bear no ethical or legal responsibility to breach confidentiality. I would not feel obliged to persuade the patient to confess to the authorities. I would discuss with the patient any internal consequences of her or his continuing failure to take full responsibility for the crime. However, if another person was convicted of the crime and remains in prison, that would complicate matters and make it urgent for the patient to right this wrong. Perhaps we could persuade the patient, at the very least, to confess anonymously, giving enough details to clear the other person.

QUESTION: "What if you are prescribing medication and are unsure about how much information to share with the patient concerning its side effects, and the patient drives as part of his or her work or uses dangerous equipment or power tools?"

ANSWER: We should make full disclosure about side effects as part of a discussion of risks and benefits of medication because patients should be part of the decision-making process. For our own protection we should document this discussion. Also, I provide a printout from the United States Pharmacopeia computer program that explains side effects of medications; it is designed for patient use. I explain the side effects of most concern, saying:

> Any person may be sensitive to any medication, or a food for that matter, and develop an allergic skin rash. If you develop a rash, stop the medicine and call me promptly. Remember that I must inform you of many side effects that are mentioned in the *Physicians' Desk Reference* and that the warnings in it have been written by the drug companies and their attorneys. I am expecting some day to read that "struck by lightening" is a side effect of some medicine. [I then go on to tell the patient about the most important specific side effects of the particular medication

prescribed.] Here is a printout of material from the U.S. Pharmacopeia for patients' use concerning [the prescribed medicine]; it is more reliable than the *PDR*. Please ask any questions about [name of the drug(s)] and remember that it's your choice after you have weighed the probable risks and benefits and the alternatives I told you about. Let me know when you start it if you decide to. Because of the possible sedating effect of [the drug], it's better to start on a weekend when you don't have to drive your car or use the forklift at work. Be sure you're alert and your reflexes are fast enough before you do either.

Note that in talking with the patient, I don't say "drug" because it has been contaminated with images of street drug use.

QUESTION: "What if the patient requests you to use a more benign diagnosis on the insurance form for reasons of confidentiality?"

ANSWER: Frequently the patient must return insurance forms to the company insurance or personnel office rather than directly to the carrier. I regard this as an improper procedure that presents a realistic threat to the patient's reputation; it could have adverse repercussions. I would honor the patient's request. However, indicating a less serious diagnosis than is justified might cause the insurance carrier to cover fewer visits. I would advise the patient to look into this possibility and then decide what is in her or his better interest.

QUESTION: "What if an inpatient on a psychiatric ward, who fears stigmatization, asks me to help her or him make up a plausible story to tell others about the reason for hospitalization?"

ANSWER: That's a legitimate request and I would honor it. After all, patients have the right to decide whom to tell about their illness. Currently, most people believe that stress-related fatigue is an honorable disability. I would suggest this to the patient.

QUESTION: "What if a patient, without justification, accuses you of misconduct, especially sexual molestation?" (Asked twice.)

ANSWER: As far as possible, it would have been better to have discerned at an earlier stage the patient's predilection for taking this kind of action; this might have been suggested during the intake interview or assessment. Then it would have been possible to take preventive measures similar to those I suggested for the physically threatening patient earlier in this chapter. Whether the patient is delusional or consciously and deliberately hateful or spiteful, it's unlikely that any of us would be able to continue the treatment. If the patient's accusations are a response to whatever interventions we make, it might be possible to continue the therapy under altered conditions. I would insist on the presence of another person, such as a co-therapist.

QUESTION: "What if I recognize that a colleague is misbehaving with patients?"

ANSWER: You put that delicately and in an even-handed way! I assume you mean that a former patient of your colleague, now your patient or known to you somehow, told you what your colleague did. If the person is now your patient, it is her or his choice about whether you report your colleague to the appropriate authority. Some states have laws that require therapists to report sexual misconduct by other professional caretakers. Because (I assume) the patient would have to be called as a witness, we should grant the patient the choice. It might be necessary for you to warn patients, if your state has such a law, *not* to reveal the colleague's name to you if the patient elects not to pursue the matter.

Real Relationship

QUESTION: "What if a situation requires that you introduce the patient to your spouse?"

ANSWER: Because my office is in my home, I do this often. I make the introduction in a matter-of-fact way. Doing so has led to no special complications. If the encounter occurs elsewhere, I make the introduction without identifying the patient as a patient.

QUESTION: "What if I and my patient or patient's family meet during a shared activity (at a party or in a gym) and I am unsure of their receptiveness to my greeting?"

ANSWER: I tend to compartmentalize my role as person and as therapist smoothly. I feel comfortable attending the same events my patients do and it requires no effort for me to behave toward them as I would toward anyone. If the patient or family seems uncomfortable and avoids me, I follow their lead and do not take the initiative in greeting them. Once you have been through these kinds of encounters several times, you will find that you become more at ease with them. And if you feel all right about it, patients and their families will too.

QUESTION: "What if I and my patient also have outside roles vis-à-vis each other, such as teacher and student?"

ANSWER: I have treated several psychiatric residents from our own program, but the residents did not have close contact with me at the time they were in treatment. That is, I was not in a role of supervisor, nor were they in a small didactic group with me. I had no problems with the dual role and did not notice that they had any either. It is important to determine very early what led them to pick you as a therapist. I have found rich transference material to deal with promptly. I can think of situations that I would avoid. Were a person already in treatment and then asked me to be her or his supervisor, I would make therapeutic material of it rather than doing it. I would advise a trainee in supervision with me or one I met with frequently in a small group setting to seek another therapist. Each of you will have to make a decision about this type of circumstance for yourself. The dual role could complicate the treatment; for this reason, unless you are confident that you can deal with the complications, it would be better to choose one role or the other.

QUESTION: "What if I encounter a patient who is in an ordinary difficulty, such as walking home in the rain? Should I offer a ride?"

ANSWER: Here again, that depends upon how you would feel about and be able to deal with the situation. I have never had this kind of experience, but I believe I would offer the patient a ride. If the patient lived a long distance from my route, I might prefer to drop her or him off at the nearest bus stop. It's important for us to avoid offering to do more than we can do graciously. Again, if you feel confident about whatever you do, the patient will also have positive feelings about it and the treatment will not be endangered.

QUESTION: "What if the patient is a member of a group that has extreme hostility toward your religion or ethnic identity?"

ANSWER: I have already cited an example (earlier in this chapter) that a colleague of mine carried off with savoir-faire. I am sure that for many of us it would be very difficult to like this patient. I favor a referral to a colleague to whom I've given an explanation of the particulars. Wouldn't it be ideal if we were able to be tolerant of vicious intolerance? Even if I was not a member of the group toward whom the patient had extreme hostility, I would have to work hard to maintain my equanimity and treat this patient competently. One danger I would have to guard against would be the tendency to go too far in the direction of overacceptance (reaction formation) and failing to speak frankly about some issue that called for such an approach.

Technical Considerations

QUESTION: "What if a young woman patient asked your advice about how to confront her father who had sexually abused her for years during her childhood?"

ANSWER: In answering this, I am assuming that no other children are currently in danger, such as the patient's younger siblings. I would initially wonder not *how* but *why*. What are the young lady's motives? What purpose would confronting her father serve? How would she feel about it afterward? What I am saying is that were you ingenuous enough to give the advice, it would be tantamount to approving the patient's doing it. And doing so might be harmful to the patient and unnecessarily upsetting to other members of the patient's family of origin who learn of the confrontation. Retribution is not a healing agent because it may cause guilt later.

Some therapists believe that it is therapeutic for patients to confront relatives who have sexually abused them. This approach may reflect a vengeful attitude toward those who

336

commit sexual abuse. Such an attitude is unhealthy; confronting the past abuser serves no useful purpose and may be stressful for the patient. It is much better for the patient to come to peace with the traumatic experiences, forgive the abuser, and get on with her or his life.

I am reminded of a lady whose family brought her to me for consultation because she was constantly accusing her husband of past unfaithfulness and current mental lechery. Both mates were in their eighties. From her history and mental status, I suspected dementia of the Alzheimer's type and advised a medical and neurological workup to rule out secondary dementia. I explained my plan to use small doses of haloperidol if nothing else turned up in the examinations. The family vetoed my plan, believing that the husband *had* cheated on his wife and deserved the "punishment" she was now giving him.

QUESTION: "What if patients ask questions about my personal life, such as if I am married, if I have children, or where I am going on vacation?" (Asked three times.)

ANSWER: In very supportive psychotherapy it may be indicated to answer most questions that do not touch on matters that are too intimate. Otherwise there are several productive alternatives. I ask patients to provide both yes and no answers, for example, to the question about whether I have children and then tell me how they would feel about it both ways. Or I may inquire about what leads them to ask at that particular time. Another choice I exercise, especially in more uncovering therapy, is asking the patient to imagine what my life is like and then exploring their productions. I explain that their responses will reveal more about them, which is the central aim of the treatment, than would my gratifying their curiosity by answering.

QUESTION: "What if a patient claimed that he is homosexual but refuses to talk about it further in therapy?"

ANSWER: What is most important for us to understand is what the patient's reasons are for not talking about his homosexuality. I wonder if he is talking about his actions, his wishes, or impulses, what sexually arouses him, or a self-perception or misperception. The first time he mentioned it I would have asked, "What leads you to believe so?" I would also wonder what the patient's goals in therapy are. If they are unrelated to his homosexuality, whatever that represents, it may not be necessary for him to discuss it further.

QUESTION: "What if the patient has trouble leaving at the end of sessions, asking one last question or lingering at the door continuing to talk?"

ANSWER: I have previously discussed this problem with terminating sessions in Chapter 5. To summarize briefly:

1. Be firm, do not answer that last question, and build a bridge to the next session. Say something like, "The clock moves and unfortunately we must both obey. Our time is up for today. We can start there next time."
2. If the patient does not start there next time, remind her or him that there's something left over from the previous session.
3. Take this opportunity to talk with the patient about the trouble he or she has with leaving.
4. Offer an explanation of the patient's difficulty if you know or can infer what is behind it.
5. End the session with an exclamation point or some humor or both by saying, for instance: "That mean old clock says we have to stop now. We both know it's difficult for you to end because it feels so rejecting. See you next week, same place, same channel!"

QUESTION: "What if a patient tells you outright that he or she lies and you can't believe anything he or she says?"

ANSWER: My favorite answer to this kind of statement is the following:

> It's your therapy, your time, and your money. If you give me bullshit to respond to, what you'll get back will be bullshit as well. It's up to you if you want to do it that way. Besides, if you have lied in saying that I can't believe anything you say, then I'll be able to believe everything you say from now on. That's an interesting mind game that I don't wish to play. I'll get paid no matter how you play it and whether you profit from the therapy or not.

A more gentle and equally effective response is something along these lines:

> I'm willing to listen to anything you have to say without concerning myself about whether you believe it to be a lie or the truth. I'll try to understand you as best I can anyway.

As the therapeutic alliance strengthens, the patient may use this complicated defensive maneuver less and less and then drop it altogether.

QUESTION: "What if the patient uses a lot of projection? How do I modify it?"

ANSWER: I have discussed this technical problem several times. To summarize:

1. Make use of it by talking with the patient in the projection. For example: "What do you think led John to do what seemed like such an evil thing to you?" [To emphasize that *I* wasn't calling it evil, I'd make quotation marks with the fingers of both hands as I said the word *evil*.]

2. Demonstrate by your thinking out loud how you would interpret what happened and thereby begin to correct the patient's cognitive distortions.
3. Strengthen other, more adaptive defenses by example and precept, such as intellectualization.
4. Help patients understand whatever protective function the projection serves, such as to rid oneself of painful feelings of shame or guilt.

How we deal with defenses will depend upon our dynamic diagnosis and the degree of support we have planned for the therapy or that segment of it.

QUESTION: "What if something a patient says reminds me of a similar personal experience? Is it appropriate to share it?"

ANSWER: I have answered this in part earlier in this chapter. Most of the time we use what occurs to us while listening to patients merely as tools to understand them, but do not directly share it. Whether or not to share this is another one of those judgment calls. At times doing so may be fitting if it provides a corrective emotional experience or contributes to the patient's progress. For example, when a couple is addressing a control issue, I sometimes tell the following story about myself:

> Early in our marriage I got fed up with the oil collecting on the tile of our swimming pool and decided to take care of it. I went to the laundry and got a big box of detergent to put into the pool to dissolve the oil before it could dirty the tile. I passed my wife on the way out and she asked what I was doing. I told her and she started to say, "If I were you, I wouldn't . . ." at which point I said that she should get out of my way and that this was my project. In my anger, I dumped the whole box of detergent in the pool. We had bubbles up to the ceiling, the street was full of bubbles, and I had to pay to have the pool repair

company drain the pool and repair the damage I'd done. See what trouble an allergy to feeling controlled can get us guys into, Jim!

Jim is a husband who is behaving in a similar manner. I find this type of therapeutic use of self very effective.

QUESTION: "What if a separated or divorced person is in individual therapy and brings his or her spouse or former spouse? I was expecting only my patient, but both are in my waiting area."

ANSWER: I'd sit right down and talk about it with them. The hour belongs to your patient. If he or she wishes to have a couple's session in place of an individual one, I would have one. To begin, I would establish a contract for that session with the couple. Before the end of the session, the three of us would decide about future sessions, if any. Did you anticipate that this might happen? If a patient talks about the possibility of a spouse or former spouse participating in the treatment, I usually encourage the patient to bring the partner along. I prefer to know ahead of time, but it's not imperative that I do.

QUESTION: "What if a family group consisting of a divorced mother and children are in family therapy, one teenaged child is angry with the father and refuses to visit him, and the father calls asking to join the family therapy?"

ANSWER: I assume that the call from the father is a surprise because the family had not mentioned the possibility. The mother has contracted with you for the hour, and it is her responsibility to discuss any change in the terms of the contract. Certainly this is an issue that the family should discuss; the children's opinions and feelings are important, but the final decision is up to the mother. Your role will be to continue to make therapeutic interventions and to refrain from giving direct advice about the father's participation. I would express pleasure to the father about his interest and tell him I would have to discuss the matter with his former wife and with their children. I'd also say that she would be in touch with him to discuss the matter.

QUESTION: "What if a patient consistently fails to put into practice what he or she has learned in psychotherapy, or fails to follow recommendations or do prescribed tasks?"

ANSWER: I have described in some detail how to facilitate patients' making constructive use of their treatment in their daily lives. Following recommendations and carrying out prescribed tasks falls under this category. The time may have come for you to have a frank discussion with the patient about the merits of continuing therapy. There are many moves that can be made before that one; I assume that you have tried many of the usual methods. I continued too long with a patient who, for reasons that were unclear to me, seemed to be fighting me at every turn. After I had exhausted all my usual approaches, I said:

> Now it's time to change your therapy. For now, I'll not make another regular appointment for you. When you have tried out one, *only* one, of the many things we've talked about in therapy, give me a call and I'll set up an appointment for you to tell me what it was like for you. No matter how it turns out, please come back and let's talk about it.

The lady never returned! I suspect that she may have done well but was unable to give me any credit for her success.

QUESTION: "What if a patient reads many self-help books and discusses their content in treatment sessions?"

ANSWER: You must understand this avoidance of issues or of your help and make whatever interventions are required to get the treatment moving, if such is indicated. I recall very clearly what my analyst once said to me:

> You are giving me a very clear and extensive review of psychoanalytic theory and technique. It's a good review for me, but it's not helping you. It's a way of keeping what's troubling you at bay.

What interventions you make will depend upon the treatment plan. If, for example, you have planned to strengthen the patient's more adaptive defenses and if intellectualization is one of these, you would join in the discussion of the material the patient brings. Through this avenue, you might be able also to enhance the patient's self-understanding by judiciously applying some of the content of these books to the patient's difficulties. I might say:

> Good, now you've hit on something that might fit your problem neatly. Let's explore that a bit in your case. What do you think about that?

QUESTION: "What if a patient uses a dream book to look up symbols to help interpret dreams?"

ANSWER: The answer to the previous question applies here as well if the patient is using the content of the book as an avoidance. As I have explained in Chapter 5, before working with my patients' first dreams, I explain that their symbols are distinctive for them and cannot be found in a dream book. I cannot recall a time when a patient did not cooperate with the procedure, once they understood it.

QUESTION: "What if a patient uses technical language (of our profession)?"

ANSWER: I prefer to use ordinary language and, unless there is some persuasive reason not to, I ask patients to define any technical terms they use. Harry Stack Sullivan spoke of the importance of words being consensually validated. Usually I ask patients to use another word even for relatively simple ones such as "depressed" or "anxious."

Transference

QUESTION: "What if the patient gives me gifts or if the patient or family brings a moderately priced gift at or after termination?"

ANSWER: If the therapy has been more expressive or analytic in its form, the patient and presumably the family will have learned that we do not accept gifts but rather make a therapeutic consideration of their motives in bringing them. There are exceptions to this caveat, even in a more analytic mode of treatment. Welcoming a patient's expression of warmth and gratitude may give the patient a growth-enhancing experience. In more supportive therapy, the question of accepting a gift is a judgment call. There are no absolute answers, but I am more likely to accept gifts as a part of the reciprocity in a more supportive relationship.

The question reminds me of the surgeon who successfully operated on the seriously ill son of the shah of an oil-rich country. As the shah was thanking the surgeon, he said that he'd be honored to send the surgeon a small gift and asked what he would like. The surgeon was unable to dissuade the shah and finally said that he would appreciate a set of golf clubs. Several weeks later a package arrived by registered mail. The surgeon opened it and was dismayed to find the real estate deeds to several country clubs.

On a more realistic note, last Christmas I accepted gifts from three patients: one was in the $150 range from a very affluent family, and the others were much more modest. It would have hurt their pride and complicated their therapy if I had not accepted these gifts. I wrote them each a note of thanks.

QUESTION: "What if the patient asks me to attend her or his wedding?"

ANSWER: Attending a patient's wedding is more personal than accepting a gift; it suggests a relationship akin to friendship. I would have to consider carefully the indications and contraindications. Were there some very persuasive clinical indication, I would agree. For example, if my refusing to attend would replicate the deep hurt of a parent who had seemed totally indifferent to the patient's significant life events, and if I had concluded that talking with this patient about this issue would be ineffective, I would attend.

QUESTION: "What if the patient talks negatively about me to friends and colleagues?"

ANSWER: Have you told your friends and colleagues that if they reported to you what the patient said, it would be necessary for you to tell the patient *who* reported *what?* If so, then it becomes possible to have a frank discussion with your patient about her or his feelings toward you. This conduct on your patient's part consists of acting out—that is, acting *outside* the treatment on feelings that belong *inside* the treatment.

Whatever has stirred up this patient's negative feelings can then be dealt with, through one of the methods I have already discussed.

QUESTION: "What if the patient says that I am insensitive or not understanding?"

ANSWER: It is certainly possible for us to be insensitive at times and, for sure, there are times when we have not understood as promptly as we might have. One time I was tape-recording sessions to use for teaching purposes. A patient accused me of having been sarcastic at a previous session. I couldn't recall that I had been, but a review of the tape proved her to be correct. In exploring a possible transference reaction, it is usually best to give the patient credit by asking for particulars and examples. If patients cannot document their feelings, then ask them to note carefully when they next feel that way and to point out what they have experienced as insensitive or what you have failed to understand. If patients' feelings are clearly based on transference, it will then be time to search for the source of it, if you do not already know.

QUESTION: "What if my long-term client becomes so dependent that he or she worries incessantly about losing me?"

ANSWER: You are not immortal! The patient may lose you suddenly and unexpectedly. I talk with patients about the reality in their existential anxieties. I wonder whether you have attended enough to what cognitive therapists have called by the felicitous term "copelessness," or if you have unwittingly contributed to the patient's dependency by expecting too little of her or him.

QUESTION: "What if the patient brings pictures of nude men or women, gives them to me, and makes a salacious remark?"

ANSWER: Do you think that the patient may be attempting to seduce you? If not, the patient may be trying to provoke either your permission or interdiction of his or her voyeuristic or other erotic activities. It's very important for you to find out what the patient is up to. One of the best ways of doing this is to glance at the pictures, hand them back or lay them down, and ask:

> What's this all about? You took the trouble to bring these pictures with you to show me. That must be important to you. Let's not let this opportunity go by without understanding what it means to you.

If the patient is not ready to face, for example, her or his homoerotic impulses toward me or others, I will accept whatever plausible explanation the patient offers. In a very supportive therapy, I might offer a generalization such as the following:

> If you're trying to tell me that you enjoy looking at these pictures, that comes as no surprise to me. Most people have these kinds of interests, but not everyone will admit it, even to himself. Am I correct about what you're trying to tell me?

Note that I'm also giving the patient a rationalization by way of an interpretation that is probably inaccurate. Patients may then offer an explanation that is more accurate.

QUESTION: "What if a patient gets upset and bolts from the therapy session?"

ANSWER: Probably you not only hit the target, you hit the bull's-eye. We've all had that kind of thing happen to us. You'll get used to it. Of course, you should examine what happened and take a look at it with the patient at the next session.

Appendix A: Reading List

Ackerman, N. W. (1958). *The Psychodynamics of Family Life.* New York: Basic Books.

Alexander, F., and French, T. M. (1946). *Psychoanalytic Therapy.* New York: Ronald Press.

Alexander, F., and Ross, H., eds. (1952). *Dynamic Psychiatry.* Chicago: University of Chicago Press.

Beck, A. I. (1976). *Cognitive Therapy and the Emotional Disorders.* New York: International Universities Press.

Berne, E. (1972). *What Do You Say After You Say Hello?* New York: Grove Press.

Boszormenyi-Nagy, I., and Spark, G. M. (1973). *Invisible Loyalties: Reciprocity in Intergenerational Family Therapy.* New York: Harper & Row.

Bowen, M. (1978). *Family Therapy in Clinical Practice.* New York: Jason Aronson.

Brenner, C. (1974). *An Elementary Textbook of Psychoanalysis.* Garden City, NY: Anchor Books (paper).

_____ (1982). *The Mind In Conflict.* Madison, CT: International Universities Press.

Bruch, H. (1974). *Learning Psychotherapy.* Cambridge, MA: Harvard University Press.

Burton, A., ed. (1976). *What Makes Behavior Change Possible?* New York: Brunner/Mazel.

Colby, K. M. (1951). *A Primer for Psychotherapists.* New York: Wiley.

Davanloo, H., ed. (1980). *Short-Term Dynamic Psychotherapy.* New York: Jason Aronson.

deShazer, S. (1982). *Patterns of Brief Family Therapy: An Ecosystemic Approach.* New York: Guilford Press.

Dicks, H. V. (1967). *Marital Tensions.* New York: Basic Books.

Fitzgerald, R. V. (1990). *Conjoint Marital Therapy.* 2nd ed. Northvale, NJ: Jason Aronson.

Flegenheimer, W. V. (1982). *Techniques of Brief Psychotherapy.* New York: Jason Aronson.

Fromm-Reichmann, F. (1950). *Principles of Intensive Psychotherapy.* Chicago: University of Chicago Press.

Frosch, J. (1990). *Psychodynamic Psychiatry: Theory and Practice.* Vols. 1 and 2. Madison, CT: International Universities Press.

Greenberg, J. (1989). *I Never Promised You a Rose Garden.* Chicago: Signet.

Gustafson, J. P. (1986). *The Complex Secret of Brief Psychotherapy.* New York: Norton.

Haley, J. (1973). *Uncommon Therapy: The Psychiatric Techniques of Milton H. Erickson, M.D.: A Casebook of an Innovative Psychiatrist's Work in Short-term Therapy.* New York: Norton.

————— (1976). *Problem-Solving Therapy.* San Francisco: Jossey-Bass.

Kohut, H. (1977). *The Restoration of the Self.* New York: International Universities Press.

Kramer, C. H. (1980). *Becoming a Family Therapist.* New York: Human Sciences Press.

Lidz, T. (1963). *The Family and Human Adaptation.* New York: International Universities Press.

Luborsky, L. (1984). *Principles of Psychoanalytic Psychotherapy.* New York: Basic Books.

Madanes, C. (1981). *Strategic Family Therapy.* San Francisco: Jossey-Bass.

Malan, D. H. (1976). *The Frontier of Brief Psychotherapy.* New York: Plenum.

Martin, P. A. (1976). *A Marital Therapy Manual.* New York: Brunner/Mazel.

Minuchin, S., and Fishman, H. C. (1981). *Family Therapy Techniques.* Cambridge, MA: Harvard University Press.

Mittlemann, B. (1956). Analysis of reciprocal neurotic patterns in family relationships. In *Neurotic Interaction in Marriage,* ed. V. W. Eisenstein, pp. 81–100. New York: Basic Books.

Napier, A. Y., and Whitaker, C. A. (1978). *The Family Crucible.* New York: Harper & Row.

Neill, J. R. (1989). *From Psyche to System: The Evolving Therapy of Carl Whitaker*. New York: Guilford Press.

Perls, F. S. (1969). *Gestalt Therapy Verbatim*. Moab, UT: Real People Press.

Pine, F. (1990). *Drive, Ego, Object, and Self: A Synthesis for Clinical Work*. New York: Basic Books.

Reik, T. (1983). *Listening with the Third Ear*. New York: Farrar, Straus, Giroux.

Saul, L. J. (1972). *Psychodynamically Based Psychotherapy*. New York: Science House.

Scharff, D. E., and Scharff, J. S. (1987). *Object Relations Family Therapy*. Northvale, NJ: Jason Aronson.

Selvini Palazzoli, M., Boscolo, L., Cecchin, G., et al. (1978). *Paradox and Counterparadox: A New Model in the Therapy of the Family in Schizophrenic Transaction*. New York: Jason Aronson.

Sifneos, P. E. (1979). *Short-term Dynamic Psychotherapy: Evaluation and Technique*. New York: Plenum.

Skynner, A. C. R. (1976). *Systems of Family and Marital Psychotherapy*. New York: Brunner/Mazel.

Slipp, S. (1984). *Objects Relations: A Dynamic Bridge Between Individual and Family Treatment*. New York: Jason Aronson.

Stanton, A. H., and Swartz, M. S. (1954). *The Mental Hospital*. New York: Basic Books.

Stierlin, H., Rucker-Embden, I., Wetzel, N., et al. (1980). *The First Interview with the Family*. Trans. S. Tooze. New York: Brunner/Mazel.

Tarachow, S. (1970). *An Introduction to Psychotherapy*. New York: International Universities Press.

Watzlawick, P., Beavin, J. H., and Jackson, D. D. (1967). *Pragmatics of Human Communication: A Study of Interactional Patterns, Pathologies, and Paradoxes*. New York: Norton.

Werman, D. S. (1984). *The Practice of Supportive Psychotherapy*. New York: Brunner/Mazel.

Whitaker, C. A., and Bumberry, W. M. (1988). *Dancing with the Family: A Symbolic–Experiential Approach*. New York: Brunner/Mazel.

Wolberg, L. R. (1954). *The Technique of Psychotherapy*. New York: Grune & Stratton.

Yalom, I. (1975). *The Theory and Practice of Group Psychotherapy*. 2nd ed. New York: Basic Books.

Appendix B:
Interview Outline

The two prime objectives of the introductory phase of interviews are, first, to set the person, couple, or family at ease; and secondly to identify patients' current contexts. Basic ways in which this can be achieved are the following:

1. Social conversation: about neutral, trivial matters such as the weather.
2. Draw a genogram of patients' present family and elicit demographic data.

History of Psychiatric Problems

The following is an outline only. Readers can find the details about eliciting significant data in the text of this book or in standard reference material.

I. Patients' Stories

    A. Onset
    B. Course
    C. Present status and trends
    D. Psychiatric history

II. Present Life Circumstances

    A. Familial
    B. Educational or occupational
    C. Social
    D. Recreational
    E. Other interests and activities

III. Possible Precipitating Events

    A. For onset
    B. For decision to seek therapy

IV. Life History

    A. Marital status
       1. *History of current marriage*
       2. *History of any past marriages or affiliations*
    B. Family history (draw genogram)
       1. *Father*
       2. *Mother*
       3. *Parental marriage or marriages*
       4. *Siblings*
    C. Education and occupation
    D. Earliest memories

    E.   Sexual development
    F.   Dreams
       1. *Recent*
       2. *Recurrent*
       3. *Nightmares*

V. Medical History and Review of Systems

VI. Mental Status

    A.   Informal
    B.   Formal

VII. Observations and Impressions

VIII. Nosologic (DSM) Diagnoses

IX. Psychodynamic Formulation

X. Treatment Plan

References

Ackerman, N. W. (1958). *The Psychodynamics of Family Life*. New York: Basic Books.
———— (1962). Family psychotherapy and psychoanalysis: the implications of difference. *Family Process* 1:30–43.
Adler, G. (1982). Supportive psychotherapy revisited. *Hillside Journal of Clinical Psychiatry* 4:3–13.
Alexander, F., and French, T. M. (1946). *Psychoanalytic Therapy*. New York: Ronald Press.
Altshuler, K. Z. (1989). Will the psychotherapies yield differential results? A look at assumptions in therapy trials. *American Journal of Psychotherapy* 43:310–320.
American Psychiatric Association (1987). *Diagnostic and Statistical Manual of Mental Disorders*. 3rd rev. ed. Washington, DC: American Psychiatric Association.
Anderson, C. M., Hogarty, G. E., and Reiss, D. J. (1980). Family treatment of adult schizophrenic patients: a psycho-educational approach. *Schizophrenia Bulletin* 6:490–505.
Arkowitz, H. (1989). The role of theory in psychotherapy integration. *Journal of Integrative and Eclectic Psychotherapy* 8:8–16.
Atwood, N. (1990). Integrating individual and family treatment for outpatients vulnerable to psychosis. *American Journal of Psychotherapy* 44:247–255.
Barton, C., and Alexander, J. F. (1981). Functional family therapy. In *Handbook of Family Therapy*, ed. A. S. Gurman and D. P. Kniskern, pp. 403–443. New York: Brunner/Mazel.
Bateson, G. (1972). *Steps to an Ecology of Mind*. New York: Ballantine.

Beck, A. I. (1976). *Cognitive Therapy and the Emotional Disorders.* New York: International Universities Press.

Beitman, B. D., Goldfried, M. R., and Norcross, J. C. (1989). The movement toward integrating the psychotherapies: an overview. *American Journal of Psychiatry* 142:138–147.

Berger, F. (1983). Alcoholism rehabilitation: a supportive approach. *Hospital and Community Psychiatry* 34:1040–1043.

Berne, E. (1972). *What Do You Say After You Say Hello?* New York: Grove Press.

Beutler, L. E. (1989). The misplaced role of theory in psychotherapy integration. *Journal of Integrative and Eclectic Psychotherapy* 8:17–22.

Binder, J. L., Henry, W. P., and Strupp, H. H. (1987). An appraisal of selection criteria for dynamic psychotherapies and implications for setting time limits. *Psychiatry* 50:154–166.

Bloch, D. A., and LaPerriere, K. (1973). Techniques of family therapy: a conceptual frame. In *Techniques of Family Therapy: A Primer,* ed. D. A. Bloch, pp. 1–19. New York: Grune & Stratton.

Bloch, S. (1977). Supportive psychotherapy. *British Journal of Hospital Medicine* 18:63–67.

Boszormenyi-Nagy, I., and Spark, G. M. (1973). *Invisible Loyalties: Reciprocity in Intergenerational Family Therapy.* New York: Harper & Row.

Bowen, M. (1978). *Family Therapy in Clinical Practice.* New York: Jason Aronson.

Brenner, C. (1974). *An Elementary Textbook of Psychoanalysis.* Garden City, NY: Anchor Books (paper).

Brown, G. W., Birley, J. L. T., and Wing, J. K. (1972). Influence of family life on the course of schizophrenic disorders: a replication. *British Journal of Psychiatry* 121:241–258.

Buckley, P. (1986). A neglected treatment. *Psychiatric Annals* 16:515–521.

Burstein, E., Coyne, L., Kernberg, O., and Voth, H. L. (1972). Psychotherapy and psychoanalysis: final report of the Menninger Foundation's psychotherapy research project. *Bulletin of the Menninger Clinic* 36:1–275.

Colby, K. M. (1951). *A Primer for Psychotherapists.* New York: Wiley.

Conte, H. R., and Plutchik, R. (1986). Controlled research in supportive psychotherapy. *Psychiatric Annals* 16:530–533.

Corney, R. H. (1985). The health of clients referred to social workers in an intake team. *Social Science and Medicine* 21:873–878.

deShazer, S. (1982). *Patterns of Brief Family Therapy: An Ecosystemic Approach.* New York: Guilford Press.

Engel, G. L. (1989). The clinical application of the biopsychosocial model. *American Journal of Psychiatry* 137:535–543.

Erikson, E. H. (1959). *Identity and the Life Cycle: Selected Papers.* New York: International Universities Press.

Falloon, I. R., Boyd, J. L., McGill, C. W., et al. (1985). Family management in the prevention of morbidity of schizophrenia. Clinical outcome of a two-year longitudinal study. *Archives of General Psychiatry* 42:887–896.

Fitzgerald, R. V. (1982). Family therapies. In *Adult Psychiatry: New Directions in Therapy,* ed. J. P. Zrull, pp. 74–101. Garden City, NY: Medical Examination Publishing Co.

_____ (1990). *Conjoint Marital Therapy.* 2nd ed. Northvale, NJ: Jason Aronson.

Fleck, S. A. (1983). A holistic approach to family typology and the axes of DSM-III. *Archives of General Psychiatry* 40:901–906.

Flegenheimer, W. V. (1982). *Techniques of Brief Psychotherapy.* New York: Jason Aronson.

Flegenheimer, W. V., and Pollack, J. (1989). The time limit in brief psychotherapy. *Bulletin of the Menninger Clinic* 53:44–51.

Foerster, K. (1984). Supportive psychotherapy combined with autogenous training in acute leukemic patients under isolation therapy. *Psychotherapy and Psychosomatics* 41:100–105.

Frank, J. (1976). Restoration of morale and behavior. In *What Makes Behavior Change Possible,* ed. A. Burton, pp. 73–95. New York: Bruner/Mazel.

Freud, S. (1905). Three essays on the theory of sexuality. *Standard Edition* 7:135–243.

Freyberger, H. (1977). Supportive psychotherapeutic techniques in primary and secondary alexithymia. *Psychotherapy and Psychosomatics* 28:337–342.

Fromm-Reichmann, F. (1959). Notes on the development of treatment of schizophrenics by psychoanalytic psychotherapy. In *Psychoanalysis and Psychotherapy: Selected Papers of Frieda Fromm-Reichmann,* ed. D. M. Bullard, p. 169. Chicago: University of Chicago Press.

Frosch, J. (1990). *Psychodynamic Psychiatry: Theory and Practice.* Vols. 1 and 2. Madison, CT: International Universities Press.

Garfield, S. L. (1978). Research on client variables in psychotherapy. In *Handbook of Psychotherapy and Behavior Change,* ed. S. L.

Garfield and A. E. Bergin, 2nd ed., pp. 191–232. New York: Wiley.

Glass, L. L., Katz, H. M., Schnitzer, R. D., et al. (1989). Psychotherapy of schizophrenia: an empirical investigation of the relationship of process to outcome. *American Journal of Psychiatry* 146:603–608.

Gottschalk, L. A. (1990). The psychotherapies in the context of new developments in the neurosciences and biological psychiatry. *American Journal of Psychotherapy* 44:321–339.

Greenberg, J. (1989). *I Never Promised You a Rose Garden*. Chicago: Signet.

Grinder, J., and Bandler, R. (1981). *Trance-formations: Neuro-linguistic Programming and the Structure of Hypnosis*. Moab, UT: Real People Press.

Gustafson, J. P. (1984). An integration of brief dynamic psychotherapy. *American Journal of Psychiatry* 141:935–944.

——— (1986). *The Complex Secret of Brief Psychotherapy*. New York: Norton.

Haley, J. (1973). *Uncommon Therapy: The Psychiatric Techniques of Milton H. Erickson, M.D.: A Casebook of an Innovative Psychiatrist's Work in Short-term Therapy*. New York: Norton.

——— (1976). *Problem-Solving Therapy*. San Francisco: Jossey-Bass.

Harvard Medical School Mental Health Letter (1989a). Families in the treatment of schizophrenia: part I. *The Harvard Medical School Mental Health Letter* 5:1–4.

——— (1989b). Families in the treatment of schizophrenia: part II. *The Harvard Medical School Mental Health Letter* 6:1–3.

Havens, L. (1978). Explorations in the uses of language in psychotherapy: simple empathic statements. *Psychiatry* 41:336–345.

——— (1979). Explorations in the uses of language in psychotherapy: complex empathic statements. *Psychiatry* 42:40–48.

Heim, E. (1980). "Supportive therapy" rediscovered?—a plea for adaptive psychotherapies (author's trans.). *Psychotherapie Psychosomatik Medizinische Psychologie* 30:261–273.

Holt, R. R. (1989). *Freud Reappraised*. New York: Guilford Press.

Jacobson, N. S. (1980). Behavioral marital therapy: current trends in research, assessment, and practice. *American Journal of Family Therapy* 8:3–5.

Johnson, A. M., and Szurek, S. A. (1952). The genesis of antisocial acting out in children and adults. *Psychoanalytic Quarterly* 21:323–343.

Jones, E. (1955). *The Life and Work of Sigmund Freud.* Vol. 2. New York: Basic Books.

Karasu, T. B. (1990a). Toward a clinical model of psychotherapy for depression. I: Systematic comparison of three psychotherapies. *American Journal of Psychiatry* 147:133–147.

———— (1990b). Toward a clinical model of psychotherapy for depression. II: An integrative and selective treatment approach. *American Journal of Psychiatry* 147:269–278.

Klerman, G. L. (1990). The psychiatric patient's right to effective treatment: implications of Osheroff v. Chestnut Lodge. *American Journal of Psychiatry* 147:409–418.

Kris, A. O. (1989). Psychoanalysis and psychoanalytic psychotherapy. In *Psychiatry,* ed. R. Michels, A. M. Cooper, S. B. Guze et al., pp. 1–13. New York: Basic Books.

Langsley, D. G. (1978). Comparing clinic and private practice of psychiatry. *American Journal of Psychiatry* 135:702–706.

Lempa, W., Poets, C., Arnold, M. A., et al. (1985). Effectiveness of supportive psychotherapy in hospitalized patients: empirical findings and practice-related consequences. *Psychotherapie Psychosomatik, Medizinische Psychologie* 35:315–319.

Lidz, T. (1963). *The Family and Human Adaptation.* New York: International Universities Press.

London, P., and Palmer, M. (1988). The integrative trends in psychotherapy in historical context. *Psychiatric Annals* 18:273–279.

Luborsky, L. (1984). *Principles of Psychoanalytic Psychotherapy.* New York: Basic Books.

Luborsky, L., Crits-Christoph, P., McLellan, A. T. (1986). Do therapists vary much in their success? Findings from four outcome studies. *American Journal of Orthopsychiatry* 56:501–512.

Madanes, C. (1981). *Strategic Family Therapy.* San Francisco: Jossey-Bass.

Madanes, C., and Haley, J. (1977). Dimensions of family therapy. *Journal of Nervous and Mental Disease* 165:88–98.

Malan, D. H. (1976). *The Frontier of Brief Psychotherapy.* New York: Plenum.

Mann, J. (1973). *Time-limited Psychotherapy.* Cambridge, MA: Harvard University Press.

Manos, N., and Vasilopoulou, E. (1984). Evaluation of psychoanalytic psychotherapy outcome. *Acta Psychiatrica Scandinavica* 70:28–35.

Marmor, J. (1979a). Change in psychoanalytic treatment. *Journal of the American Academy of Psychoanalysis* 7:345–357.

———— (1979b). Short-term dynamic psychotherapy. *American Journal of Psychiatry* 136:149–155.

Masserman, J. (1976). Unpublished lecture, section on psychotherapy VII. World Congress of Psychiatry. Honolulu.

Mittlemann, B. (1956). Analysis of reciprocal neurotic patterns in family relationships. In *Neurotic Interaction in Marriage,* ed. V. W. Eisenstein, pp. 81–100. New York: Basc Books.

Mohl, P. C. (1987). Should psychotherapy be considered a biological treatment? *Psychosomatics* 28:320–326.

Napier, A. Y., and Whitaker, C. A. (1978). *The Family Crucible.* New York: Harper & Row.

Nicholi, A. M., Jr. (1988). The therapist–patient relationship. In *The New Harvard Guide to Psychiatry,* ed. A. M. Nicholi, Jr., pp. 10–11. Cambridge, MA: Belknap Press.

Ornstein, A. (1986). "Supportive" psychotherapy: a contemporary view. *Clinical Social Work Journal* 14:14–30.

Papp, P. (1980). The Greek chorus and other techniques of paradoxical therapy. *Family Process* 19:45–57.

Paul, N. L. (1967). The role of mourning and empathy in conjoint marital therapy. In *Family Therapy and Disturbed Families,* ed. G. H. Zuk and I. Boszormenyi-Nagy, pp. 186–205. Palo Alto; CA: Science and Behavior Books.

Perls, F. S. (1969). *Gestalt Therapy Verbatim.* Moab, UT: Real People Press.

Perry, S., Cooper, A. M., and Michels, R. (1987). The psychodynamic formulation: its purpose, structure, and clinical application. *American Journal of Psychiatry* 144:543–550.

Perry, S., Frances, A., Klar, H., and Clarkin, J. (1983). Selection criteria for individual dynamic psychotherapies. *Psychiatric Quarterly* 55:3–16.

Peteet, J. R. (1982). A closer look at the concept of support. *General Hospital Psychiatry* 4:19–23.

Pilkonis, P. A., Imber, S. D., Lewis, P., et al. (1984). A comparative outcome study of individual, group, and conjoint psychotherapy. *Archives of General Psychiatry* 41:431–437.

Pine, F. (1986). Supportive psychotherapy: a psychoanalytic perspective. *Psychiatric Annals* 16:526–529.

———— (1987). The four psychologies of psychoanalysis and their place in clinical work. *Journal of the American Psychoanalytic Association* 36:571–596.

Pinney, E. L., Jr. (1981). Supportive therapy for a patient requiring penis amputation. *Psychosomatics* 22:715–719.

Rapoport, R. (1962). Normal crisis, family structure, and mental health. *Family Process* 2:68–80.

Rasmussen, A., and Messer, S. (1986). A comparison and critique of Mann's time-limited psychotherapy and Davanloo's short-term dynamic psychotherapy. *Bulletin of the Menninger Clinic* 50:163–184.

Reik, T. (1983). *Listening with the Third Ear.* New York: Farrar, Straus, Giroux.

Rhoads, J. M. (1988). Combinations and synthesis of psychotherapies. *Psychiatric Annals* 18:280–287.

Richard-Jodoin, R. M. (1989). The "holding function" of the therapist in the treatment of borderline patients. *Journal of the American Academy of Psychoanalysis* 17:305–312.

Robinson, L. A., Berman, J. S., and Neimeyer, R. A. (1990). Psychotherapy for the treatment of depression: a comprehensive review of controlled outcome research. *Psychological Bulletin* 108:30–49.

Saul, L. J. (1972). *Psychodynamically Based Psychotherapy.* New York: Science House.

Selvini Palazzoli, M., Boscolo, L., Cecchin, G., et al. (1978). *Paradox and Counterparadox: A New Model in the Therapy of the Family in Schizophrenic Transaction.* New York: Jason Aronson.

———— (1980). Hypothesizing—circularity—neutrality: three guidelines for the conductor of the session. *Family Process* 19:3–12.

Sifneos, P. E. (1979). *Short-term Dynamic Psychotherapy: Evaluation and Technique.* New York: Plenum.

Sifneos, P. E., and Greenberg, W. E. (1988). Patient management. In *The New Harvard Guide to Psychiatry,* ed. A. M. Nicholi, Jr., pp. 589–592. Cambridge; MA: Belknap, Press.

Skynner, A. C. R. (1976). *Systems of Family and Marital Psychotherapy.* New York: Brunner/Mazel.

Slipp, S. (1984). *Object Relations: A Dynamic Bridge between Individual and Family Treatment.* New York: Jason Aronson.

Smith, M. L., and Glass, G. V. (1977). Meta-analysis of psychotherapy outcome studies. *American Psychologist* 32:752–760.

Stanton, M. D. (1981). Strategic approaches to family therapy. In *Handbook of Family Therapy,* ed. A. S. Gurman and D. P. Kniskern, pp. 361–402. New York: Brunner/Mazel.

Stierlin, H., Rucker-Embden, I., Wetzel, N., et al. (1980). The *First Interview with the Family.* Trans. S. Tooze. New York: Brunner/Mazel.

Stone, A. A. (1990). Law, science, and psychiatric malpractice: a reply to Klerman's indictment of psychoanalytic psychiatry. *American Journal of Psychiatry* 147:419–427.

Strupp, H. H. (1986). The nonspecific hypothesis of therapeutic effectiveness: a current assessment. *American Journal of Orthopsychiatry* 56:513–520.

Tolsdorf, C. C. (1976). Social networks, support, and coping: an exploratory study. *Family Process* 15:407–417.

Watzlawick, P., Beavin, J. H., and Jackson, D. D. (1967). *Pragmatics of Human Communication: A Study of Interactional Patterns, Pathologies, and Paradoxes.* New York: Norton.

Vaillant, G. E. (1971). Theoretical hierarchy of adoptive ego mechanisms. *Archives of General Psychiatry* 24:107–117.

Weed, L. L. (1989). New premises and new tools for medical care and medical education. In *International Symposium of Medical Informatics and Education,* ed. R. Salamon, D. Protti, and J. Moehr, pp. 22–30 Victoria, Canada: University of Victoria.

Werman, D. S. (1984). *The Practice of Supportive Psychotherapy.* New York: Brunner/Mazel.

Whitaker, C. A., and Bumberry, W. M. (1988). *Dancing with the Family: A Symbolic–Experiential Approach.* New York: Brunner/Mazel.

Winston, A., Pinsker, H., and McCullough, L. (1986). A review of supportive psychotherapy. *Hospital and Community Psychiatry* 37:1105–1114.

Wohl, J. (1989). Integration of cultural awareness into psychotherapy. *American Journal of Psychotherapy.* 43:343–355.

Wolberg, L. R. (1954). *The Technique of Psychotherapy.* New York: Grune & Stratton.

———— (1965). The technic of short-term psychotherapy. In *Short-Term Psychotherapy,* ed. L. R. Wolberg, pp. 127–200. New York: Grune & Stratton.

Yalom, I. (1975). *The Theory and Practice of Group Psychotherapy.* 2nd ed. New York: Basic Books.

Index